THE ERA OF
THE MUCKRAKERS

The University of North Carolina Press, Chapel Hill, N. C.; The Baker and Taylor Company, New York; Oxford University Press, London; Maruzen-Kabushiki-Kaisha, Tokyo; Edward Evans & Sons, Ltd., Shanghai; D. B. Centen's Wetenschappelijke Boekhandel, Amsterdam.

BENJAMIN ORANGE FLOWER, "THE EDITORIAL DEAN OF DEMOCRACY,"
FOUNDER AND EDITOR OF THE "ARENA."

THE ERA OF
THE MUCKRAKERS

By

C. C. REGIER, Ph.D.

GLOUCESTER, MASS.

PETER SMITH

1957

To My Children
Donald, Virginia, and Frank

PREFACE

IT HAS been the endeavor in this volume to present in readable form an interesting and picturesque phase of recent American history. The period covered is, roughly, the first decade of the twentieth century. The source from which most of the information has been derived is the popular magazine. In order to understand how the magazines came to engage in muckraking, a dozen of the leading periodicals of the last decade of the nineteenth century were carefully examined. The results of this phase of the investigation will be found in the first four chapters, but particularly in Chapter III.

The statement has been made that the muckrakers and their work do not deserve dignified historical treatment. Whether or not the present study can be called dignified, the reader must judge for himself; but if it sheds any new light on the period under consideration, it can—from the historical point of view—be justified.

In some ways, it seems to the writer, conditions in this country are today very similar to those of thirty years ago. There is corruption in every type of government unit, from the small town or county up to the federal government. The buying and selling of votes is so common in certain sections that newspapers comment on it as a matter of course. And behind all this, today as thirty years ago, is business. The treatment that the laborers receive in some of the coal fields of Kentucky, West Virginia, and Pennsylvania is almost beyond belief. There is still the old problem of power, or the activities of the public utilities companies. Then there are new problems—the gangs, prohibition enforcement, corruption in unemployment relief, broadcasting, and the treatment of the so-called radicals. The list could be extended almost indefinitely. Are we not in need of exposures today? Or do we know enough of the sordid facts? Shall we follow Lincoln Steffens in his late deductions and conclude that the rich *ought* to control not only the economic but also the political destinies of the land? Or are we hesitating before the thoroughgoing task which more and more people are beginning to realize must be undertaken sooner or later?

For help and encouragement in the preparation of this book, the author is indebted to many individuals. It was begun at the suggestion of Professor Arthur M. Schlesinger, who also manifested a keen interest at all stages of the work. Harry Elmer Barnes has assisted with encouragement and useful suggestions. Nearly all the leading muckrakers have furnished information or suggested points of view, either through correspondence or in personal interviews, notably Samuel Hopkins Adams, Ray Stannard Baker, C. P. Connolly, Will Irwin, S. S. McClure, John S. Phillips, Charles Edward Russell, Lincoln Steffens, Mark Sullivan, Ida M. Tarbell, and George Kibbe Turner. Mrs. Henry B. Veatsh of Evansville, Indiana, has furnished information about her uncle, Benjamin O. Flower, as well as the photograph of him which appears in this volume. Professor and Mrs. Roscoe H. Vining of New River State College have read the proof. My greatest indebtedness, however, is due to Professor Granville Hicks of Rensselaer Polytechnic Institute. Not only has he given valuable literary assistance, but he has contributed from his rich store of knowledge, especially in the chapters which deal with literature.

I have constantly striven for accuracy of statement, but in a work of this nature, where the information has been gleaned from hundreds of sources, it may well be that some mistakes have crept in. Nor is it to be supposed that the muckrakers—of whom a large majority are still living—will all approve of the manner in which the material is presented. Their political and economic philosophies diverged rather widely.

While no use has been made of footnotes, the reader will find it possible to find exact references by referring to the bibliography in the back of the volume.

C. C. REGIER

July, 1932

TABLE OF CONTENTS

LIST OF ILLUSTRATIONS

THE ERA OF
THE MUCKRAKERS

CHAPTER ONE

THE NAME AND THE NEED

IT WAS President Roosevelt, with his gift for apt if not always accurate phraseology, who popularized the term "muckraking." In 1906, at the laying of the cornerstone of the office building of the House of Representatives, he said, "In Bunyan's *Pilgrim's Progress* you may recall the description of the Man with the Muck-rake, the man who could look no way but downward with the muck-rake in his hands; who was offered a celestial crown for his muck-rake, but who would neither look up nor regard the crown he was offered, but continued to rake to himself the filth of the floor." He went on to say that this figure typified some of his contemporaries, men who refused to see anything that was lofty, persistently fixing their eyes on vile and debasing things. That there was filth he admitted, and he commended the men who scraped it up, but he declared that the man who did nothing else was certain to become a force for evil. "I hail as a benefactor," he asserted, "every writer or speaker, every man who, on the platform, or in book, magazine, or newspaper, with merciless severity makes such attack, provided always that he in turn remembers that the attack is of use only if it is absolutely truthful."

Though Roosevelt had distinguished between sound and sensational exposures, he had been vague enough in his language to make it difficult to understand precisely who was the object of his attack; and the point has never been satisfactorily cleared up. One prominent writer of the day wrote the President, deploring the whole speech. Roosevelt immediately replied that he had had in mind, not this particular writer, for whom he professed great admiration, but a well known newspaper owner. Lincoln Steffens called on him the next morning and said, "Well, you have put an end to all these journalistic investigations that have made you." To this Roosevelt replied that he had no such intentions and that he had not had Steffens in mind. It was David Graham Phillips' attack on "poor old Chauncey Depew," he said, that had aroused him to wrath. And to make the problem even more confusing, Phillips' friends declare that Roosevelt told Phillips the latter was quite wrong in assuming that he was the writer in question.

Whatever the true purpose of the speech may have been, the term was speedily attached to all reformers who were engaged in denouncing corruption, whether or not they deserved the odium explicit in the President's application of the epithet. And in time the expression lost most of its unsavory connotation and was even accepted by the reformers themselves. Today the fact that the term came to be used indiscriminately may be regarded as an advantage, for it would be almost impossible to distinguish the good from the bad and the sane from the sensational in such a way as to satisfy everyone. Classification becomes arbitrary, and we do much better if we simply define muckraking as the exposing of evils and corruption for the real or ostensible purpose of promoting righteousness and social justice.

Muckraking, in any sense of the word, was the inevitable result of decades of indifference to the illegalities and immoralities attendant upon the industrial development of America. In the latter part of the nineteenth century colossal fortunes were falling into the hands of the fortunate, and those who could not wait for them to fall were reaching up and grabbing them. Old laws failed to serve new purposes, and most legislators lacked the intelligence, even if they possessed the will, to regulate the dizzy processes of industrial expansion. Even the financier who wished to be law-abiding realized that legal paths were too indirect to serve his purpose, and it was easier to dole out bribes to politicians, who were far from loath to share in the orgy of acquisition. The control of mineral lands, of water power, or of municipal franchises might mean the accumulation of gigantic fortunes in a short time, and it was no wonder that sharp-eyed business men, eager for wealth and power, ingeniously evaded or flauntingly defied the inadequate and feebly enforced laws of the land. "The United States," said William Archer writing for the *Fortnightly Review* in May, 1910, his impressions of America, "is like an enormously rich country overrun by a horde of robber barons, and very inadequately policed by the central government and by certain local vigilance societies."*

Everything seemed chaos in this bitterly competitive world, but there was one tendency that no one could mistake—the movement toward industrial consolidation, which had been apparent since the late seventies. Ninety-two large corporations were organized in the eighteen months after January 1, 1899, and this was by no means exceptional. In the later phases of this mêlée the real Titans were two groups of powerful financiers, the one led by John D. Rockefeller, the other by J. P. Morgan. The Standard Oil group counted among its vassals railroads such as the Missouri, Kansas and Texas, the Delaware, Lackawanna and Western, and the Chicago, Milwaukee and St. Paul. It had an alliance with the National City Bank of New York, and it was in touch with gas and electric companies and with the great life insurance companies. The Morgan group had lined up the

* See Bibliography for complete periodical references.

Philadelphia and Reading, the New York, Lake Erie and Western, the Lehigh Valley, and other railroads. Morgan himself organized the Federal Steel Company and the National Tube Company.

The first years of the new century witnessed the acceleration of the growth of these corporations; in 1904 the capitalization of four hundred and forty large industrial and transportation combinations amounted to nearly twenty and a half billions. These industrial giants controlled more or less successfully the production of tobacco, petroleum, sugar, linseed oil, iron and steel, copper, beef, starch, flour, candy chewing gum, candles, ice, glucose, crackers, whiskey, anthracite coal, fertilizers, tin cans, farming tools, locomotives, writing paper, school furniture, sewer pipe, glassware, rubber goods, buttons, leather, electrical supplies, and many other commodities that played an important part in American life. Some of them, the Standard Oil Company, the livestock and dressed beef combinations, the coffee and steel trusts, for example, secured great advantages over their rivals from railroad favoritism; and the tariff wall afforded shelter for the growth of the steel, tin plate, sugar, and leather combinations, and a dozen others.

One of the most conspicuous of these so-called trusts, the United States Steel Corporation, was formed in 1901 in order to avoid a threatened competitive war among certain steel manufacturers. The value of the tangible property thus brought together was estimated by the United States Commissioner of Corporations at $700,000,000, but the company issued securities to more than twice that amount, and the financiers who organized the corporation were handed the neat sum of $62,500,000. Ninety-five per cent of the railroads had, by this time, passed into the control of six groups, dominated by fourteen individuals, of whom E. H. Harriman was the most ambitious and the most energetic.

Among banking interests the same concentration took place. It became doubtful whether any great business enterprise, demanding large capital, could be started without the aid either of the Morgan or of the Standard Oil banking interests. Some years later (1911) the Pujo Commission of Congress found that the "members of four allied financial institutions in New York City held 341 directorships in banks, insurance companies, railroads, steamship companies, and trading and public utility corporations, having aggregate resources of $22,255,000,000."

Industrial expansion undoubtedly had enriched the country, but the greater number of citizens never knew the difference. Frank Parsons, writing in the *Arena* in August, 1901, stated that the per capita wealth of the country had increased from $200 to $1,200 during the nineteenth century and these figures agree substantially with the best estimates we have. But he also maintained that one half of the people owned practically nothing; that one-eighth of them owned seven-eighths of the wealth; that 1 per cent of the population owned 54 per cent of the wealth; that one family in every hundred was able to buy out the other ninety-nine and still have something left over; and that one two-hundredth of a per cent, or 4,000 millionaires, had 20 per cent of the total wealth, or more than 4,000 times their fair share. This great concentration of wealth, together with the disappearance of the public lands, made exceedingly slight any opportunity the working man might have to achieve economic independence.

With the building up of the great fortunes went the building up of a new public opinion. In some strange way the intoxication which accompanied the acquisition of wealth affected those who had not, as well as those who had. The psychology of business not only clouded the judgment of the entrepreneurs and financiers; it also threatened to become the national way of thinking. When people talked about success, they meant business success, and when they wished to compliment a movement, whether industrial, religious, or educational, they called it businesslike. The men of money pointed to the growth and prosperity of the country, insisting that they and their methods were responsible for these wholly desirable conditions. And the men without money, not uninfluenced, one presumes, by the hope that some day they might reap their share of the rich rewards, accepted the philosophy of the financiers and calmly acquiesced in their actions. The acquisitive instinct was glorified until it was regarded as a beneficent deity, devoted to the greater good of the country and not unworthy of the worship it received. When business men did anything humanitarian, such as providing rest-rooms for their working girls, they excused themselves by saying it was "simply to augment output."

Inevitably the government reflected the indifference of the people. William Allen White, in *The Old Order Changeth*, tells us that an extra-constitutional government passed over the country from East to West, and was dominant from 1897 to 1903. In the city, in the county, in the state, and in the nation there were two governments, a constitutional government and a business government. The constitutional government punished crimes of violence, crimes directed against individuals, but, far from punishing, it protected crimes of cunning directed against public rights. Indeed, the authorities theoretically elected to serve the people regarded themselves as the guardians of business, and it was in the interests of business that laws were enacted, interpreted, and administered. There was one jurisdiction for private business and one for public business. As Mr. White humorously pointed out, there are two sides to every lawsuit, and "it was just as easy to see the railroad's side as it was to see the other side, so the mass of federal decisions for years favored the railroads." In any strict sense the courts were corrupt, for, as Walter Lippmann insists in *Drift and Mastery*, "The attempt to serve at the same time two antagonistic interests is what constitutes 'corruption'. " But, judged by the standards of the times, men were true to their ideals. Everybody wanted business to be prosperous, and everybody looked at problems from the business point of view. Nothing reveals more bluntly the political and social philosophy of the time than the way in which the Supreme Court interpreted the word "person" in the Fourteenth Amendment as applying to corporations. Between 1890, when this interpretation was first made by the Supreme Court, and 1910, this court rendered 528 decisions on the Fourteenth Amendment and only nineteen concerned the Negro race, while 289 related to corporations.

Naturally the commercial philosophy which permitted an alliance between business and government permeated other American institutions, and, according to Edward A. Ross, reacted unfavorably upon the character and integrity of the American nation. In a volume entitled *Sin and Society*, published in 1907, Professor Ross offered a passionate indictment and a not inaccurate picture of contemporary society. In particular he called attention to the hiatus between private and public morality. He pointed out that the men engaged in business were often kind-hearted, pure, fond of their families, hospitable to their friends, and generous to the poor. These virtues lulled the conscience of the sinner and blinded the eyes of the onlookers. They were, moreover, the virtues extolled by the Puritan code of morality, which had always emphasized personal righteousness rather than social vision. The impersonal corporation, Professor Ross noted, enabled men to commit with clear conscience crimes which their whole training would have forced them to abhor if such crimes had been direct consequences of their own acts. It was true that industry was as reckless of human life as it was of natural resources. Some five hundred thousand workers were either killed or badly maimed every year, and yet an inventor declared that he could sell a time-saving invention in twenty places but a life-saving device in none. Stockholders did not mean to wear out children, to maim workmen, to defraud customers, to pollute the ballot, or to debauch public officials; yet, thanks to the impersonality of the corporation and to the narrowness of the moral code, they frequently brought about these evils, and worse.

It was the purpose of Professor Ross's book to point out that our sins had become social rather than personal, and, in a striking passage, he brought out the difference between the old criminal and the new:

> Unlike the old-time villain, the latter-day malefactor does not wear a slouch hat and a comforter, breathe forth curses and an odor of gin, go about his nefarious work with clenched teeth and an evil scowl. . . . The modern high-power dealer of woe wears immaculate linen, carries a silk hat and a lighted cigar, sins with a calm countenance and a serene soul, leagues or months from the evil he causes. Upon his gentlemanly presence the eventual blood and tears do not obtrude themselves.

He also pointed out that the modern villain could not be eliminated by a husky punch on the jaw from some handsome hero:

> If you want a David-and-Goliath fight, you must attack the powers that prey, not on the vices of the lax, but on the necessities of the decent. The deferred-dividend graft, the "yellow-dog" fund, the private-car iniquity, the Higher Thimblerig, far from turning tail and slinking away beaten like the vice-eaters, confront us rampant, sabre-toothed and razor-clawed.

And he feelingly described the opposition which the reformers and muckrakers were certain to meet:

Drunk with power, in office and club, in church and school, in legislature and court, they boldly make their stand, ruining the innocent, shredding the reputation of the righteous, destroying the careers and opportunities of their assailants, dragging down pastor and scholar, publicist and business man, from livelihood and influence, unhorsing alike faithful public servant, civic champion, and knight-errant of conscience, and all the while gathering into loathsome captivity the souls of multitudes of young men. Here is a fight where blows are rained, and armor dinted, and wounds suffered, and laurels won. If a champion of the right will prove he is a man and not a dummy, let him go up against these.

And it was in some such crusading spirit that many of the muckrakers approached their none too pleasant task. They had to overcome an incredible public inertia, but they found the fields in which they worked not wholly unprepared for the seed they were about to sow. Men had admired "the malefactors of great wealth," to employ the Rooseveltian phrase, and they had acquiesced in their dubious methods, but there had always been prophets to sound a note of warning; and discontent and distrust, though dormant, dwelt in the hearts of many. The growth of monopoly shocked some of those who talked glibly of prosperity; and the arbitrary exercise of power, together with the ostentatious display of luxury, aggravated the suspicions aroused by the sudden increase and concentration of wealth. The dominant currents at the turn of the century ran contrary to American traditions of morality and of liberty, and it was inevitable that public resentment should smoulder beneath the surface of public indifference.

the END

CHAPTER TWO

THE RISE OF THE POPULAR MAGAZINE

PUBLIC resentment for the thirty years previous to 1900 expressed itself in such ways as the granger movement, the silver "crusade," and populism. It was largely political, and found little support in the respectable press. By 1904 there was a ringing chorus of abuse and attack in the newspapers, and especially in the popular magazines. The muckrakers did not mildly call attention to evils; they thundered their denunciations in bold-face, italics, and large sized caps. They avoided generalities, and gave names and dates. No respecters of persons, they threw their bricks at the wealthiest and most powerful citizens of the land. Suave senators, socially eminent millionaires, bland clergymen, and erudite college presidents were ostentatiously drawn and quartered in periodicals that went into half a million homes.

Pure sensationalism some of this was, but much of it was the result of a real passion for social justice and an honest desire to set the truth before the people. The leading muckrakers were not cheap journalistic specialists in billingsgate; they were intelligent, educated, honest men and women. But they were nauseated by the spectacle of grab and graft presented in these United States. They were enraged at the corruption in municipal, state, and national governments. And they were shamed and sickened by the complacency of the majority of citizens, who remained utterly indifferent to the purulent condition of the political and industrial order. They were fighting for principles, and they did not hesitate to hit hard and often.

And yet the zeal of the muckrakers would have mattered but little if it had not happened that there was a medium ready through which they could reach the country. Before 1880 the four important magazines in the country were primarily literary in tone and purpose: *Harper's*, *Scribner's*, the *Century*, and the *Atlantic*. *Harper's* had been established in 1850 and had reached a circulation of 130,000 in the first three years of its existence. For fifty years, from 1869 to 1919, Henry Mills Alden was editor-in-chief. Various regular departments such as the "Editor's Easy Chair"—made famous by William Dean Howells—and the "Monthly Record of Current Events" offered comment on and information about the happenings of the day, but the greater part of each issue was devoted to literary subjects. *Scribner's*, also, under the direction of Edward L. Burlingame, was primarily belletristic, devoting some space each month to current affairs but occupying itself chiefly with literature and especially with art. The *Century*, which was started in 1870 but did not acquire its present name until 1881, when it came under the aegis of Richard Watson Gilder, attracted many of the leading writers of the day but paid little attention to economics, religion, or education. The *Atlantic*, founded in 1857 with James Russell Lowell as its first editor, surveyed a wider range of subjects than its contemporaries, printing articles on nature, travel, biography, and similar themes of polite interest, but it seldom touched on the subjects that were closest to the lives of American citizens.

These four periodicals were models of the sedate, exclusive, and not wholly indigenous culture of the latter part of the nineteenth century. One of them sold for twenty-five cents, and the others for thirty-five cents. They appealed to cultivated America, and they had no competitors. Then, with the eighties, astute young men began to realize that there was an enormous reading public in America which the Olympian quadrumvirate was not touching. This public had outgrown *Godey's Lady's Book* and the like; it was ready for something different. What the new interests were, it was the problem of these young men to discover.

By 1890 three magazines were feeling their way toward success in the new field: the *Ladies' Home Journal*, *Munsey's*, and the *Cosmopolitan*. The first of these was already marking off the special area in which its popularity was soon to be unmistakably established. The other two, both of which sold for twenty-five cents a copy, were making slower progress to their goal.

Munsey's had been established in 1889 as a weekly. Frank A. Munsey, seething with ambition, had fretted away in a Maine telegraph office until at last, in 1882, he had gone to New York with little capital other than his energy and his ideas. When his original plans failed, he succeeded in interesting a publisher in a project for a juvenile magazine. This paper, *The Golden Argosy*, later called simply *The Argosy*, was launched in December, 1882. Five months later the publishing house failed, and Munsey shouldered the magazine alone. Struggling along for a time, barely making both ends meet, he at last ventured all on a great advertising campaign. Momentarily success was his. With his own stories and with the work of Horatio Alger, Edward S. Ellis, Harry Castlemon, Oliver Optic, and other juvenile writers of the time, he built up, by 1887, a circulation of 115,000 copies.

Then the tide turned; subscribers fell off, and advertising could not win them back. Deciding that something must be done, Munsey issued his new weekly for adults. This proved less successful than he had anticipated, and in 1891, when his fortunes were at low ebb, and when he seemed to have two dying magazines on his hands, he made *Munsey's* a monthly. At first the change availed little. Mr. Munsey studied the situation carefully, trying to discover why there were so few magazine readers in the United States. He decided that the newer monthlies were copying too closely the four established magazines. He decided also that twenty-five or thirty-five cents a copy was more than the average person was willing to pay. What was needed, he thought, was a lighter, more entertaining magazine, selling at a reasonable price—"a magazine of the people and for the people, with pictures and art and good cheer and human interest throughout."

In the meantime John Brisben Walker had taken over the *Cosmopolitan.* He had been to West Point, had seen military service in China, had been a candidate for Congress, and had developed some valuable mining interests. In 1889 he ran across a magazine which had been founded by a clergyman in Rochester and had devoted itself to recipes, uplifting short stories, and a decorously domestic atmosphere. Walker took the *Cosmopolitan,* introduced new features, such as a department on social problems edited by Edward Everett Hale, and tried to secure better writers. But in general he found, as Munsey had found, that very drastic changes must be made if the new reading public was to be reached.

While Munsey and Walker were working their way toward a new type of magazine, a new enterprise swept down upon the public. S. S. McClure, during eight years of work with his syndicate, had made contacts with most of the best-known authors in America and abroad, and had gained a fairly accurate knowledge of what the people wanted. In June, 1893, *McClure's* appeared, rich in that lighter type of reading which Munsey had seen was necessary, and selling at fifteen cents a copy—the lower price which Munsey had wished to introduce. In content and in price the new magazine appealed to the public; the era of the cheap magazine had begun.

The very next month Walker countered by reducing the price of the *Cosmopolitan* to twelve and a half cents, though he raised it to fifteen in December. But the most amazing counter-attack came in October, when Munsey, not only to meet competition but also to carry out the ideas he had already developed, slashed the price of his magazine to ten cents a copy. At the moment he had two moribund magazines on his hands, and was more than a hundred thousand dollars in debt. But he saw an opportunity to regain all he had lost, and he took it.

Unfortunately, he immediately met an unexpected obstacle. The American News Company, which practically monopolized the periodical business of the country, opposed the ten-cent magazine because it would reduce their profits. Munsey, unabashed, decided to go over their heads, appealing direct to the news dealers. He sent out his circulars to the dealers, and redoubled his advertising campaign. Representatives of the American News Company offered to bargain with him, but they refused to meet his demands, and he rejected their proposals. The first issue appeared, moved slowly at first, and seemed a failure. Munsey had pitted himself single-handed against one of the strongest organizations in the country, and apparently he had been defeated, as much stronger predecessors had been defeated. But the sales grew, new editions had to be printed, and finally the issue reached the forty thousand mark. Sixty thousand copies of the November number were sold. And so the circulation grew until it had reached seven hundred thousand copies monthly.

McClure's soon dropped to ten cents, and a little later the *Cosmopolitan* followed suit. But in time the competition among these three magazines depended less on price-cutting than on the quality of the contents. McClure, utilizing his familiarity with British writers, secured the best work of Kipling, Anthony Hope, and Conan Doyle, and also cultivated many of the promising young American writers. Walker also secured contributions from Kipling and Doyle, and published serials by H. G. Wells, Camille Flammarion, and William Dean Howells. Theodore Roosevelt, Henry James, James Russell Lowell, Mark Twain, Agnes Repplier, and Frank Stockton all wrote for the *Cosmopolitan* during the nineties.

All the magazines leaned heavily on illustrations, employing popular artists, reproducing famous paintings, publishing series of photographs. *McClure's* drove up the circulation thirty thousand in a single month by publishing a collection of pictures of Napoleon. Both the *Cosmopolitan* and *Munsey's* had departments devoted to art. In September, 1893, the *Cosmopolitan* devoted practically an entire issue to the World's Fair, making photographs a leading feature.

Gradually the three magazines took on individual characteristics. *Munsey's* prided itself on general interest rather than special features. It entertained, the while it gave its readers the feeling that they were *en rapport* with currents of thought in the world capitals. *McClure's* sought to present the most discussed writers of fiction and to keep people abreast of the newest developments in science and world affairs. In order to secure lively articles on rather complex subjects, McClure had to build up a staff of specially trained writers, and it was this staff which stood him in such good stead in the muckraking days.

The *Cosmopolitan* was slower in finding its field, but in the latter years of Mr. Walker's editorship it created a place for itself by developing a new type of journalism. The older magazines had been impersonal, and their editors had been reticent. But in the nineties such periodicals as the *Chap-Book*, the *Philistine*, and the *Lark* made considerable impression because of their direct and personal appeal.

Walker, with his vast and heterogeneous group of readers could not, of course, strike the intimate note that was so successfully sounded by the little magazines, but he did try to establish a new kind of relationship with the *Cosmopolitan's* constituency. In order to make the readers feel an immediate interest in the magazine, he devised a series of ventures in which they were to regard themselves as sharers. He sent, for example, Julian Hawthorne to India to find out the truth about that country on behalf of the *Cosmopolitan's* readers, whose special commissioner he was supposed to be. Walker also began signing articles himself, and on occasion chatted informally with subscribers.

But the most remarkable experiment in extending the magazine's functions was the founding of the Cosmopolitan University. In 1896 and 1897 a number of articles appeared on the subject of education. These stimulated some general discussion and led to the familiar complaint that too many people were denied the benefit of a higher education. Walker suddenly had a brilliant idea, and, apparently without weighing the difficulties, announced that the *Cosmopolitan* would found a university, secure competent instructors, and undertake to minister to the needs of the masses. To head the enterprise he secured Andrews, who had just resigned as president of Brown University because of objections to his attitude toward free silver, but Andrews had to withdraw because he was asked to reconsider his resignation. After great difficulty, Dr. E. N. Potter was placed in charge.

In the meantime registrations had been pouring in. In order to register, a person had only to state his previous education and promise to do faithful work in whatever courses he elected. Instruction was, of course, to be carried on by correspondence. Thousands took advantage of this offer, and the sum appropriated proved ridiculously inadequate. There was not time to organize the teaching staff, and the mere secretarial work was overwhelming. By May of 1898 twenty thousand men and women had registered. The plan had to be made less ambitious, and finally was abandoned altogether.

Walker insisted that this project was purely an expression of his conception of the relation of a magazine to its readers, but the sceptically minded pointed out that it was not without advertising value. It served, certainly, to call attention to the *Cosmopolitan*, though the magazine failed to build up the large circulation enjoyed by its rivals. In 1900 *Munsey's* was decidedly the leader, demonstrating the extent to which its founder had understood the minds of the American people. *McClure's* was second, and was laying the foundations for its tremendous success in the early years of the new century. The *Cosmopolitan*, though third, was abundantly prosperous. Clearly, the cheap magazine had come to stay. *Everybody's* and *Pearson's* were founded in 1899, and there were several new and successful ventures after 1900.

Side by side with the growth of the popular magazine of this type came the development of another kind of magazine, more serious than *Munsey's* and *McClure's*, but less literary than the *Atlantic* and the others of the sedate quartet. The *Arena* was founded in 1889, the *Review of Reviews* in 1890, and the *Yale Review* in 1892. To some extent, in the shaping of public opinion these periodicals took the place of the newspapers, which were beginning to subordinate the editorial function to the reportorial. If their circulation figures remained smaller than those of the cheap magazines, their influence was probably even greater.

Of all these magazines, that which was to play the pioneer rôle in muckraking was the *Arena*, which Benjamin O. Flower founded in 1889. Flower, whom Charles Zueblin called "the editorial dean of democracy," was born on October 19, 1858, in Albion, Illinois. His parents moved to Evansville,

Indiana, and there the boy received his primary and second-
ary education, afterwards attending the University of Kentucky. From the first he was attracted to a literary career,
and at the age of twenty-two he was editor of the Albion
American Sentinel. Later he established the *American Spectator*,
and at various periods he was connected with the *Coming
Age*, the *New Time*, and the *Twentieth Century Magazine*. His
most significant work, however, was done as editor of the
Arena in the early years of the reform movement.

During a great part of his life Flower was ill, but he was
an indefatigable reader and worker and gave little thought
to his health. Somewhat naïvely he believed that if people
would but see the evil effects of their acts they would themselves mend their ways, and his faith probably accounts for
the aggressive and optimistic tone of his editorials. He was
never personal in his denunciations, but nothing could deter
his courageous spirit from making an attack that he believed
to be just. He was sensitive to beauty in any form, loved
painting, sculpture, and literature, and always kept flowers
in his office. Generosity was almost a vice with him, and his
faith in the people he trusted could hardly be shaken even
though they imposed upon him criminally. Hamlin Garland
has called him "a very good man," and the justice of the
characterization cannot be questioned. Like many other
good men, however, he had no head for business, and he
was frequently in financial difficulties. He died in 1917.

The magazine which this courageous and talented man
founded continued under his editorship from 1889 to 1896,
when John Clark Ridpath took charge. In 1897 a "stroke
to the people" was offered by reducing the price to $2.50 a
year, and a special appeal was made to the farmers. In the
same year an editorial stated that the mission of the paper
was to place before the people facts which the "plutocratic"
press withheld from the public for its own sordid purposes.

In 1898, when Paul Tyner became editor, the magazine had nearly one hundred thousand readers. Tyner stated that the *Arena* was "an absolutely independent review," whose aim was to tell the truth and to present facts and arguments on various sides of important questions. A year later he laid down the editorship for the purpose of devoting himself entirely to the practice and teaching of metaphysical healing. He was succeeded in the editorial chair by John Emery McLean, formerly editor of *Mind*. McLean made a few changes but none of great importance. A little later Flower felt himself so completely out of sympathy with the purposes of the journal that he severed all connection with it, but in 1904 he again became sole editor and sought to make it once more "one of the great conscience forces in the English-speaking world." In such wise it happened that he was editor of the *Arena* not only during the decade of preparation but also in the years that witnessed the most determined efforts of the muckrakers. He contributed more than two hundred and fifty articles to his journal during the arduous years of his editorship. Perhaps no one else voiced more fervently the sense of injustice and the possession of high hopes and aspirations. "Let us agitate, educate, organize," he urged in 1900, "and move forward, casting aside timidity and insisting that the Republic shall no longer lag behind in the march of progress." The *Arena* frankly aimed at social, economic, and political reform, and unhesitatingly exposed corruption. It is significant, however, that Flower's exposures and warnings were in general terms, and that the *Arena* seldom mentioned corporations and individuals by name. The true muckrakers were not so restrained.

Much less outspoken than the *Arena* were the *Review of Reviews* and the *Outlook*, but both magazines contributed to the growing public interest in current affairs. The *Review of Reviews*, which was founded in London by W. R. Stead, was intended to be an international review, covering the best thought of the world. Its circulation grew rapidly, and in 1892 Albert Shaw began to publish an American edition, containing editorial comment on the affairs of the world, digests of the leading articles of the month, cartoons, book reviews, and independent articles.

The *Outlook* grew out of the *Christian Union*, which Henry Ward Beecher had founded. When Lyman Abbott, who had been associated with Beecher, became editor-in-chief, he broadened the scope of the weekly, making it a well-rounded periodical instead of a purely religious journal. Abbott, after engaging in reconstruction work following the Civil War, made a survey of American problems and decided that the most important was the industrial problem. This subject he studied for himself, and he secured liberal economists and progressive ministers to write about it in his magazine. Thus he made the *Outlook* a strong force in the development of the social gospel. He was interested in other social problems as well, and the editorials and articles he published helped to shape the rising sense of dissatisfaction with politics and industry in America. The *Outlook's* position was invariably in the middle of the road, a fact on which Dr. Abbott prided himself. In an editorial published in 1897 he said it was characteristic of the magazine to believe in immortality of the spirit and in change of the form—in the old religion and a new theology, the old patriotism and a new politics, the old philanthropy and new institutions, the old brotherhood and a new social order. To citizens of a certain type, especially those closely affiliated with the churches, the *Outlook* brought tidings of change, paving the way for the rise of a movement of protest, exposure, and reform.

It is Mr. Munsey's estimate that the ten-cent magazine, between 1893 and 1899, increased the magazine purchasing public from 250,000 to 750,000. At the same time the more serious non-fiction magazines had been cultivating an interest in politics and economics. Thus three new factors had entered American life: at least half a million people were buying magazines who had never bought them before, which indicates an increase of perhaps two million in the number of magazine readers; a certain number of the people were turning to magazines for the kind of editorial guidance which they had once received from their newspapers; and, finally, the popular magazine had arrived, founded for the sake of profit, consecrated to the task of giving its readers what they wanted, and capable of going to almost any lengths to stimulate their interest.

CHAPTER THREE

THE RESTLESS EIGHTEEN-NINETIES

BEGINNING in 1901 and 1902, rising to its full force in 1903 and 1904, and lasting until 1911 or 1912, a passion for change swept the country. Jarred for once out of their calm satisfaction with life in this benign land, men started examining the institutions they had built, and suddenly realized that they fell somewhat short of the assumed perfection. Men who in another era would have been denounced as knockers and defamers were acclaimed as heroes and servants of the Republic. Muckraking became a paying business, enlisting the most skillful pens the nation could boast. We have always had a literature of discontent, of course, but at no other time has it assumed such proportions or enjoyed such esteem.

Since one does not expect a nation to be converted over night from affable acquiescence to vehement dissent, one studies the eighteen-nineties for the antecedents of this critical examination of American life, and discovers in the magazines of the period indications of the tendencies that were so conspicuous in the next decade. The first thing one notes in examining the leading periodicals is the predominance of fiction; the good American citizen still preferred a pleasant short story or a comfortably sentimental serial; but one also notes that there were five prominent journals that published no fiction whatsoever and that the others devoted a certain amount of space to articles of general interest. A rough estimate of the contents of some of the magazines of the decade shows that the number of stories printed in *Harper's* almost equals the total number of articles. *Scribner's* and the *Century* printed a somewhat smaller proportion of stories, but about one-fourth of all their articles dealt with art and literature, while one-sixth or less concerned government, politics, economics, sociology, religion, and education. The *Atlantic* printed fewer stories, and about one-fifth of its articles dealt with current problems, and another fifth, with history and biography.

In the cheaper magazines we find fiction still in the lead, but we note that political and social problems receive considerable attention. *McClure's* printed almost as large a proportion of stories as *Harper's*, but it gave much more space to history and biography than it did to literature and art. More than one-fourth of all the articles in the *Cosmopolitan* during the decade were discussions of current issues. And in the non-fiction magazines, the *Arena*, the *Forum*, the *Review of Reviews* and the *North American Review*, we observe that the majority of the articles touch very closely the critical issues of the day. The *Arena* cannot be regarded as typical, but it is interesting to note that for the ten-year period under consideration 13 per cent of its articles concerned government and politics, 30 per cent were on economics and sociology, 15 per cent were on religion, and 4 per cent dealt with education. Only 10 per cent treated literature and art, while 2 per cent are to be classed as history and biography, 6 per cent were scientific, and 3 per cent were concerned with foreign affairs. The remaining 17 per cent cannot well be classified. The averages for the twelve outstanding magazines of the period show that about one-third of all contributions, including stories, dealt with controversial questions.

[In 1890, when the McKinley Tariff Act was passed, the magazines began to discuss the whole question of free trade versus protection. In particular the *North American Review* occupied itself with this question, securing articles from such friends of the tariff as James G. Blaine and from such exponents of free trade as William E. Gladstone. The *Forum*, of January, 1891, printed an article, "The Coming Billionaire," by Thomas G. Shearman, on the concentration of wealth, a subject which also agitated contributors to the *Arena* and the *Nation*. Mr. Shearman estimated that seventy names represented an aggregate of $2,700,000,000, and an average of $37,500,000, and that there were at least fifty other men in the country who possessed ten million apiece. He stated that the average annual income of the one hundred richest Americans was $1,200,000, while four-fifths of the families of the country did not earn more than $500 a year. The *Nation*, commenting on the same situation, pointed out that a millionaire was for American youth what Roland was for the youth of the Middle Ages, the object of admiration, the ideal of achievement, and the model of conduct.

Social theorizing was in the air, and the works of Henry George, Edward Bellamy, and Henry Demarest Lloyd were widely read. Goldwin Smith, writing in the *Forum* of August, 1890, an article entitled "Prophets of Unrest," criticized the various proponents of reform, especially Bellamy, and predicted imminent catastrophe.

There is everywhere in the social frame [he wrote], an outward unrest, which as usual is the sign of fundamental change within. Old creeds have given way. The masses, the artisans especially, have ceased to believe that the existing order of society, with its grades of rank and wealth, is a divine ordinance against which it is vain to rebel. They have ceased to believe in a future state, the compensation of those whose lot is hard here. Convinced that this world is all, and that there is nothing more to come, they want to grasp at once their share of enjoyment. The labor journals are full of this thought. . . . The gov-

erning classes, unnerved by scepticism, have lost faith in the
order which they represent, and are inclined to precipitate ab-
dication. Many members of them—partly from philanthropy,
partly from vanity, partly perhaps from fear—are playing with
the demagogue and, as they did in France, dallying with revolution.

The *Arena* noted the same unrest, though, of course, with
different emotions. In 1890, the year that Smith's article
appeared, an editorial declared that a national catastrophe
was certain to come "unless some more equitable adjust-
ment of the social problem be speedily reached." It pointed
to the tremendous sale of *Progress and Poverty* and *Looking
Backward*, to the organization of single tax and Socialist societies, and to the constant agitation in the magazines. A little
later William Dean Howells, writing in the *North American
Review* (February, 1894), asked, "Are we a plutocracy?"
Everyone, he asserted, who believes in the capitalistic system, whether he is a rich employer or an aspiring laborer,
is a plutocrat. He pointed out that the wage-earners deserved
only a qualified sympathy, for most of them believed in the
wage system and were dreaming of the time when they
would give wages to others.

In the next decade it was the urban middle classes who
took up the hue and cry against corruption in government
and industry, but in the nineties the active agitators were
chiefly the farmers of the West and the laborers of the East.
Populism was growing in the West, and many of the magazines discussed this phenomenon. Some writers regarded it
with alarm, declaring that the farmers were ignorant fanat-
ics, but others saw in the movement the natural outcome
of the hard conditions prevailing in the Middle West. Flower,
writing in the *Arena*, acclaimed the movement, maintaining
that its great aim was to establish freedom and to preserve
the Republic. Albert Shaw, editor of the *Review of Reviews*,

was himself a westerner, and he understood public opinion in the West as few editors did. He tried to explain the situation to his readers in the East, and in 1894 he published a number of letters from people in the West. He himself wrote in July of that year, "The Coxey Movement, the rise of the People's party, the income tax, the demands of the Farmer's Alliance, and the silver question have led to much discussion of a so-called 'new sectionalism' that is arraying the West against the East."

The hard times of 1893, marked by the comedy of "Coxey's army" and the tragedy of the Pullman strike of 1894, brought discontent into the open. The *Nation* blamed the Republican party, with its policy of high protection, for much of the unrest, and many of the magazines were inclined to look on the Coxey movement, however farcical it might be, as a serious symptom. The *Chautauquan*, on the other hand, declared that the views advocated by Coxey and Carl Brown, his lieutenant, were a "mingling of blasphemous insanity and political incendiarism."

In 1895 certain "insurgent" congressmen addressed a call to the Democrats of the nation, stating that President Cleveland did not represent the majority of the party, and urging the radicals of the West to capture the party leadership. The radical Democrats, the Populists, and the National Silverites only needed a leader to weld them into a formidable political force, and that leader appeared in William Jennings Bryan. The *Arena* threw its influence unhesitatingly on the side of Bryan, urging the people to forget party prejudices and to array themselves against the double-headed party of plutocracy and centralized wealth. If there ever was an hour, said Flower in the November issue of that year, when freemen should refuse to sell their birth-right, when they should be vigilant workers for home, freedom, prosperity, and the Republic, that hour had come. The election of

Bryan, he wrote, would mean the rejuvenation of democracy and the salvation of republican government from a lawless plutocracy.

Few periodicals were willing to go as far as the *Arena*, but many of them looked with some trepidation on the growth of monopoly and the ideals of a money-mad civilization. In September, 1899, the *Outlook* published an article entitled "The Shadow on American Life," giving the impressions of a foreigner, Ian Maclaren (John Watson), the well known Scotch author. Maclaren praised Americans for their patriotism, their love of education, and their sense of righteousness in every national crisis, but he found one shadow which gravely affected the dignity and beauty of American public life, and that was the strength of the "secular spirit," the tendency to give an undue place to the value and influence of wealth. With a few exceptions, he wrote, Americans bow the knee to the golden calf of wealth. It was his opinion that in two fields especially, government and the church, money should not control, but he stated that in America it was common talk that one state legislature was the obedient tool of a great railway company and that other legislatures and municipal governments were under the control of other corporations. If one half of the charges were true, he said, then the secular spirit in its grossest and most offensive form was staining political life. And he found similar evidence that money dominated the church. The value of a preacher, he recorded, was usually estimated from his financial abilities, and he said it was commonly assumed that a preacher could be drawn from any church by the offer of a large enough salary.

Historians and even United States senators became alarmed at the growing power of wealth, and much was written about a "money power" or an "invisible empire" that threatened civilization itself. Senator William M. Stewart of Nevada, writing an article entitled "The Great Slave Power" in the *Arena*, May, 1898, charged the Rothschild money syndicate with conspiring to enslave the human race. It already controlled England and the rest of Europe, he asserted, and was rapidly gaining in Asia. Japan was a bankrupt appendage of the British Empire, and would sink back into the miserable condition from which she had so recently emerged. China was being enslaved, and India and Egypt were already in slavery. In the United States, he continued, this syndicate was trying to destroy democracy and enslave the people. The only fear which it entertained was that the American people might yet be aroused to assert themselves by the use of the ballot and might thereby regain the financial independence of the United States and deal a deathblow to the scheme of universal slavery.

The next month (June, 1898), the *Arena* published another sensational article, this time from the pen of John Clark Ridpath, who chose the title, "The Invisible Empire." Ridpath called attention to what he believed to be a significant coincidence. On January 28, 1898, the payment of the national debt according to contract came up in the United States Senate. A resolution was to be voted on, declaring that all the bonds of the United States issued or authorized to be issued under certain acts of Congress were payable, principal and interest, at the option of the government in standard silver dollars. To this resolution Henry Cabot Lodge of Massachusetts offered an amendment, providing that all such debts should be paid in gold. The vote was twenty-four to fifty-three against the amendment. The supporters of the resolution claimed that a gold dollar in 1898 was worth more than twice as much as the dollars in which the debt had been contracted. On April 15 the Senate voted on Cuban independence, with the vote standing sixty-seven in favor and twenty-one opposed. All but two of the twenty-one opponents of independence had favored gold payment.

Ridpath seized upon these two facts and made them the basis for alleging that the people of this country were no longer under the government of the American Republic but were under the Invisible Empire. He mentioned the nineteen senators by name and informed his readers that these gentlemen constituted the "American Committee of the Invisible Empire." Not a nation in the world, he declared, was exempt from the dominion of this "universal monarchy." Ridpath wrote with great seriousness and ended his article with this appeal:

Men of my country! Men of the world! You can accept this situation if you want to accept it. If you have no more love of freedom, no more patriotism, no more sense than to accept it, why then accept it, and be slaves forever. If nothing will arouse you, why, then, sleep, sleep! But remember that there is no sleep in the Invisible Empire.

Many people believed the sensational charges made by Stewart, Ridpath, and others; and impatient reformers complained of the difficulty of awakening the sleeping conscience of the people to a realization of the "essential immorality and injustice of the present social conditions." Benjamin Flower and his *Arena* constantly pointed to the desperate condition of the poor, and ridiculed all talk of prosperity while it remained true that one person out of every ten who died in New York was buried in Potter's Field. Flower advocated coöperation as the remedy for "our monstrous economic order," but other reformers argued for government ownership, and Frank Parsons had a long series of articles in the *Arena* in which he sought to show the advantages accruing to citizens of various European countries from government ownership of the telegraph.

Magazine writers often lamented the fact that the moral forces of the country were not organized, and in 1893 Ben-

jamin Flower suggested the organization of a "League of
Love" or a "Federation of Justice," which should be open
to all people who wished to promote the interests of humanity irrespective of race or creed. The suggestion seemed to
bear fruit, for a Union for Practical Progress was organized
on a nation-wide scale. Many cities had local clubs, and
these the *Arena* encouraged by printing suggestions for con-
ducting meetings and for organizing the moral forces of the
community. Successful groups, such as the Baltimore Union
for Public Good, were described in the *Arena*, and the New
York *Voice* and other papers coöperated by printing bibli-
ographies and suggestions for discussion. Professor Thomas
Elmer Will wrote an article for the national committee of
the Union for Practical Progress in which he explained the
methods which were to be employed in organizing and promoting social reform work. The program which he outlined
for six months suggests the scope of the Union's activities:

June: Child Labor.
July: Public Parks and Playgrounds.
August: Prison Reforms.
September: Municipal Reform.
October: The Problem of the Unemployed.
November: Best Methods for Combating Political Corruption.

In 1898 a new League of Social Service was formed in
New York for the purpose of uniting the efforts of the al-
ready existing organizations in the field of social service.
Jane Addams, Washington Gladden, Edward Everett Hale,
and Alice Freeman Palmer served on the advisory council,
and Dr. Josiah Strong was president of the organization.
Another organization of which the *Arena* approved was the
National Conference of Social and Political Reforms, which
met in Buffalo in July, 1899. Here there assembled Socialists,
Individualists, Single-taxers, Silverites, Direct-legislationists,
Green-backers, Populists, Democrats, and Republicans for

the purpose of finding a practical plan for united action in order to bring about certain radical reforms. The Conference went on record as opposing the encroachment upon academic freedom in educational institutions; it established a free school of economics; it adopted a practical plan for a referendum of the independent reform vote which should make it possible for the people to unite at the polls; it established an instrument of enlightment in the Social Reform Union; and it sent to the people an address written by George D. Herron and agreed to by the Conference.

Economic and political problems were chief among those that agitated the public and furnished material for magazine articles, but education and religion came in for their share of attention. Toward the end of the decade the dismissal of several professors, presumably because of radicalism, sharpened the interest in education and raised the whole question of academic freedom. One of the first cases to arouse popular attention was the dismissal of Professor Edward W. Bemis from the sociology department of the University of Chicago. It was charged that this dismissal was the result of statements of his that the railroad presidents and other corporation leaders considered dangerous to their business.

In 1897 President E. Benjamin Andrews resigned from Brown University because the board of trustees informed him that the institution had already lost gifts and legacies on account of his views on bimetallism and went on to suggest that it would be difficult to secure pecuniary support unless he ceased promulgating views which appealed most strongly to the passions and prejudices of the public. This communication was dated July 16, 1897. On the following day Andrews resigned rather than surrender his liberty of utterance. In the public discussion that followed, the gold-standard men and the monopoly people generally sided with the trustees, while the educators defended academic freedom. Twenty-four professors of Brown University sent a dignified "open letter" to the corporation. The editor of the *Arena* praised President Andrews' manly stand in the cause of the people and severely censured the trustees for their action. "The battle is on in this country between the Man and the Dollar," he wrote. "It is a fight to the finish. You are one of the champions of the Man. Brown University seems to be wedded to the Dollar." President Andrews withdrew his resignation and did not retire from the university until the year following.

The next bit of excitement came when President Thomas Elmer Will, Professor Frank Parsons, and Dr. Duren J. H. Ward all withdrew from the Kansas State Agricultural College, presumably because their radical tendencies in political science, economics, and religion had aroused opposition. Much more interest, however, attached to the resignation of Professor George D. Herron from Grinnell College, then known as Iowa College, where a chair of Applied Christianity had been specially created for him seven years earlier. His teachings and his public utterances disturbed so many people that a majority of the trustees and supporters of the college regarded his affiliation with the institution as detrimental. On October 13, 1899, he resigned, explaining his course of action in a carefully prepared message to the board of trustees:

It is certainly true [he said] that the doctrines of property which I hold are subversive to the existing industrial and political order. I do believe that our system of private ownership of natural resources is a crime against God and man and nature; that natural resources are not property, and cannot be so held without destroying the liberty of man and the basis of the religion of Christ.

Dr. Herron went on to say that since sincere friends of the college seemed to believe that his presence on the faculty jeopardized the financial well-being of the institution, he preferred to resign. In accepting his resignation the trustees expressed their high regard for Professor Herron and their appreciation of his ability to understand their position. They continued:

Whatever may be the ultimate and ideal truth as to the private ownership of natural sources of wealth, to us it seems clear that the most promising course for promoting the ultimate right is at present to impress on men their present duty rightly to use what wealth shall properly come to them under the present organization of society and in the world in which they now live, rather than to spend much time and force in directly attacking systems that can be best changed but slowly in the interest of a scheme which if ideal, has never yet been shown to be practical in a highly organized society.

As so often happens, the issue of academic freedom was complicated, in the case of Dr. Herron, by other factors, which, however, were not mentioned in the magazine discussions. And at all events the issue was sufficiently clear-cut to deserve a general consideration. The *Arena*, in its issue for October, 1899, published several articles on the subject, including a vigorous attack on the colleges by Willis J. Abbot, and a mild defense of academic policy by Professor Albion W. Small of the sociology department of the University of Chicago. Abbot maintained that American colleges almost invariably fought shy of a teacher who believed in the redistribution of wealth or the destruction of monopoly, and declared that enough professors had been ejected from faculties to prove the case against the college. Professor Small, on the other hand, took issue with the statement of the Buffalo Conference that "there is not a single institution of learning in this country in which the teaching of economics and sociology is not muzzled by the influence of wealth in the case of private endowments, or of partisan politics in the case of State universities." The title of his article, "Limits Imposed by Responsibility," suggests his tone. He argued that we could never have absolute freedom of speech, and voiced the opinion that among responsible Americans none were freer than university professors. He also said that he knew of no well substantiated case of dismissal because of economic views.

Two years later Thomas Elmer Will, writing in the *Arena*, made a stinging attack on the colleges, offering a list of some fifteen professors who, according to him, had been discharged because of radical opinions. He called his article "A Menace to Freedom: The College Trust," and he began by declaring that the plutocracy was arming for the coming conflict, and was seeking to debauch the public conscience in order to weaken the forces of righteousness. The press, he stated, was already largely in the hands of the moneyed interests, and the next objective was to capture the colleges. The colleges were a menace to the plutocracy, he explained, for free investigation was all that was necessary to expose the rottenness of the existing economic order. Realizing the danger, the great financiers had sent out orders to bring the colleges and universities into line, with the result that countless teachers had lost their positions and had been placed on the blacklist.

The menace to academic freedom seemed so great to certain reformers that they attempted to create a college which should be free from the influence of millionaires. In the spring of 1900 Dr. George McA. Miller took charge of Avalon College, a small, struggling institution in Trenton, Missouri, on a ten-year contract. Walter Vrooman, founder of Ruskin Hall in Oxford, England, hearing of Avalon, decided to visit it, and as a result he coöperated with President Miller. The school was renamed Ruskin College, and it became the center of the Ruskin Hall movement in America. The

aim was to offer education in the industries as well as in
the arts and sciences, and to make it possible for a student
to earn his own way. The faculty of the new college included
men who had served in the best universities and colleges of
the country, and among them were four former college presidents. In 1901 there were three hundred students, with
every indication of an increased enrollment the next year.
In 1903, however, Ruskin College joined with several other
institutions to form Ruskin University of Chicago, which
had, in its first year, a faculty of 250, a total resident enrollment of 2,500 students, and 8,000 correspondence students.
J. J. Tobias served as president, and Dr. Miller as dean.

Articles on academic freedom could be counted on to interest magazine readers, but popular interest in religion was
even keener. The rise of science, the introduction of higher
criticism, and the study of religions other than Christianity
combined in the last half of the nineteenth century to dis-
turb the orthodox. Not only did ministers and theologians
debate with animation the new challenges to faith, but men
and women everywhere interested themselves in the new
ideas, and the popular magazines published many articles
explaining and endorsing or condemning the changes that
were taking place. And who will say that the "moral awakening" of the first decade of the twentieth century was not
partially due to the fact that people had ceased to be interested in theology and had turned their attention to practical, ethical, human affairs? A break with orthodoxy in one
field often leads to liberalism elsewhere.

The *Arena*, as might be expected, encouraged free expression of liberal tendencies, and in the very first issue, December, 1889, the Reverend Minot Savage, a well known
Unitarian minister, published an article called "Agencies
that Are Working a Revolution in Theology." In the same
year the editor of the *Chautauquan*, commenting on the dis-

cussion of the authorship of the Pentateuch, stated his belief that Moses wrote these books but placed himself on record as favoring complete freedom in the application of scientific methods to the study of the Bible. Somewhat later (December, 1895), Goldwin Smith wrote for the *North American Review* an article sensationally entitled, "Christianity's Millstone," in the course of which he declared that a theology based on the faulty science, the distorted history, and the primitive morals of the Old Testament was positively harmful. This indictment brought forth many replies, several of which asserted that Professor Smith was behind the times. The *Nation* said that the documentary hypothesis was doing for theology what the theory of evolution had done for natural science, and the Toronto *Week* expressed the opinion that no Christian scholar of note held to the doctrine of verbal inspiration attacked in Smith's article. Newman Smyth, writing for the *Century* in the same year (June, 1895), tried to explain what scholars meant by the term "higher criticism," and sought to demonstrate how modern study of the Bible had enhanced the value of the Scriptures. As a result of all this discussion men and women came more and more to think of the Bible as a human document, differing from other books in degree perhaps but not in kind.

The conflict of opinion over the higher criticism, however, was far less intense than the struggle which had resulted from the publication of Darwin's *Origin of Species* in 1859. By 1890 the theory of evolution was widely talked about, and the man in the street, quite as much as the theologian, took sides for or against the Darwinian hypothesis. Liberal ministers welcomed the new scientific views and tried to show the relation of science and Christianity. St. George Minart discussed the subject in the *Cosmopolitan*, and Lyman Abbott had a series of thirteen articles on the "Theology of an Evolutionist" in the *Outlook* for 1897. Though he ran true to

form in clinging to what he regarded as the Christian funda-
mentals, he made concessions to science that deeply grieved
his more conservative brethren.

James Freeman Clark had published the first volume of
his *Ten Great Religions* in 1871, and in 1886 the twenty-second
edition appeared. Such books as this, together with the
World's Parliament of Religions, held in connection with
the Columbian Exposition in Chicago, brought people to
an understanding of other religions and tended to broaden
their conception of Christianity. F. Herbert Stead, discussing
the Parliament in the *Review of Reviews* for March, 1894, expressed the opinion that the contact with other faiths which
took place at the Exposition was certain to deal a deathblow to the fierce hatred and intolerance that had formerly
prevailed.

Another subject not infrequently discussed in the magazines was psychical research and spiritualism. Thousands
of people believed in spiritualism because it was comforting,
and, since the "spirit" messages were usually far from orthodox, and since the adherents of psychical research frequently
broke away from the churches, the tendency of the movement was to undermine orthodox theology.

In religious controversy the storm center of the decade was
Colonel Robert G. Ingersoll. In two articles entitled "Why
Am I an Agnostic?", published in the *North American Review*
in 1889 and 1890, he expounded his views of science, his
attitude toward the churches, and the case for the rejection
of miracles. He maintained that Christianity was based on
miracles and that the destruction of belief in the miracu-
lous would of necessity mean the downfall of the Christian
churches. To these assertions Lyman Abbott replied in a typical article published in the issue of the same magazine for
April, 1890. The next month Archdeacon Farrar presented
his views on "Ingersollism," sharply criticizing the famous

agnostic for his dogmatism and showing him to be an amateur in theology. Ingersoll continued to publish articles, frequently writing on men with whose views he sympathized, Thomas Paine, for example, Renan, and Tolstoy. In 1899, the year of his death, the *North American Review* published his last article, "The Agnostic Side." In this he eloquently expressed the more positive aspect of his teachings, closing with these words:

Preach, I pray you, the gospel of Intellectual Hospitality— the liberty of thought and speech. Take from loving hearts the awful fear. Have mercy on your fellow men. Do not drive to madness the mothers whose tears are falling on the pallid faces of those who died in unbelief. Pity the erring, wayward, suffering, weeping world. Do not proclaim as "tidings of great joy" that an Infinite Spider is weaving webs to catch the souls of men.

After his death there appeared many estimates of the man and of his probable influence on humanity. Some thought he had done harm, but others believed his denunciations were beneficial. A friend, Henry M. Field, declared that a bold argument for a false theory sometimes helps us to discover the truth.

Indubitably Ingersoll had contributed much to the animated discussion of religious problems that went on in the nineties. He in America and Huxley in England had made forthright attacks on the church, but they had won the respect of many of their opponents. Huxley died four years before Ingersoll, and both occasions brought forth the opinion that the expression of agnosticism might prove of benefit to Christianity. The Kansas City *Star*, for example, summed up in the following paragraph views that had been widely expressed:

It is a question whether the churches have lost a friend or an enemy in the death of Professor Huxley. His attacks upon the preachers never weakened one whit the basic principles of the

Christian system. But what they did do or helped to do was to explode those narrow and intolerant dogmas which offend reason and which have always been harmful to the church. Conduct and character have taken precedence of belief and adherence to fixed forms of worship. The church is stronger for the change, and the world is vastly better.

Ingersoll and Huxley were not the only agnostics; indeed agnosticism seemed to be so common that J. Frederic Dutton, writing in the *Unitarian Review*, named and described four species: irreligious agnosticism, which is crude, ignorant, and lazy; religious agnosticism, which is tender, humble, pious, emotional; painful agnosticism, the product of a struggle against doubt ending in defeat; and scientific agnosticism, which is not demonstrated but accepted, and is not a conviction but a convenience.

The problem of immortality troubled many. Lester Ward, writing for the *Forum* in September, 1889, expounded the anthropological conception of the manner in which belief in the supernatural and in immortality arose. Goldwin Smith, writing for the same journal some years later (July, 1896), presented the case for and against belief in immortality, reaching the scarcely original conclusion that we do not know. In January—June, 1896, the venerable English statesman, William E. Gladstone, reviewed the orthodox arguments for the immortality of the soul in a series of six articles entitled "The Future Life and the Condition of Man Therein," which appeared in the *North American Review*.

The rise of pessimism and scepticism disturbed many authors. Gamaliel Bradford, now well known for his biographies, described for the *Atlantic Monthly* of March, 1892, what he termed modern pessimism. The modern pessimist, he said, does not rail at nor curse God; he does not despise man or parade his gloom before mankind; he repudiates the dogmatism of most agnostics. The American pessimist, Bradford continued, is fully as sceptical as his European fellow, but he is less brutal, having inherited from his Puritan ancestors "a fastidious scrupulosity of conscience." He has no vices, is gentle, tender, mild, and infinitely tolerant. He seldom talks about his troubles, but he listens patiently to the troubles of others. A not dissimilar attitude was set forth by Junius Henri Browne in a *Forum* article, January, 1897, which he entitled "The Philosophy of Meliorism."

Despite the alleged prevalence of agnosticism, scepticism, pessimism, and the like, the churches were gaining rapidly in membership, the majority of the people were orthodox, and the campmeeting and revival were not given up. Magazine writers not infrequently declared that more emotionalism and a more fervent evangelism were necessary to save men from the blighting influence of science, but in general the tendency was toward liberalism. The editor of the *Chautauquan*, as early as 1890, expressed his approval of the changes that were quietly taking place, and hailed the death of dogmatism. Two years later he again noted the advance of the churches toward a more liberal position, but he deplored the vast amount of theological controversy. This, he wrote, might be good and necessary, but he pointed out that people cannot live on debate and action; the army of the Lord must move forward. The next year, 1893, he expressed the opinion that liberalism was at work throughout American life, in politics as well as in religion. He envisaged the breaking down of denominational lines and cited examples that pointed in that direction. Preachers were exchanging pulpits, and members of different denominations were meeting to consider their mutual problems. The Christian Endeavor movement, which was interdenominational, had built up a tremendous membership.

The editor of the *Chautauquan* also noted that the churches were becoming more interested in social reform. In the *Forum* of November, 1892, Jane Addams expressed her conviction that in social settlement work lay the hope of a renaissance of Christianity, of a united Christendom bound together by a desire to serve humanity. The *Nation* also noted the fact that many ministers were preaching about social reform.

Time and again, as has been said, the churches were aroused by controversies resulting from the new ideas that were gaining strength. The case of Charles A. Briggs of Union Theological Seminary was the source of much dissension in the Presbyterian church. Professor George D. Herron, because of his ideas of applied Christianity, provoked opposition throughout the Congregational denomination. Other church bodies had their stormy petrels. And the magazines freely passed judgment on the rights and wrongs of these cases, persistently discussing in popular terms the cardinal principles of Christianity. Catholicism came in for its share of discussion, and the *Forum*, the *North American Review*, and other periodicals published articles on the confessional, on Catholic theories of religious education, and on the questions raised by the rapid growth of an authoritative religion in a free country.

The tendency throughout the nineties was away from orthodox theology—indeed, away from theology altogether. Men were shaken out of their complacency and forced to face the results of science and of the historical criticism of the Bible. Denominationalism weakened, and a spirit of cooperation developed. The mood of the moment was hospitable to change, and by the end of the century liberalism was in the ascendant. In the cities the number of the unchurched grew, but on the whole the churches were increasing in membership. As has often been noted, the decline of interest in the world-to-come favored the growth of interest in the affairs of earth, and men who disagreed in theology could often work together for the betterment of mankind.

Both the critics and the defenders of Christianity subscribed to lofty ethical codes, and even the agnostics were anti-ecclesiastical rather than anti-religious.

Religious currents of the nineties, then, contributed to the development of an alert public opinion, not wholly adverse to change and reform. In education similar tendencies were stirring college presidents and professors, and the very practical question of academic freedom had awakened public interest in what was going on. In government and industry old standards still dominated, but toward government and industry a new public attitude was developing. Charles Henry Eaton, after having made a careful comparison of the *Forum* in America and the *Nineteenth Century* in England, for the decade preceding 1898, in an article entitled "A Decade of Magazine Publication" (*Forum*, October, 1898), reported that the great movements of the age were economic and political. He observed that our ideals and ways of life had been largely commercialized, but he stated that the subjects which had received most attention during the decade under consideration were those that had to do with the improvement of our social and political order. And our survey of the leading American magazines confirms his conclusions, for we have seen that there was much dissatisfaction with our national life, and that even those who regarded American institutions with the greatest placidity could not wholly escape the animated discussion of political, economic, religious, and educational problems that went on in the daily papers, in books, on street corners, and, most of all, in the magazines.

CHAPTER FOUR

THE OLD AND THE NEW IN LITERATURE

ENOUGH has been said about currents of popular interest in the eighteen-nineties to indicate that the decade was marked by an active and growing restlessness, despite the appearance of surface calm. In the literature of the period we find both the calm and the restlessness, and we note once more that most of the discontent existed among western farmers and eastern laborers. That the great middle classes must have taken at least a moderate interest in political and economic problems has been demonstrated in the preceding chapter, but the discrepancy between literature and life shows that before 1902 that interest did not go very deep.

The extent to which the literature of the period was optimistic, sunny, gentle, and rather myopic is indicated in some remarks of that amiable critic, Hamilton Wright Mabie. In the *Forum* for January, 1889, Mr. Mabie, surveying the literary achievements of the past two decades, stated that this literature had not made a deep impression on the life of the country. It had been admirable in form, sound in tone, and often charming in style, but it had lacked depth of feeling and seriousness. It had shrunk from deep conviction, strong feeling, and great emotion, leaving a gulf between the seriousness of American life and the lightness and grace of American writing.

Our literature [he wrote] has lost the note of discovery, the audacity of spiritual adventure, the courage of great faiths and passions: it is in danger of becoming a recourse of polite society, instead of an expression of vital experience and a dominant force in national life. It has struck some deep notes with great clearness and resonant power; but it must continue to strike such notes; and it must put behind the clarity of its vision the vitality and sheer human force of rich and deep experience. . . . A great deal of the literature of the last two decades would have been admirable as a subsidiary literature; it has been inadequate as representative literature.

If Mabie could criticize contemporary letters in terms that were, for him, extremely harsh, we have no difficulty in realizing the low state to which literature had fallen; and yet there were plenty of people to defend the old school and attack the new. Professor Richard Burton, for example, writing in the *Forum* for April, 1895, an article with the significant title, "The Healthful Tone for American Literature," declared that the chief menace to literature was the negative spirit that brooded over modern literary efforts. He looked with horror on the "art-for-art's-sake" doctrines of the French, which, he warned, would create a schism between art and ethics, for literature, if it followed these doctrines, would seek only to be artistic and true to life. Such an attitude he regarded as morbid and cynical, and he explained the naturalistic tendency by calling it a result of the loss of faith which had followed the weakening of organized religion. America, he said, was not as other countries, for which he thanked God. Our religious convictions were broader, more enlightened, more Christ-like than ever before in history, and as a result our writers were comparatively free from the faults of the realists. The negative, cynical, pessimistic spirit belonged, with us, to the critics, not to the creators. Our literature, he concluded, was sound at heart, and our littérateurs were eager to do work which would be sane, broad, truthful, and wholesome.

Burton's description of his contemporaries was accurate enough, whatever we may think of his attitude toward them. In the first part of the decade the dominant note was still that of sectionalism. There was a literature of New England, a literature of the South, and a literature of the West. The writers of these schools were colorful, interesting, and altogether charming in their portrayal of local scenes and provincial types, but their books seldom touched upon the sterner realities of even the provincial scene. And still further removed from the vicissitudes of life in a changing world were the romancers, the authors of the innumerable books on far countries, imaginary kingdoms, and ancient days.

By and large, then, the literature of the day offered a diversion from the facts and problems of American life, and nothing more. There were writers, however, who took an interest in the struggles that went on about them, and considered these struggles suitable themes for their novels and dramas. William Dean Howells, for example, was not afraid to deal with the relations of capital and labor, as he did in *A Hazard of New Fortunes,* nor was he hesitant about expressing his social philosophy in *A Traveller from Altruria,* which he published in 1894. Politics attracted more than one novelist, and as early as 1881 Shapley wrote *Solid for Mulhooley,* while in 1883 appeared Vicker's *The Fall of Bossism,* and in 1885 F. Marion Crawford's *An American Politician.* A few political novels appeared in the nineties: *The Boss,* by D. M. Means; *The Money Captain,* by Payne; and, best known of all, *The Honorable Peter Stirling,* by Paul Leicester Ford. Bellamy's *Looking Backward* stimulated the writing of other Utopian books, and in 1893 came Olerich's *A Cityless and Countryless World,* followed by Welcome's *From Earth's Center* in 1895, and Lubin's *Let There Be Light* in 1900.

The nineties also produced a little group of realists, among them Stephen Crane, Ambrose Bierce, and Harold Frederic. But these writers, though they helped to shake middle-class complacency, seldom touched directly on social problems. It was otherwise with Hamlin Garland, who began his literary career in 1890 with the publication of a play, *Under the Wheel*, and a volume of short stories, *Main-Travelled Roads*, and who combined the literary traditions of Howells with a strong argumentative tendency of his own. The play tells the story of a poor city family that goes West, attracted by the enticing posters of the real-estate promoters. Subsequent scenes reveal the characters of the play in a comfortless hovel on the prairie, where they are laboring desolately to earn a bare living and to pay the interest on the mortgage. *Main-Travelled Roads* is dedicated "To my father and mother whose half century of pilgrimage on the main travelled roads of life has brought them only pain and weariness." In such stories as "The Return of a Private," "Under the Lion's Paw," and "Up the Coulee" Garland tells with bitter realism certain heart-breaking incidents in the dull, grim lives of the pioneer farmers of "the middle border." One detects no propaganda in these stories, but there can be no question that behind the stark realism lies Garland's suppressed bitterness. A second volume of short stories, *Prairie Folk*, reveals something of the lighter side of farm life, but the material is from the everyday life of the prairie, and the people are worn with toil. *Rose of Dutcher's Coolly*, a novel published in 1895, is distinguished by the same uncompromising honesty, and certain of the other novels, notably *A Spoil of Office*, while less commendable as literature, provide a valuable study of the origins of Populism.

In the years just at the beginning of the new century the number of novels on political and social problems suddenly increased. In 1900 Josiah Flynt wrote *Powers that Prey*, a study of crime, and H. K. Webster made speculation the subject of a novel called *The Banker and the Bear*. In 1901 Flynt published a second novel, *The World of Graft;* Basil King wrote a novel on divorce, *Let Not Man Put Asunder;* C. W. Chesnutt, the distinguished Negro writer, brought forth *The Morrow of Tradition;* Gwendolen Overton, in *The Heritage of Unrest*, called attention to the Indian problem; and Frank Norris published *The Octopus*. Two novels on labor problems, Webster's *Roger Drake, Captain of Industry*, and Mr. Freeman's *The Portion of Labor*, appeared in 1902.

Of the novelists who were writing just at the time when muckraking was beginning Frank Norris was by far the most important. Norris, after experimenting with various forms, hit upon the idea of writing a great three-volume epic of the wheat. The first volume, *The Octopus* (1901), recounts the struggle between the wheat-growers and the railroads in California. Much of the book is highly moving, and the reader comes to understand something of the life on the great wheat ranches. The second volume, *The Pit* (1902), deals with speculation in wheat in Chicago. It is less stirring than its predecessor, but the sections which describe the stock exchange are vivid and often exciting. Norris, who did not live to write the third volume, cannot accurately be described as a muckraker, but he was sensitive to some of the more obvious injustices of the economic order, and he was keenly alive to the literary possibilities of the agricultural and industrial life of America.

In the decade from 1900 to 1910 the vast majority of the important novels were concerned with social problems of one kind or another, but in the preceding decade, as we have shown, "rococo romance," to borrow Carl Van Doren's phrase, and "local color" held sway. The novel that dealt with government or industry—indeed, the novel that faced realistically any aspect of American life—was the exception.

And one suspects that the literature of the period reflects rather accurately the middle-class mind. Here and there were people who were awake to the evils of the social order, but it was easy for the majority to lull their consciences to sleep with thoughts of prosperity, aided by an occasional vicarious adventure into the land of romance.

CHAPTER FIVE

THE BEGINNINGS OF MUCKRAKING

THE YEARS 1900, 1901, and 1902 witnessed the real beginnings of the muckraking movement. We have already seen that conditions in the nineties paved the way for the literature of criticism and exposure, and now we shall take note of the men and the magazines who began the actual attack on vice and corruption. Some differences between the nineties and the following decade are important. In the first place, the earlier period produced only a single high-class, dignified journal of protest, the *Arena*, whereas after 1903 nearly a dozen popular magazines were engaged in the work of exposure. In the second place, such criticisms as were expressed in the nineties were phrased in general terms and seldom specified the persons and corporations being attacked; the later writers were always specific and were sometimes insultingly personal. Finally, it was the proletarian and the discontented farmer that were moved by discontent before 1900, but it was to the middle-class citizen that the muckrakers made their appeal.

Muckraking is nothing new. Ray Stannard Baker has suggested that Jesus was one of the greatest muckrakers, and it is certainly true that Luther valiantly exposed what he regarded as corruption in the Catholic church of his day. S. S. McClure points out that DeFoe and the pamphleteers of his time performed in the eighteenth century the service which the muckrakers performed in the beginning of the twentieth. Much of the literature of the early Abolitionists bordered on muckraking—*Uncle Tom's Cabin*, for example, and particularly Helper's *The Impending Crisis*. Henry George was a master of muckraking, and the works of Edward Bellamy and Henry Demarest Lloyd may be classed with the literature of exposure.

Muckraking, then, had its literary antecedents in the distant as well as the immediate past, but the point which distinguishes the era of the muckrakers from preceding eras, the point which reveals the secret of the great success which the muckrakers enjoyed after 1903, is the fact that the popular magazines, which had built up great circulations, devoted themselves whole-heartedly to the business of exposure. The beginnings were gradual. In 1900 it was as true as it had been for the preceding decade that the *Arena* was the only periodical in the field. The next two years witnessed other magazines making tentative ventures into muckraking; in 1903 muckraking came into vogue; and in 1904 and 1905 the magazine-reading public was treated to perhaps the most sensational publications that respectable periodicals ever undertook.

Two important articles appeared in the *Arena* during 1900. In June Frank Parsons discussed the question of freedom for the Philippines, declaring that imperialism was a greater danger even than monopoly; and in October of the same year Clinton Rogers Woodruff undertook to expose the election frauds of 1899 in Philadelphia. Woodruff revealed that in February, 1899, three names appeared in the assessor's list in a certain division. These names were placed on the ballot at the election of that month and were duly declared elected. In November three men were imported from Washington, assumed these names, went to boss Samuel Salter of the division, and obtained from him all the paraphernalia of election which he had previously—though illegally—obtained from the county commissioners. One of these men later turned state's evidence, exposing the whole fraud. Another man admitted that he had voted thirty-eight times in the election of 1898.

Though *Munsey's* was never a muckraking magazine, in 1900 it published several articles that clearly indicated the trend of public interest. Two of these dealt with the trusts. In the January issue Senator William E. Chandler, lamenting the disappearance of competition, pointed out that large-scale production reduces the cost of commodities, but that under monopoly conditions the benefits accrue not to the consumers but to the managers and stockholders. He stated that the only way to prevent society from falling into the hands of an opulent oligarchy was for the state legislatures to act. Arthur E. McEwen, writing in the same issue, January, 1900, asserted that the corporations were without morals or scruples, and that unless they were restricted they would establish the worst kind of socialism—the "communism of pelf." The trusts themselves, he declared, had taught the only method that could be used against them—united action. He summoned his readers to cease thinking about their private affairs and take steps to check the rise of monopoly. In conclusion he expressed the view that people were favorably disposed toward municipal ownership of public utilities.

In *Munsey's* for May, 1900, Bird S. Coler discussed the relation of business to politics, taking as his text the failure of the Third Avenue Railroad Company of New York. This company, Coler said, had not hesitated to make use of political influence in obtaining franchises and securing favors and exemptions. It gained what it wanted, but the politicians, in return for the favors they had granted, made such heavy demands on the company that it failed, and the people lost millions of dollars. Coler was inclined to place the blame for such a situation on the financiers. "They are wholly responsible," he wrote, "in so far as they create temptations that are too strong for the weak man in public life to resist. . . . There is but one safe and permanent remedy. . . . That remedy is a thoroughly aroused public sentiment that will not tolerate wrongdoing in public or private life, and will not hesitate to attack and destroy any political power that breeds or excuses crime."

The same evil was made the subject of an editorial in the June, 1900, *Century*. The editor called attention to the efforts of public service corporations to extend or confirm the privileges they enjoyed. These companies, he pointed out, were greatly over-capitalized, but little was said about this watered stock. He insisted that they should not be permitted to levy tribute upon the public for stock which represented no expenditure. In summarizing the situation he declared that the injustice of these corporations and the perfidy of many city officials were furnishing material for one of the darkest chapters in our political history.

The year 1901 passed rather quietly, though the *Arena* continued its agitation. The *Arena* article of the year that attracted most attention was B. O. Flower's "A Program of Progress," which appeared in the January issue. He began by assuring his readers that in the two preceding years the country had moved away from the ideal of free government more rapidly than in any previous decade of our history. He demanded a return to the Declaration of Independence, limitation of private monopoly, government ownership of natural monopolies, direct legislation, compulsory arbitration, and the employment of the unemployed. In July the same editor wrote "The Eternal Vanguard of Progress," an attempt to encourage reformers who were disheartened by the seeming listlessness and indifference of the people. He enumerated some of the progressive leaders who, in their various walks of life, were laying strong foundations for a better social order. Among others he mentioned Edwin Markham and Ernest Crosby, poets; John Ward Stimson and John Joseph Ennecking, artists; William T. Stead, a journalist; Frank Parsons, Thomas Elmer Will, Edward Bemis, John R. Commons, and Richard T. Ely, professors; and Samuel Jones and Tom Johnson, prominent civic leaders. He particularly called attention to Mayor Johnson of Cleveland, referring to the mayor's program of municipal ownership of public utilities. The *Arena* also published during 1901 a series of articles in which Frank Parsons showed that in many ways the "great movements of the nineteenth century" had favored the freedom and happiness of the common people; in the distribution of wealth, however, the movement was against the people.

The *Cosmopolitan* for April, 1901, contained John Brisben Walker's four-page article in large type, reporting a great financial combination of the J. P. Morgan, Rothschild, and Rockefeller houses, with a total combination of $3,400,000,-000. Discussing this combination, which, it was alleged, had taken place on March 3, 1901, Walker wrote:

March third marked the beginning of the most wonderful revolution in the world's history. This will be a bloodless revolution and will eventually carry its blessings to the most remote parts of the earth. Governmental divisions will cease to exist except as a means to carry out mandates decided upon in the executive offices of the world's commercial metropolis. We are living in what is without doubt the most interesting period of the world's history. Will Messrs. Rockefeller and Morgan, having reduced production to scientific lines, proceed to the analysis of the problem of distribution? They must.

The same faith that great good might yet come out of the monopolies appeared in more than one article of the period. Ray Stannard Baker, for example, writing in *McClure's*, November, 1901, described the Steel Trust with admiration rather than with distrust. Richard T. Ely, on the other hand, had warned readers of the *Cosmopolitan*, August, 1901, that they must watch the Steel Trust lest it rob them of their liberties.

Municipal corruption, which was to be the subject of many articles a little later, came in for its share of attention in 1901. Josiah Flynt discussed in *McClure's*, April, May, and June of that year, the connection between the New York police and the criminal elements in the city. Frank Moss discussed the corruption in New York politics, in the *Cosmopolitan*, November, 1901, and Percy Stickney Grant, writing in *Everybody's*, November, 1901, held the rich responsible for a large share of the vice and crime of the city.

In 1902 the *Arena*, while bewailing the indifference of the masses, courageously prosecuted its attack on imperialism, monopoly, and corruption. A news report to the effect that the Declaration of Independence, when circulated among Filipinos, had been suppressed by American officers and called by one of them "a damned incendiary document," made Flower see red. The coöperative movement of the Rochdale Society in England, on the other hand, gave him an opportunity to set forth his constructive program. The report of the Steel Trust for the year furnished the text for a sermon against monopoly and the protective tariff. Always courageous, always alert, Flower kept on pounding away against the evils he saw about him.

And Flower might well have begun to take heart in 1902, for that year gave evidence of the storm that was to burst with incredible fury in the years that followed. *Everybody's* (August, 1902), printed a story by Frank Norris, which showed how speculation in wheat ruined both the producers and the ultimate consumers. Norris also contributed to the same magazine (September, 1902), a frank description of the life of miners in the coal region in time of strike. David

Graham Phillips contributed to *Everybody's*, November, 1902, an article on the machine politics of David B. Hill. Mary Manners wrote a series on the life of "The Unemployed Rich," in *Everybody's*, 1902, and Bessie and Marie Van Horst described the experiences of working women, also in *Everybody's*, 1902.

Other magazines were awake to what was going on. *Collier's* printed a series of articles on both sides of the Philadelphia coal strike, securing contributions from operators and from sympathizers with the miners. Ernest Howard Crosby wrote for the *Independent* of May 1, 1902, on the dangers of aristocracy. But the chief sensation of the year was furnished by the October number of *McClure's*, which printed an article by Claude H. Wetmore and Lincoln Steffens on "Tweed Days in St. Louis," and announced that in the next issue it would begin the serial publication of Ida M. Tarbell's "History of the Standard Oil Company."

With the Steffens and the Tarbell articles *McClure's* inaugurated the policy which it followed with great success for a period of years, and the era of the muckrakers had begun. In January, 1903, Mr. McClure wrote:

> We did not plan it so; it is a coincidence that this number contains three arraignments of American character such as should make every one of us stop and think. "The Shame of Minneapolis," the current chapter of the Standard Oil, Mr. Ray Stannard Baker's "The Right to Work," it might all have been called "The American Contempt of Law." Capitalists, workingmen, politicians, citizens—all breaking the law or letting it be broken. Who is there left to uphold it? . . . There is no one left—none but all of us.

McClure's had stumbled on muckraking without premeditation. For years S. S. McClure had been winning a reputation as one of the shrewdest, most ingenious editors in the country. Eccentric, imaginative, enthusiastic, he was constantly seeing opportunities for brilliant articles. He had secured such fiction writers as Rudyard Kipling and O. Henry when almost no one else knew their names; he had obtained exclusive stories about such inventions as the wireless telegraph and the Roentgen ray before the scientific world had heard of them; he had cultivated the popular interest in biography by securing entertaining writers and by introducing plenty of illustrations. With tremendous energy, McClure hastened hither and yon, discovering unknown authors, investigating unexplored subjects of potential interest, communicating something of his own enthusiasm to everyone he met, and devoting all his tremendous resources of imagination and energy to making his paper one that the American people would want to read.

Slowly McClure built up a staff that would round out his own qualities. In John S. Phillips he had early found an associate who combined calmness, good judgment, and tact with no slight editorial gifts. Miss Ida M. Tarbell he had employed to do biographies for him, and he came to appreciate her abilities as an investigator as well as a writer. Ray Stannard Baker had come to the staff as a young journalist with an interest in writing short stories. And Lincoln Steffens had brought to the magazine a mind trained both in the universities and in the offices of leading New York newspapers.

When these people gathered together to discuss policies, the electricity of brilliant ideas was in the air. McClure would come with a score of projects, and he would grow indignant and desperate as they were one by one picked to pieces by his associates. Perhaps only one out of twenty plans would actually stand the test of such analysis, but the results of that single acceptable suggestion would, months later, be attracting readers throughout the country.

At some such meeting as this, Miss Tarbell, more than three years before the articles appeared, proposed that, in

Top left: S. S. McCLURE, FOUNDER AND EDITOR OF "McCLURE'S MAG-
AZINE." *Top right:* IDA M. TARBELL. *Bottom left:* JOHN S. PHILLIPS,
ASSOCIATE EDITOR OF "McCLURE'S," 1893-1906; EDITOR OF THE
"AMERICAN MAGAZINE," 1906-1916. *Bottom right:* LINCOLN STEFFENS.

view of the importance of an interest in the trust problem, it might be well to tell the story of a representative monopoly. McClure was sceptical of the value of the historical approach, but he allowed himself to be convinced, and Miss Tarbell began the laborious task of consulting all the Congressional investigations, court records, and other documents which threw light on the growth of the Standard Oil Company. It was merely coincidence that the first of her articles was ready at just about the time when Steffens, who had long been considering a series of stories on subjects of current news value, received Claude Wetmore's account of happenings in St. Louis. And it was also a coincidence that Baker, whose interest in labor problems began while he was still in college, began at this particular time to write about these problems in *McClure's*.

It was coincidence, and yet the fact that these three writers were simultaneously occupied with related subjects indicates that there was something in the air. The response to the articles demonstrated that the American people were less indifferent to public questions than had been supposed, and McClure realized that now he had found a field with great possibilities for his magazine. Though not himself in any way a reformer, he became, through the functioning of his editorial good sense, a tower of strength to the liberal movements of the day. The circulation of *McClure's* mounted to half a million, and its influence was such that a keen English observer, William Archer, was convinced that McClure paved the way for President Roosevelt. One difficulty that McClure encountered in his efforts to procure good articles was the fact that the reporters usually knew little about the subjects they were to discuss. He decided, therefore, to pay his writers for their study and not for the amount of copy they turned in. A member of the staff would collect enough material to write a book and then condense it into an article. In two years' time Mr. Baker furnished eight articles; Lincoln Steffens, in a somewhat longer period, wrote ten; and Miss Tarbell spent five years in the preparation and writing of the eighteen articles on the Standard Oil Company. Not one of the articles cost McClure less than $1,000, and fully half of them cost $2,500 apiece. Each of Miss Tarbell's articles, he records in his autobiography, cost about $4,000. One gains some impression of the difficulties of the work, and also of the thoroughness with which it was undertaken, from McClure's statement that in twelve years he was able to secure only four persons whom he deemed competent for the position of staff writer.

After October, 1902, *McClure's* took first rank among the journals of exposure and reform, although the *Arena* continued to publish articles that were competent, dignified, and courageous. Other magazines soon took up the work, and in 1903 muckraking became militant and in 1904 sensational. The literature of exposure became popular and profitable, and for nearly a decade magazine readers were presented with a series of attacks on American institutions that was calculated to disconcert the most complacent.

CHAPTER SIX

THE SHAMELESS CITIES

ONCE muckraking was fairly started, it covered practically every aspect of American life. Inasmuch, however, as "Tweed Days in St. Louis" (by Claude H. Wetmore and Lincoln Steffens in *McClure's*, October, 1902), has already been referred to as marking the opening of a new epoch, and inasmuch as Lincoln Steffens may be regarded as in some respects the real founder of the muckraking movement, it will not seem amiss to consider as a separate topic the exposure of municipal corruption.

Lincoln Steffens, who was born in San Francisco and educated in the schools of that city, at the University of California, and at the universities of Berlin, Heidelburg, Leipzig, and the Sorbonne, began his journalistic career as a reporter for the New York *Evening Post*. Allan Nevins, in his history of that newspaper, states that Steffens was one of the best journalists New York ever had, and he rose rapidly in the profession. He was a police reporter when Roosevelt was a police commissioner, and the friendship between the two began at that time. Later he was city editor of the *Commercial Advertiser*.

Steffens, then, had had an unusual academic training and a notable career in journalism when, at the invitation of John S. Phillips, he became managing editor of *McClure's*, in 1901. S. S. McClure, however, on his return from Europe, informed Steffens that he did not know how to edit a magazine, and told him to get out of the office and start reporting. Steffens went to Chicago, looking for copy, and there received the tip to go to St. Louis. It was his idea that the public never received an accurate impression of what was happening from the newspapers, simply because it was impossible to understand a story that was spread out over weeks and even months. He believed that magazines could bring all the facts together, make a unified and comprehensible story, and interest and help the public. He had no idea of muckraking; he was interested in a journalistic experiment.

In St. Louis he found the kind of material he had been looking for, and he secured Claude Wetmore to write the story. He was not, however, satisfied with what Wetmore did. Wetmore was too close to the events he described, saw them as too extraordinary, left out too much that was important. Steffens rewrote the story, and, to satisfy Wetmore, both names were signed to it. That decided Steffens that he must write his own stories, and he went to Minneapolis for material. It was "The Shame of Minneapolis" (*McClure's*, January, 1903), that put the series on the map.

In Minneapolis a politician named Ames had been twice elected mayor by the Republicans and twice by the Democrats. Immediately after his fourth election (1901), Steffens asserted, Ames began to gather about him a group of plunderers and opened the city to all kinds of criminals. He made his brother, Colonel Fred W. Ames, chief-of-police, and he appointed an ex-gambler, Norman W. King, as chief of detectives. King's primary function, Steffens discovered, was to invite thieves, gamblers, pickpockets, confidence men, and other criminals to Minneapolis, and to arrange with them for the division of the spoils of their trades. Prisoners from the city jails were freed to assist in collecting revenues for the gang. Irwin A. Gardner, a medical student, was made a special policeman and was given the task of collecting money from the prostitutes. One hundred and seven of the more decent of the two hundred and twenty-five policemen were dismissed. "Coffee John" Fitchette was made captain, and his sole duty was to sell places on the police force.

Steffens also told how Minneapolis had been saved from the Ames gang, largely through the efforts of one Hovey C. Clarke. Clarke was foreman of the grand jury that met in April, 1902, and he collected evidence at his own expense, rejecting bribes and defying threats against his life. One member of the gang after another was indicted and convicted, and Mayor Ames fled to Indiana after having been indicted for extortion, conspiracy, and bribe-offering. On November 4, 1902, a new administration was elected.

Two months later (March, 1903), Steffens wrote again about St. Louis, having made a second visit in order to see for himself. There, he asserted, conditions were even worse than they had been in Minneapolis. He told how Colonel Edward R. Butler, the political boss of both parties, charged for every kind of municipal service, trafficking openly in franchises and municipal rights and property. Steffens described the Central Traction deal of 1898. Robert M. Snyder asked for a franchise to lay tracks all over the city, regardless of the existing lines. The street railway company offered Butler $175,000 to defeat the measure in the city council, but Snyder spent $250,000 in bribing individual councilmen, and he secured the franchise, which he thereupon sold to his rival, the street railway company, for $1,250,000.

In the same article Steffens told of the Surburban Traction deal of 1899. It happened that the St. Louis Suburban Railway Company, after promising a very considerable sum of money for a franchise, was prevented from getting it because of an injunction, and they therefore refused to pay the money promised. The boodlers asserted that they had delivered the votes, and they very rashly tried to sue for the bribe money.

This brought the matter to the attention of Joseph W. Folk, circuit attorney for the fourth district, and he promptly brought before a grand jury nearly one hundred persons, including councilmen, delegates, officers and directors of the railways, and bank presidents. When he secured the conviction of the first grafter who came up for trial, the ring broke, and certain politicians and financiers left the state in something of a hurry.

The February grand jury had this to say of members of the St. Louis house of delegates:

We found a number of these utterly illiterate and lacking in ordinary intelligence, unable to give a better reason for favoring or opposing a measure than a desire to act with the majority. In some no trace of mentality or morality could be found; in others a low order of training appeared united with a base cunning, groveling instincts, and sordid desires. Unqualified to respond to the ordinary requirements of life, they are utterly incapable of comprehending the significance of an ordinance and are incapacitated, both by nature and training, to be the makers of laws. The choosing of such men to be legislators makes a travesty of justice, sets a premium on incompetency, and deliberately poisons the very source of the laws.

When Folk, a promising young lawyer of St. Louis, was nominated for the attorneyship by the machine, it was taken for granted that he would serve those who had supported him. Of course he said he would enforce the laws if elected; that is what they all said—until they got into office. But Folk, who was new and inexperienced in politics, actually meant what he said, and during the four years that he was circuit attorney he uncovered more corruption than had ever been exposed before at any one time or place. Up to that time no public man in Missouri had ever been indicted for boodling. Folk brought forty such indictments and convicted twenty men. Of these, twelve were released by the supreme court upon technicalities, the other eight went to the penitentiary.

While Steffens was still in St. Louis a high official of the Gould railroad system suggested to him that he "do" Pittsburgh next. The Wabash Railroad, the official stated, had long been seeking a terminal there, but the Pennsylvania Railway controlled the city and protected the monopoly. He promised that the information which the Gould people had collected about this city would be secretly put at his disposal. Steffens agreed, but only to find that the promised assistance was not forthcoming. The relations between the two railroad companies were apparently improving. He had to find his own material. In his recent *Autobiography* he states his predicament thus: "I have travelled since in many foreign countries; I have never been in any place where I felt so like a foreigner, so lonely, unwelcome, and ridiculous, as during those first dreadful days in Pittsburgh." After a while, however, he found an adequate source of information. A certain merchant reformer by the name of Oliver McClintock had watched the letting of city contracts for years and had kept the accounts, until he had a large pile of damaging information. This he put at the disposal of Steffens, who read it with the purpose of tracing the methods and practices of the grafters, and to get an outline of the invisible government. He could use only a small part of this mass of information in his article, but it was worth something to know that there was plenty of ammunition that could be used in court in a possible libel suit. Steffens claims that all American cities have their McClintocks, who know and can prove what is going on; but the muckrakers and the periodicals of exposure are lacking. The article which appeared in *McClure's*, May, 1903, showed that in petty police graft and in big business corruption Pittsburgh was like New York, St. Louis, and Minneapolis.

Philadelphia came next. Here a reform charter—The Bullitt Charter—had just been put into effect. Under it much
power was centered in the mayor, and he was responsible
to the voters. But Steffens soon noticed that the form of government did not matter, and that the charter did not determine the actual government. So convinced was he of this
that he never thereafter read the charter of a city or the constitution of a state which he studied. He found that the new
charter had no reform purpose, as far as the political bosses
were concerned. The state boss, Senator Matthew S. Quay,
had had trouble with the boss of Philadelphia, and so he
induced the state legislature to pass the Bullitt Charter to
get rid of the city boss. He then appointed Israel W. Durham, a ward politician, boss of the city; and the two controlled the machines of both the old political parties, just
as before the reform. The mayor, the council, and the elected
officers represented business—the same businesses that had
corrupted the former government.

Under the new mayor, Ashbridge, there was a veritable
orgy of political impudence and corruption. Respectable
citizens who came to the polls to vote found that their names
had already been voted on by machine repeaters; all the
names of the signers of the Constitution of the United States,
of the new charter, and of the membership lists of the swell
clubs were voted by the gang; and one grand "steal" or "job"
after another was pulled off in rapid succession. John Wanamaker made a public offer of two and a half million dollars
for a street railway franchise, but the mayor *gave* it away.
The people were stunned and did not know what to make
of it or how to deal with the situation. Steffens, in desper-
ation, called on the city boss himself for an explanation of
what he regarded as bad politics, and the boss not only received him but answered his questions. He said: "If we did
any one of these things alone the papers and the public could

concentrate on it, get the facts, and fight. But we reasoned that if we poured them all out fast and furious, one, two, three—one after the other—the papers couldn't handle them all and the public would be stunned and—give up. Too much." The Bullitt Charter, he claimed, was a good thing for the politicians. It was the best that the reformers could do, and now that the politicians took it and went right on with their business it would take the heart out of reform forever.

This interview developed into something that was almost friendship between the two men. The boss frequently sneaked up to the room in the hotel where Steffens stayed, "just to chew the rag." He did not offer any information, but still the muckraker gained a better understanding of the management of the city government from him, and the boss learned something about the philosophy of government and politics. He began to appreciate his opportunities for doing the city some good, and wished that he had either his youth or health back. Steffens expresses himself thus in his recent book:

He saw the job, and it tempted him, as the same prospect attracted many such political and business leaders. I have had many similar experiences since with big, bad men and I find that, if they are big enough and bad enough, they seem to be as eager to do great good as great evil. They simply are not asked to do good; the drift of things, the rewards, the applause and education, are all the other way. "Iz" Durham, whom the reformers and the good people of Philadelphia despised, was, man for man, better than they were; he was the best man I met in that town, the best for mental grasp, for the knowledge of life and facts in his line, and—he had one other advantage which is something akin to honesty but must be described in other terms. The New Testament puts it the most clearly and briefly. Jesus said that He could save sinners; the righteous He could not save.

This boss—like other political bosses and some big business men and thieves—knew that he was a sinner, and made
no attempt to justify himself. When he lay dying he wired
Steffens to come to him; he wanted to know just what it was
that was so "rotten wrong" about his doings. Steffens told
him bluntly it was disloyalty; treason to the common people
who trusted him and supported him with their votes and
whom he betrayed to the selfish and corrupt business interests. The dying boss, who had always prided himself upon
his loyalty to his friends and his promises, was stunned and
convinced. After a long silence he said, "Say, I sure ought
to go to hell for that." Steffens found it advisable to remind
him that God probably was as merciful as a good boss.

The Philadelphia article appeared in *McClure's*, July, 1903,
and from Philadelphia Steffens went to Chicago, to give his
readers, in *McClure's*, October, 1903, the benefit of a sensationally wicked story. The stuff was all there: "the police
graft, the traffic of authority with criminals, gamblers, prostitutes, liquor dealers, all sorts of thieves, and some sorts of
murderers. The evil of Chicago was obvious, general, bold.
. . . The New York Tenderloin was a model of order and
virtue compared with the badly regulated, police-paid
criminal lawlessness of the Chicago Loop and its spokes."
But to his surprise he found that the political machine did
not work. He finally went to the political boss of Illinois,
Billy Lorimer—later United States senator—and asked him
what was wrong with his machine, "the bummest political
organization" he had ever seen. Lorimer asked him whether
he had seen that "son of a bitch, Fisher." He had not, but
he soon discovered that Walter L. Fisher—later member of
Taft's Cabinet—was the leader of the Chicago Municipal
Voter's League, which made it its business to investigate
the records of all the candidates for office, and to support
those who had good records and to oppose the others. The

League used the methods of practical politics. Each ward was studied separately, and then dealt with according to the actual situation there. Fisher performed like a regular political boss, browbeating and controlling a various lot of politicians in the interest of the whole people of Chicago, and the big financial interests which sought riches out of the resources of the city had to render some service. It was no fundamental reform, but it produced a temporary betterment. The country had not expected that Chicago should be held up as an example of a city that was reforming herself.

In 1904 Steffens turned to the study of state governments. In order to understand the system in Ohio he investigated two cities there, a northern and a southern, Cleveland and Cincinnati, and he told the story, "Ohio: A Tale of Two Cities," in the July *McClure's*, 1905. Cleveland was at that time engaged in its joyous experiment in good government under Tom Johnson, who, according to Steffens, combined intelligence, courage, strength, will power, humor, and leadership with a knowledge of economics above all the politicians of his day. He had been a street railway magnate, and he had done his share to corrupt politics in Cleveland. Then one day on a train he bought a copy of Henry George's *Social Problems*, and read it. This convinced him that he was on the wrong track; that great wealth came unearned to individuals and companies who owned land, natural resources, and franchises; that it was society which made these natural monopolies valuable, and that society should have the benefit from them. Gradually he sold out his business and went into politics. He tried to apply in Cleveland the Henry George theories, and to set there an example for other cities to copy. He was sure that the evils from which municipalities suffered were not politicians nor big business, but privileges—franchises, etc. To him "privileged business" was the devil, and his plan was to abolish all privileges by introducing a system of public ownership and operation of all public-service utilities and the taxation of land values. He was elected mayor twice, and the political campaigns which he waged in his picturesque way became a school in economics for the city. His plans were ultimately defeated by state interference, but while it lasted it was—in Steffens' opinion —the best city government in the country. There was no police corruption, and the men who assisted Johnson in the management of the city's affairs liked their work and took pride in it.

Cincinnati had a very different sort of boss. There George B. Cox had developed one of the most perfect political machines, by which he controlled both Republican and Democratic parties. So efficient and all-pervading was it that Steffens found only one or two men in the whole city who dared to criticize the machine above a whisper, and few cared to be seen publicly in his company. The machine was built on the solid ground of privileges. Not to coöperate with the machine hurt a man's business. Steffens decided early in his investigations that he would have to depend on Cox himself for the protection of what he had to write, for he knew that he could not count on witnesses to defend a case of libel. They would not testify. So he often called on the boss in his office over a saloon to report to him the stories of graft and corruption that he was discovering. Usually Cox would say they were lies. Then the muckraker would go over the ground again and tell him that those stories were true with the exception of some inaccuracies which he had corrected. In the meantime detectives followed him at every step. After he had collected twenty or thirty true stories against Cox and his machine—all of which he had reported to the boss—he wrote his article on Cincinnati. In this, however, he made use of only some eight. So while the public thought Steffens was hard on the boss, the latter thought

he was let off easy. At their final interview Cox boasted that
he was the only one who divided the spoils in his city; and
he was proud of his machine.

On the whole, Cincinnati was not unhappy. A few men
were angry at the prevailing conditions, but the rest were
in the system for profit or fear. What there was to be obtained by supporting the machine is well brought out in the
following paragraph:

The bums get free soup; the petty criminals "get off" in court;
the plain people or their relatives get jobs or a picnic or a friendly
greeting; the Germans get their beer whenever they want it;
the neighborhood and ward leaders get offices and graft; "good"
Democrats get their share of both; shopkeepers sell to the city
or to politicians or they break petty ordinances; the lawyers get
cases, and they tell me that the reputation of the bench is such
that clients seek lawyers for their standing, not at the bar, but
with the ring; the banks get public deposits and license to do
business; the public utility companies get franchises and "no
regulation"; financiers get canals, etc., they "get blackmailed,"
too, but they can do "business" by "dividing up"; property
owners get low assessments, or high; anybody can get anything
in reason, by standing in. And anybody who doesn't "stand in,"
or "stand by," gets nothing but trouble. And there is the point
that pricks deepest in Cincinnati. Cox can punish; he does punish, not with physical cruelty, as a Czar may, but by petty an-
noyances and "trouble," and political and business ostracism.
The reign of Cox is a reign of fear. The experience that made
my visits there a personal humiliation was the spectacle I saw
of men who were being punished: who wanted to cry out; who
sent for me to tell me facts that they knew and suffered and
hated; and these men, after leading me into their back offices
and closing the door, dared not speak. They had heard that I
was shadowed, and they were afraid. Afraid of what? They were
afraid of their government, of their Czar, of George Cox, who
is not afraid of them, or of you, or of me. Cox is a man, we are

American citizens, and Cincinnati has proved to Cox that Americans can be reduced to craven cowards.

These articles, as indicated above, all appeared in *McClure's*. Steffens depended largely, except in the case of Pittsburgh, on materials that had been brought out in the courts. As he saw the same phenomena recurring in these various cities, he became more and more convinced that there were underlying causes. He began to believe in the possibility of a science of politics. In time he found he could predict, once he knew the state of corruption a particular city had reached, what stage it would next develop. As he realized that the politicians were not themselves to blame but were the victims of a system, he commenced blaming business men. He made the revolutionary discovery that whenever a bribe is taken, a bribe must have been given. But as he studied further, he decided that the business men were as much victims as the politicians.

What he wanted to do more than anything else was to make people see that corruption could not be laid at the door of any particular party or group. He found that he had succeeded in waking people up, but he discovered that they were looking to him to provide them with simple remedies. When he was asked how to deal with corruption, he replied flatly:

As if I knew; as if we knew; as if there were any one way to deal with this problem in all places under any circumstances. There isn't and if I had gone around with a ready made reform scheme in the back of my head, it would have served only to keep me from seeing straight the facts that would not support my theory. The only editorial scheme we had was to study a few choice examples of bad government, and tell how the bad was accomplished, then seek out, here and abroad, some typical good governments and explain how the good was done;—not how to do it, mind you, but how it was done.

After he had written on the cities, Steffens wrote on state governments. He left *McClure's* with the group that founded the *American*, and wrote on various political topics. On leaving the *American*, he was associated for a time with *Everybody's*, and for a few weeks represented a newspaper syndicate in Washington. When the war broke out in 1914, Steffens was in Europe, studying municipal conditions there and finding the same cycles he had observed in America. Forced to abandon this work, he decided to make a study of revolutions and went to Mexico to watch developments. Then, when the Russian revolution came, he hastened to Russia to see if revolutions followed any definite laws. Since the war he has spent much of his time in San Remo, Italy, but recently he has returned to this country, and in 1931 published his charming and stimulating *Autobiography*.

One of the topics on which Steffens wrote for the *American* was the situation in San Francisco, which he described in a series of articles called "The Mote and the Beam," which appeared in 1907. San Francisco, indeed, attracted much attention: George Kennan and Mrs. Fremont Older had articles in *McClure's;* Charles Edward Russell, in a series of articles, covered the subject for *Hampton's* in 1910; Frederick Palmer wrote about it for *Collier's;* and later Mr. Fremont Older went into the subject in considerable detail in *My Own Story*.

The situation in that city was unpleasant and disillusioning. During the late nineties James D. Phelan, a rich Irish gentleman, was the mayor of the city. His administration was honest, but he was accused of being friendly to the employers and hostile to the workers. Abraham Ruef, a young and talented Jewish university graduate, took advantage of this discontent and organized a labor party which elected Eugene R. Schmitz, an orchestra leader and a member of the Musicians' Union, for mayor. This labor administration proved to be as bad as any business government had ever been, using the same methods for the same ends. As Frederick Palmer wrote in *Collier's* (January 12, 1907), what happened was "the betrayal of the common interest of all the people to the special interest of some of the people; the conversion of a representative democracy into a government representative of a privileged class, and the class preferred was Business."

It was against Abraham Ruef's carefully constructed political machine that the reformers worked. Ruef had builded so skillfully that his ring controlled the council, and anybody who wanted favors from the municipality had to do business with him. Fremont Older, editor of the San Francisco *Bulletin*, Rudolph Spreckels, a progressive young capitalist, and ex-Mayor James D. Phelan led a campaign to expose and destroy the corrupt political ring. In spite of their efforts Mayor Schmitz was reëlected in 1905.

Older decided to get outside help. He went to Washington to sound Francis J. Heney, a native of San Francisco and a young lawyer who was at the time making a reputation for himself by prosecuting the land fraud cases in Oregon for the federal government. Heney was willing to help but he wanted William J. Burns of the United States Secret Service, who was assisting him in Oregon, to go along. President Roosevelt consented. The next problem was to raise $100,-000 for the prosecution. This Phelan and Spreckels took care of. The latter insisted that the prosecution should not stop until William F. Herrin, chief attorney for the Southern Pacific Railroad and political boss of California, was convicted.

The graft prosecution started early in 1906. District Attorney Langdon coöperated by appointing Heney as his deputy. For this act the assistant mayor—Gallagher (Schmitz being absent)—removed Langdon from office and appointed

Ruef himself to the office of district attorney. The court re-stored Langdon, for the "best people" were still with the reformers. Late in the year Schmitz and Ruef were both in-dicted. At this the privileged interests became alarmed. From the east came Patrick Calhoun—a relative of John C. Calhoun, a "wise" man of the world who had financial, political, and social connections in many parts of the country and who was president of the United Railroads of San Fran-cisco. His plan was to make it a class fight, Capital against Labor. By bribing some of the labor leaders he created a street railway strike. Coming immediately after the great fire this strike threatened business with utter ruin. Gangs of professional strike-breakers were imported. Rioting followed. Then, openly and conspicuously, Calhoun put down the disorder. He was the hero of San Francisco. The "best people" turned against the graft prosecution.

In spite of discouragement the prosecution went on. By threat of exposure Golden M. Roy, who was on the inside of the ring, was persuaded to tell what he knew. To frighten him into silence Ruef introduced an ordinance into the Board of Supervisors making it illegal for any girl under eighteen years of age to visit a skating rink without her mother. If this became a law it would ruin Roy's skating rink business. Roy cleverly planned to trap the Supervisors on this same scheme. He would invite them to his back room and offer them each five hundred dollars to vote against the ordinance. This was carried out—with Burns and others in an adjoin-ing room watching the whole procedure. Three Supervisors fell into the trap. On promise of immunity for telling what they knew, they confessed. Then the other fifteen Supervisors confessed; and finally Ruef confessed on a similar promise of immunity. In his case, however, the judge demanded that he plead guilty on one charge, for which he should be sen-tenced to one year in the penitentiary. Ruef than went before the Grand Jury and gave evidence against himself, Schmitz, Calhoun, and others. After this Calhoun was indicted.

Calhoun, it seemed, had paid $200,000 to Ruef for the purpose of obtaining a franchise for an overhead trolley for the United Railroads. It was taken for granted that this sum was paid as a bribe to the Supervisors. Ruef insisted that nothing had been said about bribing, and that it had been paid to him as an "attorney's fee." As a result the prosecution claimed that Ruef "fell down," and so the immunity contract with him was broken. First Schmitz was convicted and sentenced to five years in the penitentiary. Then Ruef was tried. The first jury disagreed. During the second trial Heney was shot through the head by an ex-convict whom Heney had barred from the jury. This created enough excitement to convict Ruef. He was sentenced to fourteen years in the penitentiary. The first big victory of the reformers.

Finally came Calhoun's trial. Calhoun would not stop at anything. On a tip from a friend Older provided himself with two plain-clothes men from the police department, who, he afterwards learned, prevented two attacks on his life. Later he was enticed into an automobile and taken for a "ride." Fortunately for him, the gunman who was to have ten thousand dollars for his job lost his nerve. He was put on a south-bound train and was rescued in Santa Barbara. It was a United Railroads scheme to dispose of this relentless prosecutor. The big witness against Calhoun was to be Jim Gallagher. Shortly before the case came up Gallagher's house was dynamited, and he narrowly escaped death. Then some flats which he owned were dynamited. It was necessary for the prosecution to reimburse him for these to keep him from falling out. Roy was offered $150,000 if he would testify that Spreckels had promised to pay large sums to Older, Heney, and Gallagher on the day that Calhoun should be convicted.

In spite of all this the jury finally stood ten to two for acquittal.

This practically ended the prosecution. The evidence against Herrin and other big grafters was less convincing than that against Calhoun. In the city election of 1909 the Calhoun forces won. Francis J. Heney, who ran for district attorney, was decisively defeated by Charles Fickert. The new district attorney dismissed all the remaining charges against Calhoun and the other defendants.

What had been gained by San Francisco and California as a result of these exposures? Nothing fundamental. The most obvious achievement was Ruef's conviction and the breaking up of his ring; but Older himself was instrumental in getting him paroled after he had served half of his net sentence. Older became convinced that Ruef's immunity contract was broken when the latter refused to tell more than the truth. Heney had given three strenuous years of his time; he became deaf in one ear as a result of the attack on him, and never received a dollar for his services. Hiram Johnson succeeded in putting the Southern Pacific out of power for a while. But neither the city nor the state was convicted of graft, and no fundamental reform resulted in either.

From a somewhat different angle S. S. McClure dealt with the effects of municipal corruption. He was led by Steffens' articles to ask whether officials elected by the methods Steffens described could protect life and property. Could a body of policemen who engaged in blackmail, persecution, and criminal practices make a community lawabiding? Could a body of aldermen who combined to loot a city govern it well? To answer these questions he made a study of homicide and criminality in American cities, and in December, 1904, he published the results of his research under the title, "The Increase of Lawlessness in the United

States." He showed that in 1881 there were 24.7 homicides for every million people in the country, whereas in 1903 there were 112 homicides per million inhabitants. The increase, he showed, had been steady, though the peak was reached during the great social unrest of 1894-1896. He pointed out that such an increase in crime was precisely what one might expect in view of the conduct of government. He assailed the "American oligarchy," which, he wrote, consisted of three classes: the saloon keepers, gamblers, and others who were in businesses that were degrading; contractors, bankers, capitalists, and the like, who stood to gain from bribery; and politicians who sought and secured offices with the aid of the other two classes. These three groups, he concluded, made the laws and institutions of the country; they polluted free government at its source; they were "the murderers of a civilization."

McClure kept his interest in this aspect of bad government, and in 1907 he resumed his agitation. He had been disappointed because Steffens' articles had not had a greater effect, and he believed that Steffens had confined himself too closely to the waste in money and the wretchedly poor public service that resulted from corruption. He therefore resolved to appeal directly to the public imagination, and in the winter of 1906-1907 he kept a file of clippings from Chicago papers in order to show, from her own journals, the criminality and insecurity of that city. Before publishing his findings, he sent George Kibbe Turner to Chicago to study conditions there and to write an introductory article. Turner's investigations proved important and his account of them, published in *McClure's* for April, 1907, led to the activities that subsequently produced the Vice Commission Report. He divided the business of dissipation into three classes. First was the liquor trade, whose receipts amounted to $115,000,000 in 1906. Second came prostitution, with a gross revenue for the same year of $20,000,000. And third was gambling, which brought in about $15,000,000.

Turner exposed the workings of these various enterprises in some detail. He stated that there were at least 10,000 professional prostitutes in Chicago, and that their average income was $2,000 a year. Much of this money never reached them, however, because they were exploited by the criminal hotels, the houses of ill-fame, the cheap dance halls and saloons, and the men who dealt in women for trade. A prostitute's career, he asserted, lasted from five to ten years, and during that time a woman was ordinarily almost continually under the influence of alcoholic stimulants, if not of drugs. He declared that the whole business was organized, from the securing of young girls to the drugging of older and less salable women out of existence. To carry on these businesses of dissipation it was necessary to buy protection, and he asserted that $200,000 was paid annually to the police. One chief of police, he maintained, had salted away $187,000 during his few years in office.

Turner's article so impressed William Archer that in his essay on "The American Cheap Magazine," published in the *Fortnightly Review* for May, 1910, he cited it as an outstanding example of the methods of muckraking, which McClure had perfected.

It condensed into a few fascinating pages [he wrote], without rhetoric or emphases of any kind, the most amazing picture of organized, police-protected vice and crime—a picture every line of which was evidently the result of a patient, penetrating investigation, and intimate personal knowledge.

McClure's own article, "Chicago as Seen by Herself," appeared the next month, calling attention to the crime wave which, as her own papers showed, was sweeping over the city. These articles by Turner and McClure made a strong impression on the public mind, and before the end of the following year Miss Tarbell could write an account of "How Chicago is Finding Herself."

Naturally New York came in for her share of exposure, and the activities of the Tammany organization were described in many articles. Turner, writing for *McClure's* in June, 1909, gave a detailed account of the way in which Tammany won elections by the use of "repeaters." From 1894 to 1909, he wrote, the Democrats had control of New York two-thirds of the time, and with one doubtful exception they never had a majority of the popular votes at a city election. They got their majorities from trained bands of repeaters, who were largely composed of professional criminals. The East Side Gang, under criminal leaders, furnished many of these. One of the leaders, "Kid" Twist, could furnish about a thousand of them, each good for from five to ten votes at the general elections, and for ten to twenty at the primaries. In 1908 one-fourth of the names in some election districts were entirely fictitious, and four-fifths of these faked names voted. Perhaps twenty thousand entirely fictitious names voted in that year—to say nothing of the names of dead people and of men who had moved away.

General Theodore A. Bingham, ex-commissioner of police of the city, also wrote for *McClure's*, November, 1909, describing his fight against the organized criminals, which had been brought to a stop by his sudden removal in July, 1909. He stated that he could not even trust the men in his own department to carry out his orders, for they knew that police commissioners and mayors were frequently changed, whereas the politicians remained. He found spies everywhere, especially on the telephones, and Mayor George B. McClellan gave every evidence of being in league with the enemy. After Bingham had organized a partially dependable force, he began war on the criminal district south of Fourteenth Street. He described conditions there in the following terms:

In this lower section of New York, the practice of law is as distinct from any ordinary practice as the customs of the criminal class are from those of ordinary society. It is formed for one chief purpose—the defense of the criminal. The principal factors in this practice are not legal at all. They consist in destroying or manufacturing evidence and postponing cases until they can be brought before a politically favorable judge. A tribe of criminal lawyers exactly suited for this practice has developed out of the slums. They might be divided into two classes, according to their use, as "fixers" or "bellowers"—the use of the first being silently to pervert justice, and of the other to cover this up by bawling a few inches away from the judge's nose a diatribe concerning the rights of man and the oppression of the poor—the stock cry of the professional criminal class and the politicians who defend them.

Mr. McClure also wrote about New York politics in an article called "The Tammanyizing of a Civilization" (*McClure's*, November, 1909), which described the way in which Tammany Hall exploited and degraded ignorant foreigners and Negroes:

Its political saloon keepers have killed unnumbered multitudes of these people through excessive drinking; its political procurers have sold the bodies of their daughters; its contractors and street-railway magnates have crowded them into the deadly tenement districts by defrauding them of their rights of cheap and decent transportation; and its sanitary officials have continuously murdered a high percentage of the poor by their sale of the right to continue fatal and filthy conditions in these tenement districts, contrary to law.

The novelists of the period were not unaware of the extent of municipal corruption, and a number of political

novels appeared between 1900 and 1910. Winston Churchill,
Booth Tarkington, and Brand Whitlock all wrote novels on
political themes, and all took a more or less critical attitude
toward American political life. Tammany Hall furnished
material for at least two narratives of the period, W. L.
Riordon's *Plunkitt of Tammany Hall* (1905) and Alfred Henry
Lewis's *The Boss* (1903). Lewis, who has been mentioned
as a chronicler of cowboy life, was also something of a muckraker, as will be noted later, and in 1904 he published his
novel of New York politics. The leading character, "the
Boss," tells the story of his rise to power. He describes his
life as gang-leader, as head of a club, as alderman, as lieutenant to Big John Kennedy, and as "the boss." Into the
mouth of this Irish politician Lewis puts the most complete
cynicism, and although the novel can scarcely be regarded
as primarily a piece of muckraking, it contributed to the
exposure of "the shame of the cities."

The social evil was repeatedly discussed in connection
with New York and other cities. Mr. Turner touched on it
in his article on Chicago; he gave a whole paper to an account of the business in New York. It was entitled "The
Daughters of the Poor," and appeared in *McClure's* in November, 1909. New York was the leading center of the
white slave trade. It developed under Tammany Hall rule.
After the red-light district was broken up in 1901 the politicians who were engaged in this business, known as "cadets,"
reorganized and reported that the cadet system had been
entirely abolished. This was not true. The Independent
Benevolent Association of New York was the chief agent
and operator in the business. It was a corporation which
was both in the business and in politics. The supply of girls
was obtained at the dance halls. The cadets, usually handsome young American Jews (or Italians), seduced the poor
and ignorant girls in various ways, but often by promise of

marriage and wealth. Turner mentioned three classes of girls from which the supply was obtained: the "greenhorn" Jewish girls, the Polish girls, and the "smart" Jewish girls who made purely commercial contracts with the cadets. Liquor and drugs played a very small part in the procuring of girls. New York furnished about half of the women in this business for the entire country, and most of them came from domestic service. Steffens wrote about the hardships of these women in his Pittsburgh article.

Disorderly houses [he wrote] are managed by ward syndicates. Permission is had from the syndicate real-estate agent, who alone can rent them. The syndicate hires the houses from the owners at, say, $35 a month, and he lets it to a woman at from $35 to $50 a week. For furniture the tenant must go to the "official furniture man," who delivers $1000's worth of "fixings" for a note of $3,000, on which high interest must be paid. For beer its tenant must go to the "official bottler," and pay $2 for a $1 case of beer; for wines and liquors to the "official liquor commissioner," who charges $10 for $5's worth; for clothes to the "official wrapper-maker." These women may not buy shoes, hats, jewelry, or any other luxury or necessity except from the official concessionaires, and then only at the official monopoly prices. If the victims have anything left, a police or some other city official is said to call and get it.

In 1910 Rheta Childe Dorr wrote several articles on "The Prodigal Daughter" for *Hampton's*.

Other criminal classes in New York were frequently written about. Alfred Henry Lewis, whose novel, *The Boss*, has been mentioned, wrote a series of articles for *Pearson's* in 1911 and 1912, using the title, "The Apaches of New York." The *Cosmopolitan* published a number of articles on metropolitan criminals, beginning in 1905 with three articles called "Confessions of a New York Detective." The anonymous author exposed the corrupt relations between politicians and the policeman, and stated that, having made his "pile," he was going to retire, partly for fear of being caught by investigations instituted at Albany. In 1907 Josiah Flynt exposed, in the February, March, April, and May *Cosmopolitan*, the evils of the pool-room, revealing the far-reaching system of gambling connected with the race-tracks and pool-rooms. He produced evidence to show that there was a gambling trust, organized with multimillionaires as directors, and having definite business agreements with telephone and telegraph companies. In the same year Jack London published "My Life in the Underworld" as a serial in the *Cosmopolitan*, and this document touched rather intimately on political corruption, the protection of criminals, and conditions in prisons. David Graham Phillips wrote on "The Delusion of the Race-Track" for the same magazine in January, 1905; Joseph Freeman Marston's "The Maelstrom of the Betting Ring" and Stephen Sutcliffe's "In a New York Gambling House" appeared in *Munsey's* in 1904; Elisha W. Kelly's "Gambling and Horse Racing" was published in *Public Opinion*, July 22, 1905; and Henry Kitchell Webster's "Cotton Growing and Cotton Gambling" was featured in the *American*.

As a result of the exposures of municipal corruption, many cities threw the old parties out of office and elected reform candidates. Some of the changes appear to have been but of short duration. An incidental result of muckraking was the development of the scientific sociological survey, such as was carried on in Pittsburgh from 1909 to 1914. These surveys, which were conducted in many cities, provided a sound basis for reform and have paved the way for important experiments in municipal administration.

CHAPTER SEVEN

CORRUPTION IN STATE POLITICS

O F COURSE the muckrakers soon discovered that corruption was not limited to the cities, and between 1904, when Lincoln Steffens wrote his series, "Enemies of the Republic," for *McClure's*, and 1910, when Charles Edward Russell published in the *Cosmopolitan* a number of articles with the general heading "What Are You Going to Do About It?" various muckrakers wrote for various magazines articles describing conditions in Pennsylvania, Montana, Colorado, Delaware, New York, and others of these United States. As early as 1903 there were articles on the Folk exposures in Missouri in the *Cosmopolitan* and in the *Independent*. The latter considered the subject of bribery editorially at least three or four times during the year, concluding that the greatest sinners in this respect were the corporations which sought special municipal privileges whereby they might enrich themselves at public expense, and supporting Mr. Choate in his statement that "the only way in which this legislative corruption can be stopped is by holding up such men publicly to opprobrium; they must be driven from the churches; they must be branded in society as men dishonest and unworthy for honest men to associate with. Not until the attack is made directly upon the directors of corporations who are responsible for this sort of corruption will it be possible to cure the evil."

As in municipal exposure so in state exposure Steffens easily ranks first among the muckrakers. In 1904 he wrote

about Missouri, Illinois, and Wisconsin; and in the following
year about Rhode Island, New Jersey, and Ohio.

In opening this series—"Enemies of the Republic"—he
stated that every time he attempted to trace to its source
the political corruption of a city ring, the stream of pollution branched off in the most unexpected directions and
spread out in a network of veins and arteries so complex
that hardly any part of the body politic seemed clear of it.
Corruption was not confined to politics, but extended into
finance and industry. Miss Tarbell had shown it in the trust,
Mr. Baker in the labor union, and his investigations of municipal government had always drawn him out of politics into
business and out into the state and the nation. The source
of sustenance of our bad government was not politicians,
the bribe-takers, but the bribe-givers, the captains of industry. The highway of corruption, he wrote, is the "road
to success."

In his article on Missouri he explained what he meant by
the "System." It was corruption settled into a "custom of
the country"; the betrayal of trust established as the form
of government. A few bribes, or even a hundred bribes,
might not be so bad, but in Missouri—as elsewhere—there
was a System of bribery—"corruption installed as the mo-
tive, the purpose, the spirit of a state government." The
"combine" was composed of dishonest legislators of both
parties who were usually in the pay of big business interests,
and were controlled by the lobby. The lobby also controlled
the honest legislators, for they represented the corporations
and big businesses which contributed to the campaign funds.
Such contributions were everywhere the first step toward
corruption. It was wholesale bribery which bought also the
honest legislator. The lobby served both the party and business.

When Folk and Attorney-General Crow exposed Missouri
it was found that it was not only state interests that were

corrupting politics, but that national concerns which operated all over the United States were also involved. Among
these were the American Sugar Refining Company, the
American Book Company, and the Royal Baking Powder
Company. Steffens had much to say about the last named
concern, to show that "good" business makes for bad politics. In its train was even United States Senator William
J. Stone.

In December, 1905, William Allen White had an article,
"Folk," in *McClure's* in which he described the system with
which Folk had to deal in Missouri. For a generation that
state had been under the domination of the Democratic
party, and the machine that was in control had no moral
sense.

The legislature met biennially, and enacted such laws as the
corporations paid for, and such others as were necessary to fool
the people, and only such laws were enforced as party expediency
demanded. The statute prohibiting murder was operative except
against persons who had served the party by stealing elections;
and the statute against larceny was operative only when it could
be shown that the offender was outside the party machine, and
stealing from private citizens. Boodling, bribe-giving, public
blackmail, legislative hold-ups, corrupt political deals and combinations carrying thousands of dollars with them flourished,
and politicians who benefited thereby were accounted shrewd.

The governors were mere "pasteboard men"; the force
that operated the machine came from without. White
claimed that fifty men in New York City formed the boards
of directors of a majority of the great railroads, the great
banks, the great life insurance companies, and the great
public service corporations. Some of these were high-salaried
lawyers who hired subordinate lawyers in every American
state and territory whose duty it was to control the courts
and the forces that make laws and courts. Through these

subordinates in the state capitals and trade centers they could dictate the election of United States senators, governors, and supreme court judges in two-thirds of the American states. This was achieved by granting railroad passes. The two men who wielded much power in Missouri were Alexander Cochran, state counselor for the Missouri Pacific Railroad, and John Carroll, counselor for the Burlington Railroad. To them the governors and legislators and politicians went for orders.

Since Folk found that the state supreme court undid again and again the work which he started in St. Louis, and since the corrupt forces made life hard for him and threatened to make it impossible for him to live in the state after his term should expire—he decided that the logical thing for him to do would be to run for governor and break up the corrupt machine. City reformers in other states made the same discovery—to protect the cities they had to reach back to the state government. In Missouri the governor was the overlord of the large cities. He appointed the majority of the police commissioners and he named the excise commissioners. In this way he could control the policemen and the saloon-keepers. It was not easy for Folk to win the gubernatorial nomination and election in 1904, but he succeeded in both, and immediately set about to reform the state. He enforced the anti-pass law and the Sunday-closing law, both of which had been dead letters on the Missouri statutes for nearly forty years. In fact, he enforced all the statute laws; and he induced the legislature to pass some new ones of a nature which the machine had consistently refused to pass for many years. Legislative corruption was eliminated, and government by corporations was overthrown. And this was achieved largely by enforcing laws which were already on the statute books. Missouri was probably the only state which had no dead letter laws in 1905.

The St. Louis of Illinois is Chicago, and just as Folk learned that he could not reform St. Louis without reforming Missouri, so the Municipal Voter's League of Chicago discovered that their city was closely linked up with Illinois. Missouri was normally Democratic while Illinois was Republican, but one state was as machine ridden as the other. In both states the business politicians of both parties coöperated in obtaining privileges and boodle.

The heart of the corrupt system in Chicago was the council. Two-thirds of the aldermen were organized into a bipartisan "combine." The bosses of the two parties had a rough working agreement. The Democrats took the city, while the Republicans ran Cook County, in which Chicago is located. The Republican sheriff, for instance, was allowed to operate his horse-racing graft without police interference, and the sheriff let the police alone in their vice graft. The Republican leaders were granted general immunity from all hindrances in their county contracts, and in return the Republican aldermen voted with the "combine" which sold out municipal legislation.

The relation between city and state was well illustrated by Chicago's fight against long-time street railway franchises. By 1895 many of the Chicago traction franchises were expiring. The corrupt municipal system was in good order and could have extended them, legally, for twenty years. But Charles T. Yerkes wanted a franchise for at least fifty years. He went to Springfield, the state capital, to get a law from the legislature. A suitable bill was passed, but Altgeld, the Democratic governor, vetoed it. Yerkes then "favored" John R. Tanner, chairman of the Republican Central Committee, for governor; and the campaign of 1896 swept him into office. By that time, however, the Democratic system in Chicago was getting out of order. The Municipal Voter's League was attacking Yerkes and his plans, and in the spring of 1897

Carter H. Harrison was elected mayor. Yerkes, therefore, decided to let the state system do the whole job for him. Instead of having a law passed that would empower the city council to extend the franchises he would have the state legislature pass bills granting the extension outright. The Humphrey bills were drafted, which provided for a fifty-year extension. This was a violation of the "Home Rule" principle and created intense resentment in Chicago. The city newspapers circulated over the state and the country people became aroused. The "Senate combine" passed the bills, but the House defeated them. Since the chief stated objection to the Humphrey bills had been their violation of "Home Rule," Yerkes substituted another, the Allen bill. This bill did not grant outright the fifty-year extension of franchises, but permitted the Chicago council to do so. The country members thought this was fair, and although Chicago protested, the bill was passed and signed. Then the proposition to carry the Allen Law into effect came before the city council. The reformers had been active and had cut down the strength of the combine, but still the grafters were in a majority and they controlled the committees. Mayor Harrison now became the key man. He had the veto power and it took a two-thirds vote to override his veto. They could not bribe him, and so he defeated this scheme of his own party. Yerkes again looked back to the state and asked only for time and no legislation. Chicago also looked to the state, and demanded the repeal of the Allen Law in the session of 1899. It asked the people of Illinois to keep out of the legislature every member who had voted for this measure; and the people responded. Of sixteen retiring senators who had voted for this act only two were reëlected; and of eighty-two representatives who voted for it, fourteen were returned. The result was that the Allen Law was repealed. The mayor and the council now could refuse to extend franchises to the street railways, but in order to be able to compel the companies to negotiate for fair terms, they had to have the power to receive back the property. This they had not, and this they demanded of the legislature of 1899. But the legislators were afraid of the subject and would not touch it. Two years later Chicago's comprehensive bill was strangled in committee. In 1903 the city was bound to have this enabling legislation, and the business and political bosses were bound to prevent it. Walter L. Fisher of the Chicago Municipal Voter's League drafted the so-called Mueller bill, and under heavy pressure the "Senate combine" passed it. William Lorimer, one of the Republican state bosses and at the time a congressman, rushed to Springfield to prevent the House from passing it; and it was buried in the Municipal Committee. He offered a substitute bill, the Lindley bill. "It is the Lindley bill or nothing," he said. Chicago decided to reject the Lindley substitute, and she commanded sufficient votes to do it; all that was needed was a roll-call. This the Speaker refused to grant. Under the law a roll-call was to be granted on the demand of five members. Lorimer had drafted six amendments to the Lindley bill. As the first amendment was offered, ninety-six members rose and shouted "Roll-call!" The Speaker would not hear. He put the amendment, swung down his gavel and declared the amendment adopted. In this way each of the six amendments was passed. Then there was a rush for the chair, and the Speaker fled through the back door. The House quickly reorganized; the Lindley bill was rejected, and the Mueller bill passed.

Chicago was on the road to reform, and she was trying to carry the state with her.

The story of Wisconsin was the story of Robert M. La-Follette. Steffens told it in a long article for *McClure's* in October, 1904, and in a briefer and more interesting chapter in his *Autobiography*. He went to Milwaukee under the impression that the then governor of the state was a charlatan and a crook. He tried to obtain his information largely from the enemies of the governor, and it was these enemies who convinced Steffens that LaFollette was an honest and courageous man who was really trying to establish good and representative government in his state. When he approached the governor with a demand for his whole story, LaFollette agreed to give it—at the St. Louis Exposition. There in a room of a hotel LaFollette took a week to tell everything about himself. To this his enemies had nothing to add, as Steffens found out later. The one big sin that LaFollette had committed was that he had taken the Republican party away from the corrupters and made it stand for the interests of the people.

In Wisconsin the reform started with the state—at the state capital. From there it worked out into the cities and the rural districts. The cities in the state, including Milwaukee, had the same bipartisan corrupt systems that prevailed in St. Louis and Chicago and elsewhere. When the corrupting interests were driven out of one party—in this case the Republican—they went over to the other party. This happened also in other states, and Steffens urged his readers to show the same independence and intelligence in their political affiliations and in their voting.

When the Republican state convention met in 1904, the Stalwarts (conservatives and corruptionists) bolted and held another convention. To this convention came Postmaster-General Payne, United States Senators Spooner and Quarles, Stalwart congressmen and federal office holders. "The broken State System was appealing to the United States System," and the Republican National Convention in session at Chicago decided in favor of the Stalwarts. LaFollette was reëlected governor, but he began to see that he would have to go to the United States Senate.

Rhode Island was "A State For Sale" (*McClure's*, February, 1905). Here the farmers—of the pure American stock —sold their votes to the bosses, who sold them to the business interests, who, in turn, gave the people a poor and corrupt and undemocratic government. The governor was a mere figurehead, without an appointing or a veto power. The legislative power was all vested in the General Assembly of two houses, which was controlled by the blind boss, General Charles R. Brayton. It was the best established and most shameless system that Steffens had seen.

The lower house consisted of seventy-two members, and the Senate of thirty-eight members—one from each town or city. Of the total population of 428,551 (in 1900), 36,027 lived in twenty towns. Thus it was easy to buy a majority of the senators. The legislators came bought from the country, and they took orders absolutely. The unpropertied citizens could vote only if they registered four months before the election, and then they could not vote on any proposition to impose taxes or to spend money.

Among the outstanding men in Rhode Island politics were, besides General Brayton, Marsden J. Perry, a capitalist, and Nelson W. Aldrich, a business man in politics. These men, by manipulating the legislature, gave to themselves perpetual franchises and irrepealable laws which were worth millions of dollars to them. Aldrich came to be not only the dominating influence in Rhode Island politics, but he was commonly regarded as the boss of the United States Senate.

Steffens came to the conclusion that the farmers were as corruptible as any other class of people. "Political corruption is not a matter of men or classes or education or character of any sort; it is a matter of pressure."

In the brief introduction to Steffens' two articles in *Mc-*

Clure's on "New Jersey: A Traitor State," which appeared in April and May, 1905, the editor of *McClure's* stated that they already knew something about political and commercial corruption and had charted some of its submerged depths, but here, he stated, "we have found ourselves at times off soundings and the leadsman has reported no bottom."

Situated between two such thriving cities as New York and Philadelphia, New Jersey was "the gateway of the continent," a natural highway of the nation. Alexander Hamilton himself seems to have been the first to appreciate this, for he was instrumental in organizing companies which took advantage of this situation. One of these obtained a charter from the state securing unto itself as private property the water front on the Jersey shore opposite New York City, which was valuable for ferry landings. Another company obtained the right to exploit the people and to operate in other states. The people were taught to use the state for private business purposes.

In 1830, when railroading was still in the experimental stage, some leading Jersey men organized the Camden and Amboy Railroad and asked the state for aid. What they wanted was a monopoly forever of the New York-Philadelphia traffic; perpetual exemption from taxation; state subscription to their stock; and plenty of time to build. It was all granted; and from then to 1873 followed a period of almost unparalleled corruption in state politics. The promoters of the Camden and Amboy foresaw that they would have to protect their monopoly rights by corruption. And they did.

The local railroad could not, however, resist the large national lines in the long run, and in 1871 the Camden and Amboy was "leased" to the Pennsylvania Railroad. The people of New Jersey were in uproar against the "foreign" monopoly, but the Pennsylvania went quietly about to own the legislature and to be the state. In this she succeeded after a long and hard struggle.

The Pennsylvania was not the only railroad with privileges doing business in the state. There were others that were also exempt from taxation. As these grew and prospered they withdrew more and more property from the state that could be taxed. In the eighties more than a fourth of the property of the state was exempt from county and local taxation. This made the burden on the citizens increasingly heavy. "Equal taxation" was therefore an issue that came up again and again, and had to be consistently defeated by the railroads.

No wonder, then, that James B. Dill received a hearing when he proposed a scheme whereby New Jersey could not only increase her business but make "foreign" business pay her taxes. His plan was to create a corporation which should invite all the corporations of the United States to come and incorporate in New Jersey at a moderate charge. In 1890 the Corporation Trust Company of New Jersey was formed, composed of influential men in business and politics, including the secretary of state. It was a graft, for the company was organized to graft upon the incorporating power of the state. The company advertised boldly and did good business. In 1891 a New York newspaper complained that during the last two years 1,626 national corporations with an aggregate capital of over $600,000,000 had organized under the New Jersey laws.

New Jersey had at last found an adequate source of revenues. In 1890 her corporations brought in only $292,000; by 1903 this source produced $2,177,297. Her debt had been wiped out, her schools were famous, and she could boast of her fine roads.

Between 1888 and 1896, when the Revision Act was passed,

the New Jersey laws were made steadily more favorable to the corporations. Charters were made perpetual, and any three or more persons might become a corporation for any lawful purpose whatever—with some exceptions, and these exceptions applied only to the state which granted the charter. In other words, New Jersey would allow corporations to do things in other states which she would not tolerate within her own borders.

Wherein did the treason of this state consist? In that she was selling out the rest of the states. The people of the United States were anti-trust. By the end of 1894 the federal government and twenty-two states had passed anti-trust laws; and precisely at that time New Jersey said in effect—in the words of Steffens—"Come to us. We'll let you do anything. You needn't stay here. Pay us for them, and we'll give you letters of marque to sail out into other states and do business as you please. The other states have made your business a crime; we'll license you to break their laws. We'll sell out the whole United States to you, and cheap; and our courts are 'safe' and our legislature is 'liberal,' and our location is convenient."

New Jersey had become the tenderloin district of the Union.

In "Ohio: A Tale of Two Cities" (*McClure's*, July, 1905), Steffens had much to say of Mark Hanna, the state boss, George Cox, the boss of Cincinnati, and Tom Johnson, the reform boss of Cleveland. All three were rich business men who knew what it meant to be in politics in order to protect business. Cox, however, was a professional politician, while the other two regarded themselves as business men in politics.

Hanna's parents moved to Cleveland in 1852, when Mark was still a boy. He married into a wealthy business family and was soon prominent in business himself. The M. A. Hanna & Co. was concerned with mines, ships, coal, oil, iron-ore and pig-iron. Then he acquired interests in banks, a newspaper, a theatre; and finally he was let into the West Side Company of Cleveland—a street railway concern. By 1882 he was president of this company, and this business forced him into politics. He wanted extensions to his line, more franchises and more privileges. To get these he went into politics, and corrupted politics. He wanted the right kind of mayor, and his share of the councilmen. These he secured by supervising—through an agent—the nominations and paying campaign expenses. The Cleveland of Hanna's day had a government by the public utility companies, a government by politicians hired to represent the privileged class. Hanna took an aggressive part in local politics only when his business interests demanded it. For that reason he never became the undisputed boss of his city.

After some years he became much interested in national politics. He organized the "spontaneous demand" for McKinley which in 1896 led to the latter's election to the presidency of the United States. Then the organizer of the National Republican machine wanted to be United States senator. But there was no Ohio vacancy in the Senate, and he had no local organization to back him. However, the vacancy was created. The President appointed the senior senator from Ohio, John Sherman, to the position of secretary of state; and by reaching an agreement with Boss Cox of Cincinnati the hostile governor, Bushnell, was induced to appoint Hanna to the vacancy.

The other new senator from Ohio was Joseph B. Foraker. He had been governor for two terms, and had the reputation of being a good orator and a courageous opponent of corporate greed and corruption. Foraker, too, needed backing, and he entered into a working arrangement with Cox. The Cincinnati traction interests wanted a fifty-year five-cent-fare franchise in their city, and Foraker wanted to be a United States senator. Both aims were achieved by the legislature of 1896. The Rogers Law provided for the franchise and Foraker was elected senator.

In 1898 Hanna's term as senator drew to a close, and this time he would have to be elected by the legislature. When it became known that his Republican enemies were forming a combination with the Democrats to beat him, he went there to take personal charge of his own fight. With him came money, the influence of the President, of the railroads, the banks, and the federal officeholders. By a narrow margin he was elected. The Rogers Law, however, was so unpopular that this same legislature repealed it.

To get his street-railway franchise renewed he had to start the fight for privileges all over again. He went to Cleveland; but he found that the Republican machine there was against him. Then he supported the Democratic candidate for mayor, and succeeded in electing him. This Democrat, Farley, was ready to do his part, and the traction people to do theirs; but before the plan was carried out, Cleveland elected Tom Johnson mayor, and that upset everything.

Johnson, as we have stated in an earlier chapter, held to the theory that the evil in government was to grant privileges to anybody. One of his first moves was to establish a Tax School, which was to investigate the inequalities and the favoritism of the tax lists, but the interests which were in danger of losing their tax privileges got out an injunction and stopped the unlawful expenditures on the Tax School. Next he tried to overcome the ridiculous undervaluation of the steam railroads, but the local and state boards of equalization refused to act, and the state supreme court held that the legislature alone could remedy the evil. (In 1903 the state tax on railroads was increased from one-half of one, to one per cent on the gross receipts.) Johnson's city board of equalization added $18,000,000 to the tax valuation of the street-railway and lighting companies. They appealed to the state board of tax remission, and got the entire amount remitted; and the legislature provided for the abolition of the Cleveland city board.

The big fight came when Johnson demanded from the street-railway people a three-cent fare and universal transfers. They would not hear of it; so he and the council established routes for competing three-cent lines and advertised for bids. Two days later the attorney-general of the state brought an ouster suit against the city of Cleveland— to oust the whole administration, and on June 26, 1902, the supreme court of the state ousted the board of control of Cleveland on the ground that it had been created by special legislation, which was unlawful. Since all the city charters of the state had been created by special legislation they were also voided by this decision, but it was so arranged that all the cities of the state could do business, all but one. Cleveland could not grant any more charters. In the fall the legislature met in special session to adopt a uniform municipal code for all the cities of the state. Hanna, Foraker, and Cox were among the dominant leaders, and this legislature adopted the Cincinnati board plan (of scattered irresponsibility) as the plan for all Ohio cities!

Being frustrated in his plans for Cleveland, Johnson ran for governor—but was defeated.

When Steffens' articles were published in book form, they bore the title, *The Struggle for Self Government*, and there was added to them a dedicatory epistle addressed to the Czar of Russia. Mr. Steffens informed the Czar that the book had been written for the encouragement of American citizens, but that they found little in it that was encouraging. On the other hand, it contained much that ought to prove heartening to the Czar. "There is proof in it," he wrote, "that the horrid conflict that has been waging between your Majesty and your Majesty's subjects is entirely unnecessary." And he went on to explain, with elaborate irony, the superiority of the American system of boss rule to the Russian imperial government. Russian subjects, he noted, were demanding a constitution, and he urged the Czar to grant their request and save himself trouble.

Sire [Steffens continued], a constitution is not only an innocent gratification to a people; shrewdly interpreted by corporation lawyers, or, as you might say, by King's counsel, a constitution may become a bulwark—of the rulers of a people. . . . Your Majesty may grant all that your people ask, and more— a representative government and a constitution, free speech and a free press, education and the suffrage,—and yet you may rule them as you rule them now, absolutely and with little more heed to their best interest. For have I not shown, sire, that we, the great American people, have all we want of all of these things, and that, nevertheless, our government differs from yours—in essentials—not so much as you thought, not so much as your people think, and not nearly so much as my people think.

While Steffens' articles were still appearing in *McClure's*, the *Arena*, in 1905, began the publication of eight articles on Pennsylvania politics. The author, Rudolph Blankenburg, a wealthy merchant of Philadelphia, covered the political history of the state from the Civil War to the time he wrote, describing a galaxy of corruptionists of whom the chief were Simon Cameron and Senator Quay. Before he had finished writing this account of "Forty Years in the Wilderness," he had already caught his first glimpse of the Promised Land. The political ring overreached itself, the public grew indignant, Mayor John Weaver championed the rights of the people, and the gang was overthrown. Mr. Blankenburg closed his series with their prayer of thanksgiving:

My heart was heavy and almost despaired when I undertook the task of writing these articles. The day of deliverance seemed far off, but, thanks to the abnormal voracity, and unheard-of arrogance and utter defiance of the laws of God and man on the part of the "organization," and thanks to an awakened public conscience the day has come, let us hope to stay.

Out of the changes which brought such joy to the heart of Mr. Blankenburg came revelations of the extravagance and graft that had characterized the previous administration. Owen Wister, writing about "The Keystone Crime" for *Everybody's*, October, 1906, and Louis Seaber, describing in the *Independent*, May 30, 1907, "Pennsylvania's Palace of Graft," made public some of the more spectacular facts concerning the building of "the graft-cankered capitol." In 1897 the old state capitol had been burned, and the legislature provided for its replacement. The building was completed at a cost of four millions, and then was furnished for the sum of nine millions. One John H. Sanderson, having obtained, in dubious fashion, the contract for these furnishings, proceeded to make the most of his opportunities. From a company which he himself had organized he purchased two thousand fixtures at a cost of $550,000; he then sold them to the state for $1,612,573.56. He received $4.85 a pound for chandeliers; wherefore he made them solid, and distributed about the edifice as many as possible, including four weighing seventy-five hundred pounds each, which adorned the House of Representatives. For painting and decorating he was paid $789,473.16; the sub-contractor who actually furnished the goods received only $174,962. And so the statistics went, until there stood forth a complete revelation of an astounding but no unrepresentative achievement in the fine art of plundering the people.

Even more sensational had been the developments in Montana, where, during the nineties, the great political rivals were Marcus Daly and William A. Clark. In 1890 Clark, who was a Democrat, felt a strong inclination to become United States senator, but he was unsuccessful in his attempts to win the state legislature. Eight years later the outlook was brighter, for the legislature was supposed to be favorable to him, and the Clark leaders announced that they were sure of fifty-four votes on the first ballot—more than a majority. Just before balloting began on January 10, 1899, Senator Whiteside obtained the floor. Holding in his hands four envelopes containing $30,000 in new $500 and $1,000 bills, he explained to the representatives and senators of Montana that this money had been given him by the Clark ring for the purpose of bribing several members of the legislature. In order to obtain this evidence, he had posed as a Clark supporter, and he had been given $5,000 as payment for his imagined services.

As a result of this revelation, only seven members of the legislature voted for Clark when the balloting began. Disheartened, on the verge of collapse, Clark met with his lieutenants in his hotel room. They had more confidence in the power of money than he, and they set to work to bribe both the legislature and the members of the grand jury which had been called to investigate the charges of bribery. They spent $431,000 in buying votes, paying from $4,000 to $50,000 a head, and they also availed themselves of such other weapons as they could find. They studied each member of the legislature, unearthed long-buried indiscretions in conduct, found out about private debts, and scanned political records. Most of the legislators succumbed either to the money or to the pressure, and on January 28 Clark was elected by fifty-four votes. The grand jury two days before had reported that there was not sufficient evidence of bribery to warrant a trial, a decision which, it was said, $10,000 apiece had helped the jurymen to reach. And on that same day Senator Whiteside had been unseated and a safe man put in his place.

The night after Clark's election most of the bars in Helena were open to the populace, and no one was allowed to order anything but champagne. It was said that Clark's champagne bill alone was thirty thousand dollars, but at the time he doubtless thought the money well spent, for neither he nor his allies believed there was a chance that the fight would be carried to Washington. It happened, however, that Clark had said, when Whiteside exhibited the bribe money, that Marcus Daly was responsible, and Daly could not let such a charge pass unnoticed. In the meantime, Whiteside brought disbarment proceedings against John B. Wellcome, Clark's chief lieutenant and the man who had done most of the bribing, in the supreme court of the state. This court was composed of three members. One of these was approached with an offer of $100,000 to drop the case, and the other two were sounded out; but all three stood firm, and Wellcome was disbarred.

On January 5, 1900, the committee on privileges and elections of the United States Senate began its investigation of Clark's election, continuing its sessions until April 6. On May 10 it unanimously decided to recommend to the Senate the adoption of a resolution voiding Clark's title to a seat. But there was still one string left to Clark's bow. He realized that if the Senate adopted the committee's report, as it undoubtedly would, then, according to law, there had been no election, and there could be no vacancy. If, on the other hand, he resigned, that would create a vacancy which the governor could fill by appointment—and he might appoint Clark to succeed himself. The one difficulty was that Governor Robert B. Smith was not a Clark man and could not be bought.

With great ingenuity and daring the Clark ring solved its little problem. Lieutenant-Governor Spriggs was at the service of the Clark faction, and he would do the trick if Smith could be eliminated. A day or two before Clark's resignation Spriggs left Montana to attend the Populist National Convention at Sioux Falls, South Dakota, where, it was assumed, he would spend at least a week. At the same time Tom Hinds, an adroit politician, persuaded Governor Smith to go to California on a vacation and to look into the title to some mining claims. An hour after the Governor left, Spriggs was notified and started at once for Helena. Clark was also informed, and he immediately made his resignation speech in the Senate—some days before the report of the committee was to be submitted. Thereupon Spriggs, in the absence of the Governor, appointed Clark to succeed himself.

Smith, naturally indignant at the turn affairs had taken, announced that the appointment was fraudulent, and wired the leaders of the Senate that he intended to ignore it. Before decisive action could be taken, however, Clark announced himself as a candidate for senator in the election that was to take place that year. He allied himself with F. Augustus Heinze, who had large copper interests in Montana and who was engaged in fighting the Amalgamated Copper Company, organized by Marcus Daly, H. H. Rogers, William G. Rockefeller, and James Stillman, the last three being Standard Oil magnates. Clark wanted political vindication and a seat in the Senate; Heinze wanted economic advantages. Heinze managed a spectacular campaign; Clark spent a million dollars; on January 16, 1901, Clark was re-elected United States senator by fifty-seven votes; and that night Helena once more had free champagne and cigars.

It was C. P. Connolly who told this sensational story in two series of articles, "The Story of Montana" and "The Fight of the Copper Kings," which *McClure's* published in 1906 and 1907. Connolly had gone to Montana in 1884, when he was twenty-one years old, and had later been admitted to the bar of that state. For four years he was prose-

cuting attorney at Butte, and he won a considerable reputation "because of the marked personal courage he displayed in political speeches during the Montana copper war,
when it wasn't any too safe to speak in boldness and when
men held themselves prepared to back every word on the
drop of the hat." Connolly knew every detail of the struggle
he described, and *McClure's* advertised his articles as "the
most thrilling fact story that has ever come out of the West."

Whereas most of the muckrakers began as journalists,
Connolly had been a business man and a lawyer, and it was
the success of the Montana articles that led him to adopt
a literary career. He wrote for various magazines, but especially for *Collier's*, for which he reported the Steunenberg
murder, the McNamara trial, and the Leo Frank case.

Mr. Connolly also wrote an article on "Boss" Barnes of
New York, and it was this article which Theodore Roosevelt quoted in the speech which resulted in the famous libel
suit. Roosevelt's victory was, then, a victory for Connolly
as well. A further testimony to Mr. Connolly's accuracy
came as a result of another libel suit, this time a suit in which
the muckraker happened for once to be the plaintiff. A
Memphis lawyer, Caruthers Ewing, speaking before the
State Bar Association of Georgia, delivered a bitter attack
against Connolly, declaring that certain articles, published
in *Everybody's* and entitled "Big Business and the Bench,"
were false and misleading. The address was reprinted in
Law Notes, which Connolly promptly sued for libel. The
case was settled out of court by awarding Connolly a sub-
stantial sum in damages. Mark Sullivan, who at one time
was editor of *Collier's*, wrote about Connolly:

Whenever in *Collier's* you find a passion for the sacredness of
a fact, that is likely to have been written by Connolly. His zest
in life was in finding the facts of a complex situation and most
of the waking hours of his existence were spent in that absorp-

tion, in a concentration of all his faculties on comparing and testing and verifying, in separating the ragged shadows from the solid substance of truth, and finally in reducing the facts to what they were as God made them.

What Connolly had done for Montana, Judge Ben Lindsey did for Colorado. In 1910 *Everybody's* published "The Beast and the Jungle," issued afterward in book form as *The Beast*. This was Lindsey's autobiography, written with the aid of Harvey O'Higgins, but it was more than a personal story: it was an irrefutable demonstration of the influence of corporate wealth over government.

Lindsey is known primarily for his work with juvenile delinquents, but his services to his state and to the nation include much besides his achievements in the juvenile court. The corporations and trusts were nowhere more ruthless and domineering than in the new state of Colorado, with its immense mineral resources. There, in the first years of the century, they seemed to control the entire government, state and local, legislative, executive and judicial. And in the capital of the state Judge Lindsey has constantly stood for clean government, serving both as reformer and muckraker, remedying conditions where he could, and calling the attention of his fellow citizens to the corruption about them.

When he became judge of the county court in 1902 he found, for example, that the county had been paying $36 per one thousand sheets for paper that was not worth four dollars, had paid six dollars for letter files that were normally priced at forty cents, and had granted one company in sixteen months $40,000 more than the material it supplied was worth. He found also that the corporations were everywhere in control. In 1905 the public utility corporations of Denver actually appointed the committee which nominated the candidates for the supreme court of Colorado. In the Cripple Creek labor trouble the governor and a hand picked

supreme court decided against the laborers in plain violation
of constitutional rights. In 1904 the supreme court super-
vised and controlled the state elections, and later investigated the ballots, throwing out thousands of votes to carry
the state for the Republicans. In 1906 the district court
granted similar writs to prevent election frauds, but this
time it was against the interest of the corporations and the
supreme court promptly reversed itself to satisfy its masters.

In his autobiography Lindsey stated that when rich corporation magnates were forced to trial they blandly smiled
at the judges and refused to testify. If, through some miscal-
culation they found themselves in jail they were immediately released by the higher courts. After the great election
conspiracy of 1904, he wrote, "the citizen of Colorado had
no more right to 'life, liberty, and the pursuit of happiness'
than a yellow dog on the streets of Denver, unless he wore
the corporation collar and tag, came to the whistle of his
master and ate scraps from his hand." By the use of the legislature, the courts, and public officials, the corporations
were establishing a power trust with "incredible rights" in
all the watersheds and power streams surrounding Denver,
without reserving to the state any rights in these natural
resources. Coal companies received from the State Land
Board for a song hundreds of acres of land that was worth
at least $2,000 an acre. Corporations in Denver secured
millions of dollars worth of franchises, and special acts were
passed in favor of the railroads and other corporations, while
laws to protect the public were almost invariably defeated
by a combination of the corporation groups in both parties.

In California it was one corporation that held sway, the
Southern Pacific Railroad. In his novel, *The Octopus*, Frank
Norris had presented a picture of the war between this railroad and the farmers, but the reality was far more amazing
than the portrayal in fiction. When E. H. Harriman became

boss of the Southern Pacific, he also became boss of California. At a dinner in Washington he announced that Congressman James N. Gillet would be the next governor of the state. He got the job. Charles Edward Russell, describing the power of this railroad in *Hampton's* in 1910, said, "It was the government and all the branches thereof, not merely directing but performing." It defeated the plans of the reformers in the legislature, it stopped the graft prosecution in San Francisco, it enabled Herrin, Calhoun, Schmitz and others to escape and it defeated Francis J. Heney at the polls. It was in the fight against the Southern Pacific that Hiram Johnson made his reputation. Steffens, Russell, and other muckrakers wrote about the situation.

The evils of Delaware politics were exposed in a series of articles in the *Outlook*, February, 1903, by George Kennan. The corruption there centered about J. Edward Addicks. In 1902 some $30,000 was distributed in crisp new five- and ten-dollar notes in Kent County alone between November first and election day. This was to bribe voters. In some instances as much as thirty dollars was paid for a single vote. Kennan estimated that Addicks spent not less than $80,000 in Kent and Sussex counties that year, and bought between seven thousand and eight thousand of the thirteen thousand votes that were cast for his legislative candidates. He had twenty-one supporters in the Delaware legislature in 1903, and there held up the state. Senator Hanna told the anti-Addicks Republicans not to combine with the Democrats, for the Union Republicans (the Addicks men) were entitled to the fruits of their victory.

Other states received their share of attention. Burton J. Hendrick wrote about the Republican party in New York, as did Charles Edward Russell and others. The relations between the Boston and Maine Railroad and the legislature of New Hampshire figured in muckraking articles and were made the subject of Winston Churchill's *Coniston*. Indeed, while the agitation against state corruption was at its height there were few commonwealths that were untouched by the literature of exposure. Some articles on the subject were published after 1910, but few of any great importance. As has been said, we may regard Charles Edward Russell's series, "What Are You Going to Do About It?" *Cosmopolitan*, 1910, with its articles on graft in New York, Pennsylvania, Illinois, and Colorado, as marking the end of the interest in this phase of muckraking.

CHAPTER EIGHT

ATTACKS ON THE FEDERAL GOVERNMENT

THE FEDERAL government was attacked less frequently, but it did not escape untouched. After having muckraked the cities and the states Steffens went to Washington. In his articles on the states he had repeatedly alluded to the national government as a part of the "system," and at last he was ready to subject it to the same sort of investigation. The city of Washington, he soon learned, was governed much in the same fashion that other cities were governed, in spite of the fact that the citizens were disfranchised and that the city was directly under the control of Congress. Public service corporations and banks controlled, and congressmen sold out to high finance.

Fortunately for Steffens, President Roosevelt was not only a liberal himself but he was a personal friend. Later we shall say something about the estimate which other muckrakers placed on Roosevelt's relations to the muckraking movement; here we are interested in Steffens' estimate of him.

When Steffens first came to the national capital with the intention of exposing the federal government, Roosevelt was unwilling to tell of his experiences with the Senate and House machines, with the federal courts, and with the forces in the government of the District of Columbia. The reason for this was that Roosevelt was trying to work and deal with them. "He was not a reformer in the White House; he was a careerist on the people's side." He was trying to wrangle some concessions from the powers that be and make them do some things for the country at large. In return for the congressmen's votes for his favorite measures he would appoint their candidates to office. Once Steffens wanted to know which had been the President's "most outrageous appointment." The answer was that he had appointed the brother of a senator's mistress to the attorneyship of a certain city. Up to that time the senator mentioned had consistently voted against Roosevelt, but since then he sometimes voted his way. Another reason for Roosevelt's reluctance to collaborate with the muckraker was his realization that he was no hero fighting for a representative democracy. "He had no economics, he never understood the political issue between the common and the special interests; neither as a police commissioner nor as a president did he grasp the difference between morality and representation."

Early in 1906, however, he gave Steffens *carte blanche*, directing all officials and employees of the government to tell him anything he might wish to know about the running of the government—not incompatable with the public interests; and he promised that the officials should not be hurt. The subject on which Steffens was especially anxious to throw light was the question as to what our federal government represented. He showed that neither house of Congress nor the executive departments were representative. In one article he stated that the President had to "bribe" congressmen—by appointments—to vote for the people's measures.

He wrote about ten weekly articles for a newspaper syndicate of about one hundred members in which he exposed his findings in Washington. The editors did not find this material sensational enough; so Steffens quit. He was through with muckraking in the old form.

One of the most sensational series of the entire campaign in fact was directed against the Senate. The author, David

Graham Phillips, was primarily a novelist. He had been educated at De Pauw and at Princeton and had served on a Cincinnati newspaper and on the New York *Sun* and the New York *World*, for which he had been a foreign correspondent and an editorial writer. In 1901 he published his first novel, *The Great God Success*, and shortly thereafter he devoted himself entirely to the writing of fiction. Although he was a conscientious worker, writing and rewriting his books, he turned out two novels a year regularly, and at the time of his assassination in 1911 he had six novels ready for publication. He did not hesitate to use his novels for muckraking purposes, and he left vigorous pictures of corruption in journalism, national government, and Wall Street. In *The Second Generation* (1907), his aim was to reveal the evils wrought by inherited fortunes, and he tried to work out an ideal solution of the problem. His best-known novel, *Susan Lenox*, published posthumously (1917), tells in great detail the life of a woman who became a prostitute, though afterwards she rose to virtue and success. It is full of typical muckraking material about police corruption, the lives of factory workers, houses of prostitution, and conditions in the tenement district.

Although he occasionally wrote articles on political subjects, Phillips was so absorbed in his novels that when the editor of the *Cosmopolitan* asked him to write a series on the Senate, he refused, suggesting that William Allen White be invited to take his place. White was too busy to accept, and the editor again applied to Phillips, agreeing to pay him any price he asked. The novelist named a sum that he believed to be out of the question, and was overwhelmed when his offer was promptly taken. He set to work at once, and was soon frantically excited about the discoveries he made. He began bringing his articles to the office, where the editorial staff was forced to delete libellous material. Good looking and fashionably dressed, Phillips had the appearance of a society man rather than a muckraker, but he was a born fighter, and he knew how to get punch into his articles.

The first installment of "The Treason of the Senate" appeared in the *Cosmopolitan* in March, 1906, and began with these words:

The treason of the Senate! Treason is a strong word, but not too strong, rather too weak, to characterize the situation in which the Senate is the eager, resourceful, indefatigable agent of interests as hostile to the American people as any invading army could be, and vastly more dangerous: interests that manipulate the prosperity produced by all, so that it heaps up riches for the few; interests whose growth and power can only mean the degradation of the people, of the educated into sycophants, of the masses toward serfdom. . . . The Senators are not elected by the people; they are elected by the "interests." A servant obeys him who can punish and dismiss. Except in extreme and rare and negligible instances can the people either elect or dismiss a senator? The senator, in the dilemma which the careless ignorance of the people thrusts upon him, chooses to be comfortable, placed and honored, and a traitor to oath and people rather than to be true to his oath and poor and ejected into private life.

Phillips selected Chauncey M. Depew for the first onslaught. Depew, he said, was secure from the finger of scorn in one place only— the Senate Chamber after the galleries had been cleared and he was alone with his colleagues. He cited the fact that the Senator from New York was a member of seventy directories, which brought him more than $50,000 a year in attendance fees alone—part of his payment for serving his master, the plutocracy.

Next came Senator Nelson W. Aldrich of Rhode Island, who was singled out for special attack because of his connection with the Rockefellers and because of his tariff legislation, which, it was charged, favored the oil and tobacco trusts. Aldrich, a Republican, was called the right arm of the interests, and Senator A. P. Gorman of Maryland, a Democrat, was called the left arm. Phillips, referring to this interest in business affairs which Democrats and Republicans alike displayed, spoke of the Senate "merger." Not all senators, he admitted, belonged to the "merger," but he accused the majority of them of membership, and he declared that the "roaring eloquence" and the "sham battles" of the body were intended to befog and blind the people.

In subsequent articles he named and characterized some of the principal members of the "merger." Spooner of Wisconsin he described as "chief spokesman" of the organization, and Bailey of Texas as "chief spokesman of the Democratic branch." Elkins of West Virginia, according to Phillips, was "a powerful second lieutenant"; he and Philander C. Knox of Pennsylvania were men of "immense wealth." The record of Joseph Benson Foraker of Ohio, he declared, showed "no act of friendliness or even neutrality toward the people in their struggle with 'the Interests.'" Henry Cabot Lodge he characterized as "the familiar coarse type of machine politician, disguised by the robe of the 'Gentleman Scholar.'" Shelby M. Cullom of Illinois had one great achievement to his credit, the Cullom Act, deliberately written to make the Interstate Commerce Commission powerless. Phillips reviewed the records of these men and of Allison of Iowa, Stone of Missouri, Senators Hale and Frye of Maine, and Vice-President Charles Warren Fairbanks of Indiana. He called attention to questionable transactions, and attempted to show how these men had gone about advancing the industrial and financial interests of the wealthy classes of the country. He concluded his ninth and last diatribe with these words:

Such is the stealthy and treacherous Senate as at present constituted. And such it will continue to be until the people think,

instead of shout, about politics; until they judge public men by
what they do and are, not by what they say and pretend. However, the fact that the people are themselves responsible for their
own betrayal does not migitate contempt for their hypocritical
and cowardly betrayers. A corrupt system explains a corrupt
man; it does not excuse him. The stupidity or negligence of the
householder in leaving the door unlocked does not lessen the
crime of the thief.

Other articles on the Senate appeared in the *Cosmopolitan*.
In June, 1906, Ernest Crosby wrote about "Our Senatorial
Grand Dukes," and in April of the same year Alfred Henry
Lewis mercilessly denounced Senator Platt of New York,
closing his article with these biting phrases:

What is he? Nothing! What has he done? Nothing! Who will
remember him? No one! . . . He is a weak, vain, troubled, unhappy, unrespected man. . . . The country owes him nothing,
for he has given it nothing; in no wise has he left his favoring
mark upon the times. One day he will die; and his epitaph might
truthfully be, "He publicly came to nothing, and privately came
to grief."

Crosby, in the article mentioned and in similar articles,
pleaded for the direct election of senators.

Naturally the senators were not pleased with these attacks,
and they were constantly on the alert to defend the august
body of which they were members. As early as 1894 Senator George F. Edmunds had described for the November
Forum the self-sacrificing labors of himself and his colleagues.
And in 1906, shortly after the appearance of the first of
Phillips' articles, George C. Perkins, multimillionaire and
three times senator for California, came to the rescue of his
afflicted associates in an article which the *Independent* published on April 12. Perkins asserted that there were not more
than ten senators who were millionaires, and that, leaving
out of consideration one senator, the average possessions of

the members did not exceed the "average accumulation of the business man, manufacturer, farmer or professional man of the New England or Middle States." He expressed his complete confidence in the virtue of his colleagues, who aspired to the Senate, he declared, simply because they coveted the honor of belonging to the most distinguished legislative body in the world. With self-righteous pride he pointed to the Senate as the barrier against tendencies that were threatening the very existence of the Republic (the word "Bolshevism" was unknown in those days), and he voiced the conviction that the then existing Senate would stand forth in history as one which had exhibited in the highest degree the qualities of fairness and impartiality and the determination to arrive at the truth.

The consequences of the attack on the Senate are difficult to determine. The *Cosmopolitan* declared that Phillips' articles were stirring the country as it had never been stirred before, but they had little effect on the political careers of the men attacked, and Phillips himself was so depressed by the savage denunciations visited upon him by various periodicals that he refused to write any more articles. Some students of the time state that Phillips purified the Senate; others point out that the bitterness of his attacks helped to discredit the whole muckraking movement; and still others say that the only effect was to undermine respect for government and thus to encourage lawlessness. It is a fact, however, that in 1913 the amendment providing for the direct election of senators was adopted, and it is only reasonable to assume that the exposures of six or seven years earlier did something to prepare public sentiment for the change.

During the Roosevelt administration there were few attacks on the federal government, aside from those directed against the Senate. Many of the muckrakers were ardent Roosevelt supporters, not only during his term of office but also when he again ran for President in 1912. Taft, however, was under suspicion from the very first. The *American* stated in October, 1908, that the great financiers were all anxious to have Taft elected, though they had remained discreetly silent lest their support antagonize Roosevelt. Other magazines voiced similar doubts. But the hostility remained latent until the beginning of the controversy between Gifford Pinchot of the forestry bureau and Richard Ballinger, secretary of the interior.

Collier's, which had at first suspended judgment, contenting itself with offering the administration friendly advice, now took the lead in denouncing the conduct of Ballinger and other government officials. This magazine was published by the company which Peter F. Collier had established. Mr. Collier, as a pioneer in the enterprise of bringing a library within the reach of the average man, built up a strong business, and in 1888 he founded a paper called *Once A Week*. Robert J. Collier, fresh from college, was placed in charge in 1896, and the name was changed to *Collier's Weekly*. With the aid of a college friend, Norman Hapgood, and of other brilliant young men, Collier built up a strong journal, which, because of the wealth of his father's organization, he was able to keep out of the hands of the financial and political interests. At the very outset *Collier's* adopted a liberal editorial policy, but it was not until 1905 that it began to publish muckraking articles. By 1909 it had a circulation of half a million copies a week, and in 1912 it passed the million mark. Although chiefly devoted to fiction, the magazine published fearless editorials, articles, and cartoons, and in the latter half of the muckraking decade it assumed the position of leadership which *McClure's* had held for the first four or five years.

It was in 1909, after an investigating committee had supported Ballinger, that *Collier's* engaged C. P. Connolly to take charge of the campaign to save the coal lands of Alaska. In the issue of November 13, 1909, the magazine published an article by L. R. Glavis, who was the author of the charges against Ballinger. This article failed to arouse the public and Hapgood suggested that Connolly undertake to write up the matter himself. Using the material Glavis had unearthed, together with his own knowledge of the situation as a whole and of the personalities involved, Connolly wrote an article which appeared in the issue of December 18, 1909. On the cover of this issue appeared a drawing of a whitewash brush, with the legend, "More Work for the Whitewash Brush." Two weeks later the House of Representatives took the appointment of the House members of the Ballinger committee out of the hands of Speaker Cannon, reserving to itself the right to select them. This was the first successful blow at Cannonism. While this campaign was going on, malicious and totally unfounded charges were made against Mr. Connolly by a government official.

Other magazines were aroused by what they regarded as an attempt to rob the people of invaluable natural resources in Alaska. *Pearson's* published, in 1909, a series by Alfred Henry Lewis, called "The Betrayal of a Nation," and in January, 1910, John E. Lathrop and George Kibbe Turner discussed the subject in *McClure's*. John L. Mathews in several articles discussed in *Hampton's*, 1909, the economic situation lying behind the controversy.

Hampton's was much concerned with all phases of the conservation movement. Charles Edward Russell once wrote that this was the best-liked and best-hated magazine ever published in America, and that its editor, Benjamin B. Hampton, showed more courage and ingenuity than any other muckraking editor. It was taken over by Hampton in 1907, and in a few years its circulation had risen from 13,000 to 440,000 a month. *Hampton's* aimed to give information on the controversial issues of the day, and it soon earned a reputation for liveliness. For three years it devoted an unusually large proportion of its space to the literature of exposure, and Hampton repeatedly asserted his faith in the value of such work. In 1909, after having stated the policy of the magazine, he wrote:

There, then, we have our platform. We are going to expose evil wherever we can; we are going to expose it calmly and truly; we are going to expose it in order that it may be replaced by good, and we are going to hold, by the very process, the loyal army of subscribers, whose standing and number command advertising. There is not going to be any let-down.

A year later he wrote: "Make no mistake. Muckraking has not gone out of date. It really is just beginning to find itself, to make itself efficient." But little more than another year had passed before Frank Orff, president and general manager of the Columbian-Sterling Publishing Company, informed the readers of *Hampton's* that the paper had been taken over by his concern. He stated that Mr. Hampton would remain as consulting editor for all his publications, that he had been given absolute freedom to conduct these magazines in the interest of the whole people of the country, and so forth and so on. But in less than a year the magazine was no more.

It was in 1910 that Hampton began writing on the need for preserving our resources. In a carefully prepared article, "The Vast Riches of Alaska," he commented on the great wealth of that territory, which he estimated at seventeen billion, and warned his readers that these incredibly rich resources might be turned over to the Guggenheims. He besought all Americans to write to their senators—or to Senator Beveridge of Indiana—recommending that the government itself build a railroad in Alaska, and that it lease the mineral lands, subject to an honest royalty. In the next issue he stated that the article had produced the desired effect and that, thanks to the widespread protest, the scheme to exploit Alaska had been at least temporarily blocked. A year later *Hampton's* again dealt with the Alaska question. Hampton said that the "big interests" had charged him with overstating the wealth of the territory. He had denied the charge, maintaining that he had secured all his figures from government sources. Immediately thereafter, he said, every official source of information in Washington was closed to the public.

During the years of its greatest activity *Hampton's* published many articles on conservation, and a few of the titles will indicate something of the tone and content: John L. Mathews' "The Trust That Will Control All Trusts" (August, 1909), and "Water Power and the Price of Bread" (July, 1909); "Mr. Ballinger and the National Grab-Bag," "The Heart of the Railroad Problem," "Aldrich, Boss of the Senate," "Oklahoma and the Indian: a Carnival of Graft," and "The Negro in Politics." When, in 1910 and 1911, the magazines were protesting against the proposed increase of postal rates, *Hampton's* contended that the purpose of the bill was purely punitive, and that it was directed against the magazines which had not supported the Taft administration. The editor ironically deplored the ruin that this measure would bring to the publishing industry, and he suggested that the administration simply name the six or seven muckraking journals it desired to punish, with *Hampton's* at the head of the list, and deprive them of the use of the mails.

Prominent among the factors in the Taft administration that aroused the indignation of the muckrakers was the autocratic power exercised by Speaker Joseph G. Cannon of the House of Representatives. The *American*, the *Cosmopolitan*, *Success*, and *La Follette's Weekly*, took part in the struggle against "Cannonism," but *Collier's*, as in the campaign against Ballinger, was the recognized leader. William Hard was one of its contributors, and Mark Sullivan, in the "Congressional Department" which he conducted, constantly noted the progress of the "insurgents" in their rebellion against "the Czar of the House." In the insurgent movement, which led to the forming of the Progressive party in 1912, *Collier's*, as well as other muckraking magazines, played an important part.

In national politics muckraking was allied with the whole liberal movement, which, in the years prior to 1914, made a vigorous fight for the democratization of Congress, the conservation of natural resources, and the restriction of big business. In the achievements of this movement muckraking undoubtedly played a large part; it opened the eyes of the middle classes, and it furnished reformers with all sorts of weapons. It is difficult to believe that such a campaign as that of 1912, in which two of the candidates stood upon extraordinarily liberal platforms, would have been possible if it had not been for the decade of muckraking.

CHAPTER NINE

THE BATTLE WITH BIG BUSINESS

N O SUPERHUMAN perspicacity was required to perceive that corruption in government was primarily a phase of the industrial development of the country and the rise of the trusts. The advantages accruing to corporations that had political power were so obvious that business men could not ignore them, and the influence of the trusts was so widespread that they could not well have kept out of politics if they had wanted to. Our whole economic history had paved the way for the growth of monopolies, and no one could deny that they were a logical—and perhaps a necessary outgrowth of the economic order. On the other hand, it was perfectly plain that the great trusts brought suffering and poverty to large numbers of people, and it was equally clear that the debauching of political life had resulted in part from the struggle to establish and maintain monopoly control of essential industries.

The question of the trusts was the greatest problem facing the American people in the two or three decades preceding the country's entrance into the World War. As is not infrequently true of economic movements, the industrial development of the nation during those years had the air of inevitability, and it seemed almost futile to combat a tendency that appeared to be inherent in the very laws of nature. Many people—especially, of course, those who profited or expected to profit by the growth of the trusts—acquiesced in the development of these organizations, even though the political integrity of the United States was threatened thereby. Others, however, realized the danger, and the agitation against the trusts revealed itself not only in countless magazine attacks but also in such official actions as Roosevelt's "trust-busting" campaign and the anti-trust legislation of his administration and that of Wilson's first term. The official remedy for the situation was government regulation, which, as has often been pointed out, had the effect of establishing the trusts more firmly than ever—and frequently had no other effect. The remedy of the Socialists and of some others was public ownership of natural monopolies, a remedy which had never been tried on a large scale. The muckrakers frequently pinned faith to one or the other of these devices, but they placed greatest emphasis on the necessity for publicity and the arousing of public spirit. And it is safe to say that if the situation has been improved —it is clear that the problem has not been solved—the activities of the muckrakers in awakening the public are largely responsible for the improvement.

Not infrequently the articles of the muckrakers were diatribes against "big business" in general and attacks on Wall Street, but the most effective work was done by those who dealt with specific corporations. The idea of publishing articles on great business enterprises was one of the many inspirations that came to the alert mind of S. S. McClure. He was not quite sure that the historical approach, suggested by Miss Tarbell, would catch the public interest, but he agreed to make the experiment. He gave Miss Tarbell *carte blanche*, and the result was a document that provided a model and set a standard for the best type of muckraking.

Ida M. Tarbell was one of S. S. McClure's discoveries. She had written a few articles for his syndicate, and, just at the time he was starting his magazine, he called upon her in Paris. He told her that he had only ten minutes to talk, but he remained two hours, and when he left he had borrowed her last forty dollars and she had agreed to write a number of articles for him. They became close friends, and when she returned to the United States, he persuaded her to write a life of Napoleon. Her researches had familiarized her with the background of the period, and she accepted the assignment. The biography, which McClure wanted to accompany some pictures he had secured, proved tremendously popular, and soon after its publication she joined the staff of the magazine.

It had never been Miss Tarbell's intention to become a writer, for, in Allegheny College, where she was one of five girls, she had resolved to devote her life to biology. After two years of teaching, however, she became associate editor of the *Chautauquan*. Then came her trip to Paris, where she spent three years in historical research and in writing. A biography of Madame Roland, on which she had been working when she met McClure, followed the book on Napoleon, and her life of Lincoln came soon after.

Such a career would not appear to be very good training for an investigator of a great corporation, but Miss Tarbell had learned how to conduct researches, and she had a certain personal interest in the Standard Oil Company. Her father had been on the spot when oil was discovered in Pennsylvania, and he became the first manufacturer of wooden oil tanks. The family went to live in Rouseville, a village on the famous Oil Creek, where it maintained its loyalty to Puritan standards amid the riotous lawlessness of the early oil days. Later the Tarbells moved to Titusville. Still later the family fortunes were severely affected by the rise of the Standard Oil Company.

Miss Tarbell has denied that her father's misfortunes in any way embittered her against the great Rockefeller trust, but it is obvious enough that the family's experience must have sharpened her interest in the ways of monopolies. She did not, however, let any personal bias affect the diligence of her research. In the dozens of suits in which the Standard Oil Company had been involved an enormous body of material had been made available. These data Miss Tarbell examined, traveling from city to city, reading files of old newspapers, spending months in the perusal of court records and government investigations. Three years had passed before she was ready to begin writing; five years had elapsed before her investigations were completed. In that time she had mastered the history of the company, penetrated the technical intricacies of her material, pieced together the evidence, and prepared herself to tell the complicated story in such a way that the average man and woman could understand it.

From any point of view the story was worth telling. In 1854 George H. Bissell, a graduate of Dartmouth College, became convinced of the commercial possibilities of the oils from western Pennsylvania that were being used for medicinal purposes. "Seneca Oil," "American Medical Oil," and other preparations were sold all over America and Europe by the hundreds of thousands of bottles. An analysis revealed that this oil was a good fuel, and the expansion of the industry began. Wells were sunk, people flocked to the oil regions, and the railroads began building near the wells. In 1864 Samuel Van Syckel opened the first pipeline with relay filling stations. By 1872 nearly 40,000,000 barrels of oil had been produced.

It was at about this stage of the game, while the industry was still competitive, that John D. Rockefeller appeared on the scene in the rôle of the guiding spirit of the South Improvement Company, a large and secret body of refiners. He was quiet, thoughtful, industrious, taciturn, and not unduly troubled by ethical considerations. Already aiming at a monopoly, he saw that the first step was to secure control in Cleveland. To do this it was necessary to get secret rebates from the railroads, a task which was simplified by the fact that the railroads were weary of the rate wars and were willing to accept any scheme that would stabilize freight rates, even though that scheme might be dishonest and criminal. As a result, the South Improvement Company received not only rebates for its own freight but also for the freight shipped by competitors. That is, if an independent concern paid eighty cents a barrel for shipping its oil, forty cents of that amount went to the Rockefeller company. Moreover, the company had complete access to the books of the railroads, and could know the destination of every barrel of oil sent out of Cleveland.

But the South Improvement Company did not last. A brilliant young lawyer by the name of Dodd aroused the people of Pennsylvania, and reverberations were heard in Congress. In May, 1872, three months after the company was organized, it was dissolved. But rebating continued, competition was eliminated, and the Standard Oil Company came into existence—and Dodd became one of its principal attorneys. In 1878 the Pennsylvania Railroad paid the company $4,456,000 in rebates, and other railroads paid proportional sums. By 1884 the trust had several thousand miles of pipe-lines, and was not only independent of the railroads but was also in a position to defy the Interstate Commerce Act of 1887, which said nothing about pipe-lines. In 1904 the trust was controlling 90 per cent of the eastern oil production, and made about $45,000,000 dividends annually, nearly 50 per cent on the investment.

"The History of the Standard Oil Company" published as a series of articles in *McClure's*, in 1902-1904, showed clearly, as Miss Tarbell intended it should, that the trusts

were necessarily based on "primary privileges." It was a
scholarly work, a genuine contribution to the study of a
great problem, and, as a reviewer in the *Arena* stated, "a
fearless unmasking of moral criminality masquerading under the robes of respectability and Christianity." Miss Tarbell followed these articles with other discussions of the subject, notably two articles on Rockefeller himself, two articles
on the Standard Oil Company and Kansas, and an article
entitled "Roosevelt vs. Rockefeller," in the *American Magazine.*

Though Miss Tarbell was not the only author who exposed the Standard Oil Company, defenders of the company
were not lacking, Chancellor James Roscoe Day of Syracuse
University being the most ardent. In his book, *The Raid on
Prosperity,* he stated that the claim that there was a down-
trodden and oppressed class in the country was "an imper-
tinence and an insult to our intelligent working people and
mechanics." "The people are not oppressed by the corporations," he wrote, "but the corporations by the people."
To his mind the Standard Oil Company was one of the
greatest benefactors the country had ever known, a boon
to the working man and a civilizing force the world over.
The steady growth of the company, he argued, was the best
answer to all who calumniated it, for he regarded it as axi-
omatic that a business which is not conducted on the highest
levels of morality never survives long. He called its directors
"high-minded" and regarded them as "incapable of dishonest practices." The federal government had brought the
company to court simply for political reasons, and the courts
rendered unjust decisions because of the long campaign of
slander.

So enthusiastic was Mr. Day that there seemed to be no
need for any further defense, but in 1908 and 1909 Mr.
Rockefeller himself published in the *World's Work* a group

of articles which he entitled "Some Random Reminiscences of Men and Events." The burden of his statements was that the company had been misunderstood. He very generously gave much credit to his associates for the achievements of the company, and he philosophized at length on philanthropy, coöperative giving, and the difficult art of getting. His articles offer an interesting comparison with Miss Tarbell's "Commercial Machiavellianism" (*McClure's*, February, 1908), in which she showed how easily one could create an up-to-date edition of *The Prince* out of the mouths of modern captains of industry.

Miss Tarbell's "History of the Standard Oil Company" was soon followed by other series on "big business," and in 1904 *Everybody's* began the publication of a document which literally swept the public off its feet. This was Thomas W. Lawson's "Frenzied Finance," not a careful historical analysis such as Miss Tarbell had written, but a great, colorful picture of the financial world, taking as its *dramatis personae* the colossi of Wall Street. For once the curiosity of the public to know what goes on behind the scenes was satisfied, and the public responded as it would respond today if a similar document should be published. *Everybody's*, which had been the house-organ of Wanamaker's until 1903, when it was purchased by the Ridgway-Thayer company, increased its circulation from 197,000 to 735,000 in 1904 and 1905.

Tom Lawson was one of the more picturesque figures of the decade, a millionaire stock-manipulator, a man with a keen sense of the dramatic and an uncanny eye for publicity. For some time he had been nursing a grudge against the financial leaders of the country, and had been brooding over the possibility of exposing their methods. Once persuaded by Mr. Cosgrave that his story would be worth telling, he threw himself into the task of writing and adver-

tising it. He agreed to furnish the articles free of charge if
the owners would spend $50,000 in advertising. This they
did, while Lawson himself spent more than five times that
amount.

In July, 1904, the first of the articles appeared, full of all
the dynamite which Lawson could pack into it and carefully rewritten by John O'Hara Cosgrave, the editor of
Everybody's. Audaciously and without mincing matters Lawson attacked the most discussed, the most feared, and quite
possibly the most admired men in America—Rockefeller,
Rogers, and their attendant divinities. Especially, however,
he attacked the "System."

> Through its workings during the last twenty years [he wrote]
> there has grown up in this country a set of colossal corporations
> in which unmeasured success and continued immunity from pun-
> ishment have bred an insolent disregard of law, of common
> morality, and of public and private right, together with a grim
> determination to hold on to, at all hazards, the great possessions
> they have gulped or captured. It is the same "System" which
> has taken from the millions of our people billions of dollars and
> given them over to a score or two of men with power to use and
> enjoy them as absolutely as though these billions had been earned
> dollar by dollar by the labor of their bodies and their minds.

The great corporations, Lawson asserted, had grown wealthy
because they knew how to "make" dollars out of nothing.
By this he meant that they arbitrarily set the value of stock at
an amount far greater than the actual investment. This fictitious value the "System" was selling to the public for good
money. His purpose in writing the articles was, he said, to
expose the machinery of the "System," and to show that
it was an artifice which tricksters had imposed upon the
people.

> All financial institutions [he stated] which in any way are en-
> gaged in taking from the people the money that is their surplus

earnings or capital, for the ostensible purpose of safe-guarding it, or putting it in use for them, or exchanging it for stocks, bonds, policies, or other paper evidences of worth, are a part of the machinery for the plundering of the people.

One of the most sensational chapters was that devoted to his account of the bribing of the Massachusetts legislature in 1896 by the Whitney machine. He declared that many of the legislators were financially involved in Bay State Gas or Dominion Coal and were eager to vote for the new charter for these industries that was before the legislature. The refusal of the governor to sign the bill in its original form utterly dismayed the legislators who had financial interests in the company or who had been bribed. The bill was finally changed to meet public demands, and great losses resulted. Lawson said that he himself had lost a million dollars, and that Towle and Patch, the lawyers who had managed the bribing, had fled to Jamaica, where they had ended their lives a few days later.

Mr. Lawson was not given to modesty, but if we are to believe his statements the articles revolutionized the country. He said that at the end of two months after the publication of the first chapter, the Standard Oil "monster" broke its old custom of silence for the first time, at the end of three months the people elected their champion as president with a tremendous majority, at the end of four months the leading insurance companies discharged their agents in great numbers and their aggregate business fell off at the rate of four and a half million dollars a week, at the end of five months $200,000,000 of what the people had regarded as real value ran into the gutter as dirty water, at the end of six months the President of the United States was able to shake the biggest trusts and combinations "until their teeth chattered and their backbones rattled like hung dried corn in a fireplace when the wind gets at it," and at the

Top left: CHARLES EDWARD RUSSELL. *Top right:* UPTON SINCLAIR.
Bottom left: DAVID GRAHAM PHILLIPS. Courtesy of Pach Brothers.
Bottom right: THOMAS W. LAWSON. Courtesy of the Litchfield Studio,
Arlington, Massachusetts.

end of seven months the City Bank of New York was hung up so that people could see it in its most contemptible transactions.

The articles brought other results as well. *Public Opinion* announced in January, 1905, the publication of a series of articles on "The Truth About Frenzied Finance." Denis Donohoe, the author, financial editor of the New York *Commercial*, sought less to controvert Lawson's statements than to reveal the somewhat unsavory record of the man. One New York banker sent a list of eighteen questions to Lawson, and stated that if he did not answer them he would be denounced. This banker indicated the effect of "Frenzied Finance" by blaming Lawson for the failure of banks, legitimate Wall Street businesses, and life insurance companies. In the course of answering these questions Lawson stated that the time might come when he would ask the people to withdraw their money from the banks, but he would do this only when he was sure they would follow his suggestion, and when it was apparent that there was no other way of crushing the "System." He made the unqualified assertion that he had a new and certain remedy for the financial ills of America, and the next year he announced that in the April issue of *Everybody's* he would reveal what that remedy was. But the April number contained only an exposure of the life insurance companies and a statement that the people were not ready for the remedy. In November he again expressed his regret that the country was not prepared for his plan, and he announced that he intended to write fiction in order to keep the people interested in finance. His first story, he said, would blow out seven-eighths of the windows in Wall Street and would make it impossible for the "System" to continue to do business in the same old way. One story, "Friday, the Thirteenth," did appear in *Everybody's*, 1906-1907, but later in 1907, Lawson announced his intention of going back to stock-gambling. E. J. Ridgway of *Everybody's* wrote to him, expressing regret at this decision, and saying that there were thousands of people all over the country who had confidence in Lawson as a leader. To this the ex-muckraker characteristically replied. After expressing sorrow for the pain he had caused his friend, he wrote:

You talk about what I owe to the people. What do I owe to the gelatine-spined shrimps? What have the saffron-blooded apes done for me or mine that I should halt any decision to match their lightning change, ten-above-ten-below-zero, chameleon-hued loyalty? The people! The very name has so sealed itself into my being, that, heeling its very appearance, of late, are myriads of fantastically appareled marionettes whose solemn graphophon-ing of "Our rights, our privileges," whose bold fronting of mirror shields and savage circlings of candy swords, make me almost die a-laughing. Forgive me, my dear Ridgway, but the people, particularly the American people, are a joke—a System joke. When in all history, ancient, modern, or budding, have the people done aught but rail or stand shivering by, like the fear-some Gobbos they are, while their enemies crucified those who battled for their benefit? Where in all history, I ask, does it appear that the people aided those who battled disinterestedly for them?

Thus ended one of the most spectacular episodes in the entire history of muckraking. Nowhere in the entire move-ment do we find a better example of mixed motives and con-fused results. Lawson undoubtedly wished to pay off an old score, and it is possible that he used the sensation his articles caused to advance his personal interests in the stock market. On the other hand, there was a strange streak of altruism in the man, a sort of messianic eagerness to deliver the com-mon people from what he regarded as their bondage. The results are equally difficult to evaluate. It is certain that the articles had less effect than Lawson thought, but undoubt-edly they did some harm and more than a little good. On the credit side of the ledger is to be recorded the fact that Lawson, despite inaccuracies in his statements, gave the people a fairly correct understanding of the workings of crooked finance. After the articles appeared, it was, as Cosgrave has said, a little more difficult for pickpockets to operate. Moreover, the publicity which Lawson gave the insurance investigations undoubtedly served to arouse general interest and helped to effect the reforms that took place.

One important result was to thrust *Everybody's*, which had hitherto stood aloof, into the very midst of the muckraking movement. The success of "Frenzied Finance" had demonstrated that muckraking was interesting to the public, and it was as a good journalistic exploit that *Everybody's* took up the movement, just as *McClure's* had entered upon it a few years before. Somewhat later the owners attempted to found a weekly with definite reform aims, but this was a failure. *Everybody's* itself, however, continued muckraking down to 1911, when John O'Hara Cosgrave resigned the editorship. Articles were published by Senator Cannon, Judge Lindsey, William Hard, Garet Garrett, C. P. Connolly, and many others.

Next to "Frenzied Finance" probably the most important series which this magazine published was Charles Edward Russell's articles on the Beef Trust, a series which began before the Lawson series had stopped. This trust had built up a tremendous monopoly, resting squarely upon railroad rebates, called in this case "private car charges." Like the Standard Oil Company, it was an almost perfect example of the way monopolies grow and function, and, touching as it did the lives of countless people in a vital way, it was inevitable that it should receive its share of attention and censure.

Russell, who was among the most persistent of the muckrakers, has often been mentioned before. He was born in

Davenport, Iowa, in 1860, and from his ardent Abolitionist ancestry he early acquired a whole-hearted sympathy for oppressed people of all kinds. After his education in the Davenport high school and at St. Johnsbury Academy in Vermont, he joined his father, who was editing the Davenport *Gazette*. At the age of twenty-one he was managing editor of the Minneapolis *Journal*, and during the next quarter of a century he held positions of responsibility on the Detroit *Tribune*, the New York *Commercial Advertiser*, the New York *World*, the New York *Herald*, the Chicago *Examiner*, and other New York and Chicago papers. Since 1904 he has devoted himself chiefly to writing articles and books, and his output has been prodigious. His books include studies of Thomas Chatterton and Wendell Phillips, several volumes on Russia, treatises on socialism, and works devoted to muckraking. His sympathy has always been with the common people, and he has maintained the critical note in his writings. During the war he actively supported the government, and in 1917 he was appointed on the Root Mission to Russia by President Wilson, while in 1918 he was in charge of the London office of the Committee on Public Information, and in 1919 he served on President Wilson's Industrial Commission. He has studied political and social conditions in Europe and Asia, as well as in the United States.

Russell called his series, which appeared in *Everybody's*, 1905, "The Greatest Trust in the World," and he began with these words: "In the free republic of the United States of America is a power greater than the government, greater than the courts or judges, greater than legislatures, superior to and independent of all authority of state or nation." He showed how the packers had acquired this power through their relations with the railroads, and he described with care the evolution of monopoly control. In the course of his articles he pointed out that the men who wielded this incredible power were personally kindhearted, well-intentioned individuals, themselves victims of a vicious economic order. To show that the perfection of the packer's organization had not meant cheaper food for the public, he quoted statistics to the effect that the value of beef cattle had declined $163,000,000 in the three years ending with January 1, 1905, whereas the retail price of meat had gradually increased.

But Russell's exposure of the Beef Trust had less effect than the work of Upton Sinclair. Born in Baltimore, Sinclair worked his way through the College of the City of New York, paying his expenses by doing all kinds of hack-work. After receiving his degree in 1897, he spent four years in Columbia University, but he did not always have great respect for his teachers, and much of his work he did by himself. In his own way he attacked one modern language after another, mastering each in a few months, and this command of half a dozen tongues has enabled him to keep abreast of the literary movements of Europe as well as those of America.

As he explained in "My Cause," in the *Independent* for May 14, 1903, he approached the world with "a heart full of love and trust," but he soon discovered that the world was far different from his dreams. His reaction to this discovery was neither cynicism nor dispair; he resolved to do what he could to make his dreams live for the generations to follow.

You do not understand [he wrote in the *Independent* article] for you have not the memory of that midnight hour when I knelt with a fire of anguish in my soul and hot tears upon my cheeks, and registered my vow: So help me Almighty God, and His angels, if I come out of this torture-house alive, never will I rest in this world again until I have served the man who comes after me. . . . Until I have made it impossible for joy and tenderness and rapture and awe to be lashed and spit upon and

trampled and mashed into annihilation as mine have been!
Until I have made this world a place in which a young artist
can live!

Later, writing in the *Cosmopolitan*, he said that his life seemed
like that of a man on a sinking ship, trying to reach the shore.
He continued: "So far as I myself am concerned, the well-
springs of joy and beauty have dried up in me—the flowers
no longer sing to me as they used to, nor the sunrise, nor
the stars; I have become like a soldier upon a hard campaign—I am thinking only of the enemy."

And in 1919, when most of the muckrakers had long since
ceased their efforts Sinclair again gave utterance to his faith
in the introduction to *The Brass Check:*

The people I have lashed in this book are to me not individuals, but social forces; I have exposed them, not because they
lied about me, but because a new age of fraternity is being born,
and they, who ought to be assisting the birth, are strangling the
child in the womb.

To the work of muckraking, then, Sinclair brought more
than a social philosophy; his determination drastically to
alter the existing order had all the emotional force of a religious mission. His first book, *King Midas*, was published
in 1901, and his second, an autobiographical work, *The
Journal of Arthur Stirling* appeared in 1903. A little later
Sinclair went to Chicago and for seven weeks lived in Packingtown, talking with workingmen, bosses, superintendents,
night-watchmen, saloon-keepers, clergymen, and settlement
workers. Before he had had time to prepare the statement
of his findings, he was drawn into a controversy in *Collier's*.
Early in 1905 the English *Lancet* made some damaging charges against the Chicago slaughterhouses. Sinclair was asked
for his opinion, and in an article entitled "Is Chicago Meat
Clean?" which *Collier's* published in its issue of April 22,

1905, he declared that the *Lancet* had vastly understated the truth. Then Dr. L. L. Seaman was asked to make an impartial investigation of the sanitary situation in the stockyards, and he reported that no tainted meat was sold by the Chicago packers. To this Sinclair replied in "Stockyard Secrets," published in *Collier's* for March 24, 1906, asserting that Dr. Seaman had not spent more than thirty minutes in the stockyards but had obtained his information from the packers' inspector.

The controversy in *Collier's* was, however, merely a preliminary skirmish. In 1906 *The Jungle* appeared. Into this novel, which records the misfortunes of a Lithuanian immigrant and his eventual conversion to Socialism, Sinclair packed all the information which he had secured during his sojourn in and about the stockyards. He described how diseased cattle were butchered, marked by the government inspectors, thrown into dumps, loaded on carts, wheeled back again, mingled with other carcasses, treated, and sold as clean meat. In relentlessly nauseating detail he told all the various ways in which the packers extracted a profit from condemned meat, and his descriptions of the conditions of laborers were almost as revolting as his descriptions of the treatment of meat. No wonder many people temporarily lost their appetite for meat after reading the novel. Sinclair once remarked that he had aimed at the public's heart, and by accident he had hit it in the stomach.

The book had a tremendous sale. For a year it was the best selling book in the United States, England, and the British colonies. It was translated into seventeen languages, and more than 150,000 copies have been sold. Only recently it has been reissued in cheap form by the Vanguard Press. Almost immediately after the publication of *The Jungle* President Roosevelt appointed a commission to investigate the packers' methods. The commission, despite the fact that the packers were aware that the investigation was going on, found conditions almost as bad as Sinclair had indicated, and the Pure Food and Drug Act of 1906 was the result.

In reply to Russell's "The Greatest Trust in the World" and Sinclair's *The Jungle*, J. Ogden Armour published in the *Saturday Evening Post*, an article in which he claimed that the charges brought against his company were absolutely false. Since Mr. Russell was not in America at the time, *Everybody's* requested Sinclair to comment on Armour's statements. Sinclair's article, "The Condemned-Meat Industry," which appeared in *Everybody's* for May, 1906, is one of the most scathing and withering articles in controversial literature. It was written, Sinclair states, in a few hours, at a white heat of indignation. Sinclair not only attacked Armour's veracity; he bolstered up with affidavits and other evidence the most unbelievable and disgusting charges against the meat industry which he had made in *The Jungle*.

Nor did the controversy end here. In *The Brass Check* (1919), Mr. Sinclair states that a year after the Roosevelt investigation the editor of the Sunday magazine section of the New York *Herald*, W. W. Harris, asked him to make another secret investigation of Packingtown and write it up for the paper. James Gordon Bennett, proprietor of the *Herald*, was in Bermuda at the time, but his consent was received by cable. It happened that Sinclair was too busy to undertake the investigation, and therefore a Mrs. Bloor and a *Herald* reporter worked in Packingtown for two months in disguise. They found conditions worse than ever, and they stated this in a long article which they prepared and for which Sinclair wrote the introduction. Before publishing the article Mr. Harris sent it to Mr. Bennett, who kept it and made no reply. Then Sinclair tried to find a place for it in some other New York paper, but without success. Nor would President Roosevelt have anything to do with it. A big meeting was arranged for Sinclair in the stockyards district of Chicago, and there he told his story to five or six thousand enthusiastic people. A group of reporters who were present admitted it was a good story, but they declared that their papers would not accept it. Sinclair urged them to turn the story in and see what would happen. They agreed, but only the Chicago *Socialist* published the reports. Later Sinclair made the same speech in San Francisco, and Fremont Older's paper, the *Bulletin*, was the only one that repeated the facts he had presented. Sinclair is also responsible for the assertion that, as a result of the publication of his "The Condemned-Meat Industry," *Everybody's* lost many pages of advertising, not merely advertisements of hams and lard but also advertisements of fertilizers, soaps, and railways. Thomas Lawson, Mr. Sinclair says, wished to publish the names of these boycotters, but the proprietors of the magazine refused. Later the advertisements came back.

Among Mr. Sinclair's other adventures in muckraking, some of which will be discussed later, were his attempts to expose the Steel Trust. He tells us in *The Brass Check* that after the publication of *The Jungle* he suggested to *Everybody's* that he investigate the glass industry, the steel industry, the coal mines, the cotton mills, and the lumber camps. His proposal was accepted, and he set to work. A little later he sent in articles on the glass industry and the steel mills of Allegheny County, but these were never published. In *The Brass Check* he asserts that few magazines ever dared to attack the Steel Trust, which, he charged, had often cheated its customers, including the government. He also recounted one of the sensational stories which he had included in the articles offered *Everybody's*. A Hungarian caught his legs under the wheels of one of the gigantic traveling cranes. To save his legs it would have been necessary to take the crane apart at the expense of several thousand dollars, and they therefore ran over his legs, cut them off, and paid him $200 damages.

In the attack on the railroads the *American Magazine* played an important part, agitating for the passing of a bill compelling the roads to install the block system to insure public safety. In *McClure's* Ray Stannard Baker exposed several of the abuses of which the railroads were guilty: favoritism in the making of rates; the use of rebates; the treatment of private cars, especially in connection with the Beef Trust; the creating of public opinion; and the destruction of industries by railway consolidation and rate discrimination—illustrated by the case of Danville, Virginia. Baker also wrote about the railroads for *Collier's*, as did Mark Sullivan and Carl Snyder. In the *Twentieth Century Magazine*, December, 1909, Carl. S. Vrooman discussed the corruption in government owned and in privately owned railroads. Charles Edward Russell, writing in *Pearson's*, argued that our railroads were highly inefficient when compared with the government owned roads of Europe, and he attributed to the poor condition of the lines the innumerable accidents which took place. The street railways also were subjected to attack. Baker, Webster, and Hendrick were among the writers who called attention to the inefficiency and corruption of the municipal traction companies, emphasizing in particular the methods by which they secured their franchises.

During 1905 and 1906 the revelation of the methods employed by certain of the great life insurance companies created something of a scandal and furnished material for more than one muckraker. *World's Work*, which never took any great share in muckraking, published, in 1905-1906, a series of six articles in which an anonymous writer, signing himself "Q. P.," exposed the corruption prevalent in the insurance business. The *Independent*, another magazine which did little in muckraking, though by no means hostile to the movement, also printed in the issue of December 30, 1906, an attack on the insurance companies. Louis D. Brandeis, the author, stated that in the fifteen years ending December 31, 1905, the workingmen of Massachusetts had paid to the so-called industrial life insurance companies a total of $61,294,887, of which only $21,819,606 had been received back in death benefits, endowments, or surrender values. Since the companies held only $9,838,000 in reserves, it appeared that, in addition to interest on invested funds, about one-half of the amount paid by workingmen in premiums had been absorbed in the expense of conducting the business and in dividends to the stockholders.

No less drastic and much more inclusive was the series which Burton J. Hendrick wrote for *McClure's* in 1906 and 1907. Hendrick declared that the whole character of the life insurance business had changed so that what had once been an honest, efficient, and necessary institution had become primarily a gambling device. He said that the Mutual, the Equitable, and the New York Life had been participating in a mad race for size, in the course of which they had made extravagant payments to agents, had advertised recklessly, had invested dangerously, and had devised unsound and unethical methods of accumulating wealth. The most questionable device of all was the Tontine or deferred dividend, contrived by Henry D. Hyde, the founder of the Equitable and the man who was chiefly responsible for the prostitution of the life insurance idea. Hyde's plan was to accumulate over-payments instead of paying dividends annually and, combining the sum thus gained with the values of lapsing members, to divide the total, which he called the surplus, after twenty years among all members who had paid their dividends regularly and were still alive. The company had full control over this fund and used it as Mr. Hyde and his trustees saw fit. Much of it was distributed among his agents in the form of commissions, and a good deal more he and his favored trustees took as booty. He and the heads of other companies who adopted his scheme used this fund to pay themselves huge salaries, to corrupt legislatures and the press, to build large financial institutions for their own advantage and at the expense of the policy-holders, and to engage in Wall Street speculation. At the end of the dividend period they paid such portion of the Tontine as had not been wasted or stolen. These deferred dividend policies were absolutely forbidden as a result of the New York investigations, and other questionable practices were checked.

Just as the insurance scandals had brought forth a considerable body of articles on the insurance companies, so the panic of 1907 provoked a number of attacks on the banks. Of these the most notable was that embodied in a series of four articles which C. M. Keys, formerly an editor of the *Wall Street Journal*, wrote for *World's Work*. Mr. Keys, after trying to explain in simple terms the mysteries of finance, currency, and banking, discussed the value of trust companies and set forth the good and the bad points about savings banks. He also exposed the manner in which the large Wall Street banks gambled on a gigantic scale, citing the profits that had come to some of them as a result of the panic.

No trust was safe from attack during this period. In 1909 Charles P. Norcross, writing in the November *Cosmopolitan*, charged the sugar trust with using rebates to build up its power, with conspiring to throttle competition, with employing false weights, with defying the law, and with corrupting legislatures. In *Hampton's*, January, 1910, Judson Welliver asserted that the sugar trust and the Mormon church controlled between them from two-thirds to four-fifths of the beet sugar of the country. "The combination," he wrote, "absolutely dominates beet sugar. It makes the market prices of sugar, distributes the territory, and completely controls tariff legislation." Two months later, in the March issue, he went on to show that the sugar trust was trying to dominate Cuba. In the same number an editorial note stated that Mr. Welliver's first article had already produced important results. It had given direct evidence upon which the government could base a suit against the trust, and the Department of Justice had corroborated *Hampton's* charges. The beet sugar industry had been freed, and the refining monopoly had been weakened. "Never before in the history of journalistic enterprise," declared the editors, "have such big and prompt results been secured from an exposure of this kind." Two months later, in the May issue, Welliver described the activities of the sugar trust in the Payne-Aldrich tariff fight.

Welliver was also one of the men who wrote against the threatened national water-power trust. President Roosevelt in his James River Dam veto message had said:

The people of the country are threatened by a monopoly far more powerful because in far closer touch with their domestic and individual life, than anything known to our experience. A single generation will see the exhaustion of our natural resources of oil and gas and such rise in the price of coal as will make the prices of electrically transmitted water power a controlling factor in transportation, in manufacturing, and in household lighting and heating.

Welliver, writing in *McClure's*, May, 1909, expanded on this theme, showing the ramifications of the General Electric Company. In a series of articles in *Hampton's*, 1909, John L. Mathews discussed the same subject, and his articles, according to Charles Edward Russell, "blocked an audacious scheme to corral the water powers of the nation." Mathews began by denouncing the apathy of the American people, and then went on to show the relation between the water-power interests and the American Cyanid Company, which had recently acquired the rights to a method discovered in Germany for extracting nitrogen from the air. Because the people had lost control of water power, Mathews asserted, they would have to pay $75 a ton for this invaluable fertilizer which they might have secured for $20. In subsequent articles he maintained that whoever controlled water power would control farming, manufacturing, transportation—and human life itself. He declared that "pork-barrel" politics dominated Congress, which had given away 1,500,000 horse-power of water to the mighty water-power monopoly, and wasted $500,000,000 on rivers and harbors appropriations.

Alfred Henry Lewis, in the *Cosmopolitan*, April, 1905, attacked the International Harvester Company, asserting that this trust, with its railroads, its steamships, and its bank allies, was managing an annual export trade of $21,000,000; was borrowing money at 3 and 4 per cent to loan at from 6 to 10 per cent; was killing competition and stifling invention; was pressing toward a monopoly; and was paying a little more than 40 per cent dividends on its capital stock of $120,000,000. "The whole," he concluded, "presents a condition of fiscal bloodsucking, permitted by the people, who are as sheep."

The muckrakers called attention not only to the trusts but also to the men who dominated them. In 1907 Charles Edward Russell wrote for *Everybody's* a series of seven articles entitled, "Where Did You Get It, Gentlemen?" He contended that the great fortunes did not indicate national prosperity, for they were the result of corruption and robbery. Describing the rise of these fortunes, he said:

The bonds are issued, the stock is floated, the syndicate is enriched, the palace arises. And every cent thus represented we furnish: we that consume the tobacco, ship the freight, grow the crops, eat the beef, hang on the straps of the Subway, we upon

whose backs is piled the whole vast mass of watered stocks, fictitious bonds, fraudulent scrip, gambling securities. And the only
profit obtained by society in all these operations is the spectacle
of five or six men accumulating vast fortunes, fortunes beyond
computation, fortunes for a few comprising the sum of available
wealth that should be for all.

And he ended the series thus:

Where did the gentlemen Get It? They Got It from us and by
means of our own witless contrivance, brethren. For do you not
suppose we can take those filching fingers from our pockets if
we try?

In the course of these articles Russell savagely attacked
Thomas Fortune Ryan, who had built up tremendous wealth
through his connection with the New York Metropolitan
Street-Railway Company. This attack cost Mr. Russell
dearly. He was a magazine writer, and his articles had been
appearing in a large number of periodicals, but after the
publication of this series he was "blacklisted in every magazine office in New York," except the three that were then
engaged in muckraking. And that blacklist, it has been
claimed, was in force as late as 1922. Later *Everybody's* was
also silenced, notifying Russell that it could use no more of
his contributions because it could not permit his name to
appear in its pages. And this in spite of the fact that he had
traveled around the world for the magazine and had been
a member of its staff! Even while the series was running the
editor of *Everybody's* decided to omit the article on the
American Tobacco Company, but Mr. Russell, receiving
a friendly tip from someone in the office, hurried back to
New York and succeeded in getting his article into the advertising section, the main part of the magazine having
already gone to press.

To the above interpretation the editor of *Everybody's* would
reply that the incident never was quite so dramatic; that

Russell had won the reputation of a firebrand and a dangerous writer whose matter carried trouble; and that his articles were, therefore, excluded for sound editorial reasons. Russell's method was to start with a text and then to pick up the facts to prove the thesis, whereas Cosgrave wanted to let the facts prove the implications. The editor constantly kept in mind the consequences—a possible day in court.

A not dissimilar series, written by Alfred Henry Lewis, appeared in the *Cosmopolitan*, beginning with June, 1908, and including articles on Andrew Carnegie, Thomas F. Ryan, J. Pierpont Morgan, the Vanderbilts, Charles M. Schwab, John D. Rockefeller, the Armours, the Swifts, E. H. Harriman, and the Astors. Lewis described these rich men coolly and dispassionately, but did not refrain from questioning the expediency of permitting such accumulations of wealth. Concerning Ryan he wrote:

Mayors are his office-boys, governors come and go at his call. He possesses himself of a party and selects a candidate for the presidency. Tammany Hall is a dog for his hunting, and he breaks city councils to his money-will as folk break horses to harness. Borough presidents and city boards are among his chattels; comptrollers and corporation counsels become the ornaments on his watch-guard.

Of John D. Rockefeller he said that he had no vices and no pleasure except that of "seeing his dividends come in." Of social intercourse he had none, and "lying" was his only luxury. The Vanderbilts, he said, were easy-going people who did as they pleased and let the world take care of itself. Describing Charles M. Schwab, he wrote, "For myself, I hope I may never find worse company than Mr. Schwab—suave, plausible, of friendly atmosphere. He built churches and played the piano and fiddle." Burton J. Hendrick also wrote articles on the great American fortunes, mostly for *McClure's*.

Throughout the period the tariff was an uneasy subject. In the *American*, 1910-1911, Miss Tarbell tried, by using the historical approach, to make this difficult and complicated matter clear to the average citizen. In a series of seven articles she surveyed the tariff legislation since the Civil War, noting the effects of high protection on some particular communities and on the conditions of labor, and particularly emphasizing the close connection between big business and tariff legislation. "Ever since 1888," she declared, "it has been the settled and openly expressed principle in political circles that your protection shall be in proportion to your campaign contribution." She showed that high protection did not protect the laborer, for wages were no higher in protected than in unprotected industries. In Rhode Island, for example, where the textile industries were highly protected, wages in 1907 ranged from $7 to $15 a week, laboring conditions were poor, infant mortality was high, and the owners showed no consideration for their employees.

This, then [she said in summary], is high protection's most perfect work—a state of half a million people turning out an annual product worth $279,438,000, the laborers in the chief industry underpaid, unstable, and bent with disease, the average employers rich, self-satisfied, and as indifferent to social obligations as so many robber barons.

After showing that duties were determined not scientifically but by a process of bargaining, she stated:

Dip into the story of the tariff at any point since the Civil War and you will find wholesale proofs of this bargaining in duties; rates fixed with no more relation to the doctrine of protection than they have to the law of precession of the equinoxes.

It was in the *American* also that there appeared some of the chapters from Upton Sinclair's novel, *The Metropolis*, in which he sought to describe the new and vulgar society which had been created by the accumulation of great fortunes. In introducing the first installment of the novel, the editor pointed out that New York society had developed into something

. . . strange, unreal, almost uncouth; gorgeous in outward appearance, whimsical and wanton in display, unprecedented in extravagance of every conceivable form. And with this grotesque luxury has developed a social temperament just as fantastic, in which, to say the least, culture, gentleness and right-mindedness are not conspicuous elements. This new and barbaric element in Society has pushed aside the older and gentler past.

In the eighteen-nineties, as we have noted, laborers here and farmers there might protest against their lot and threaten revolt, but the average middle-class citizen looked with complacency on the industrial expansion of the age, admiring, envying, and seeking to emulate the amassers of great wealth. In the first decade of the new century, however, a new sentiment arose. Every great enterprise was under suspicion, and every great fortune was subjected to attack. The popular magazines, devoting themselves to the literature of exposure, published scores of articles on our industrial life, articles that ranged from the rankest sensationalism to the calmest factual survey. In legislation as well as literature the new mood found expression, and a president of the United States became a leader in the attack on the trusts. Exposure and reform, hand in hand, dominated the decade. What they achieved must be left for discussion in a subsequent chapter.

CHAPTER TEN

THE MUCKRAKERS AND THE UNDER-DOG

EXCEPT in so far as muckraking was purely sensational, there lay behind it a real and often passionate sympathy for the under-dog. By and large the muckrakers were neither doctrinaire reformers nor hard-boiled economists; they were newspaper men with a generous interest in human nature, considerable confidence in American democracy, and a sportsmanlike desire for fair play. They were for the workers and against oppressive employers, and in general they favored trade unionism.

Among the more diligent practitioners of unsensational muckraking, we can find no more representative figure than Ray Stannard Baker. After graduating from Michigan State College, Baker became a reporter on the old Chicago *Record*. In college he had been interested in economics, and as a journalist he sought to familiarize himself with the human and practical problems which economic theory so often overlooks. One of his early assignments was to go to Canton, Ohio, to interview Coxey, who was leading his famous army to Washington. Baker stayed with Coxey's Army, marching with it day by day until it had reached its goal. Interviewing each member, he learned how that strange horde had been assembled, and gradually he came to understand the minds and hearts of the poverty-stricken. He remembered the extravagant crowds that had gathered to enjoy the lavish spectacles of the World's Fair, and he contrasted with them the

ragged cohorts straggling over the Alleghenies in the hope
of forcing an indifferent government to come to their aid.
On his return to Chicago, Baker was regularly sent out to
report labor disturbances, and the great Pullman strike soon
came to give him another lesson in practical economics. In
Pullman he found men and women starving in the model
homes erected by the company, and his accounts of the many
tragedies he observed led to the establishment of a relief
bureau. In the Debs trial he appeared as a witness.

Baker became more and more fascinated by the human
side of great industrial problems, but at the same time he
aspired to a literary career. Some of his stories appeared in
McClure's, and it was not long before Mr. McClure tele-
graphed him, as he did so many young men whose work
attracted his attention, to come to New York. Thus, in
1897, Baker associated himself with that lively group of men
and women who were making *McClure's* the most talked-of
magazine in America. He continued writing stories and did
various special features, but in time he returned to his favorite field, the labor problem. No one could have been
more sympathetic than he with working people, but any
type of oppression was abhorrent to him. Although he had
often spoken in defense of labor unions, he found it necessary
in 1903, just at the time when the Tarbell and the Steffens
articles were marking the inauguration of a muckraking
policy, to attack the conduct of certain labor organizations.
In his first article he discussed the manner in which labor
unions, during the coal strike, prevented non-union miners
from working; in another he attacked the corruption of
various labor leaders, showing how labor and capital had
sometimes worked together to secure a monopoly; and in
subsequent articles he dealt with the way in which workers
had on occasion been betrayed by their leaders.

Baker continued with *McClure's* for several years, writing

on all manner of topics, and always displaying the same ardor for justice and the same curiosity about people. In 1906 he was one of the group who left *McClure's* to take over the *American Magazine*, with which he was associated as long as its original policy endured. For the *American* he wrote many articles of exposure, and he also wrote "Adventures in Contentment" and similar sketches under the name of David Grayson. Though he had been extremely friendly with Roosevelt, Baker chose to support Wilson in the campaign of 1912, and he became closely identified with his administration and with the man himself, whose biography he later wrote.

Baker was one of the men who wrote about the industrial warfare in Colorado, discussing the employers' association and the widespread lawlessness. A more vivid account of the struggle, however, was that contained in "The Confession and Autobiography of Harry Orchard," which appeared as a serial in *McClure's* during 1907. Orchard was a member of the Western Federation of Miners, and was in close touch with the "inner circle" of that organization. At his trial he appeared as the chief witness for the state, confessing to eighteen murders, including that of ex-Governor Frank Steunenburg of Idaho, who had aroused the fierce hatred of the miners by his handling of the strike. Orchard related, without mincing matters, how unions were conducted, and how they met violence with violence and corruption with corruption.

This sensational autobiography was provided with an introduction and notes by one of the later recruits to muckraking, George Kibbe Turner. Turner, who had been for many years connected with the Springfield *Republican*, and who had written considerable fiction, was added to the staff of *McClure's* soon after the departure of Baker and his associates on the *American*. Coming from the strait-laced traditions of New England journalism, Turner, as he says, "registered very acutely the brilliant but erratic movements of McClure." His first job was a write-up of the Galveston commission form of government, an article which was intended to display the more constructive side of muckraking. Soon after, he was assigned to the Orchard case, and later he studied the vice problem in New York and Chicago, as has already been noted. Among the people who were associated with Mr. Turner during his period of service on *McClure's* were Will Irwin, Willa Cather, Burton J. Hendrick, and Cameron Mackenzie. Like Baker and most of the other muckrakers, Turner took special interest in the human and personal side of his work. Orchard, he records, was the most religious man he had ever known.

Other people wrote about Colorado, notably C. P. Connolly in *Collier's* and George Creel in *Harper's Weekly*. Creel's articles, which appeared in 1914, some time after the cessation of hostilities, discussed the attitude of the press toward the struggle. He showed that the newspapers had often employed the most despicable methods to destroy the people's confidence in the labor leaders. Mother Jones, an eighty-two year old friend of the workers, was branded as a prostitute and the keeper of a house of prostitution. Tikas, the "peacemaker," was brained by a militia lieutenant while a helpless prisoner, and was stigmatized as a brothel hanger-on. The grossest infamies were circulated about Judge Ben B. Lindsey and the committee of miners' wives who went to Washington to plead their cause. The laborers were often treated brutally and in utter disregard of the laws, and then falsehoods about them were spread broadcast through the country.

Upton Sinclair was intensely interested in the same factor in labor disputes, and in *The Brass Check* (1919), he had considerable to say both about Colorado and about the West Virginia coal strike. Sinclair stated that Ivy L. Lee—"Poison Ivy," as the miners called him—was Rocke-feller's thousand-dollars-a-month press-agent. This public relations counsel, as he is now entitled, was responsible, Sinclair charged, for much of the misrepresentation of the Colorado situation. Sinclair also charged the Associated Press with having concealed and misrepresented the out-rageous treatment which the West Virginia miners received at the hands of the Baldwin-Felts Detective Agency.

The condition of women in industry interested many writ-ers of the period, and *McClure's* and *Everybody's* published numerous articles on the subject. The subject of child-labor attracted even more attention, however, and enlisted the sympathies of Edwin Markham and John Spargo. Markham, who has been called "the poet of the muckrakers," was born in Oregon, and, after receiving his education in San Jose and at Christian College at Santa Rosa, where he majored in modern literature and Christian sociology, taught in vari-ous capacities in a number of California towns and cities. It was while living in Oakland that he wrote his most famous poem, "The Man With the Hoe," which Charles Edward Russell calls "the greatest poem of the age—the most splendid of all utterances for man." At a time when the majority of Victorian poets were clinging to the con-ventional Victorian subjects, Markham made an effort to bring verse into some kind of relation with contemporary life, and in this respect he is regarded as having been an important force in contemporary poetry. He is still writing, and his poetry and prose still bear witness to the staunch sympathy with the oppressed which led him to ally himself with the muckrakers.

Markham's one direct contribution to the literature of ex-posure is the series of articles which he wrote for the *Cosmo-politan* in 1906 and 1907, under the title, "The Hoe-Man in the Making." He described the conditions under which children were working in mills, glass factories, sweatshops, coal mines, candy factories, and box factories, filling his articles with dramatic appeal, laying hold of his reader's emotions, and rousing the desire for fair play. John Spargo also wrote about children, estimating that there were three million underfed school children in the country. His articles, which originally appeared in the *Independent* in 1905, were expanded into a book, *The Bitter Cry of the Children*, for which Robert Hunter, author of *Poverty* (1905) wrote the introduction.

Another subject that interested the muckrakers was the industrial status of the Negro. The increased sensitiveness to injustice led various writers to see that the black race had not been miraculously freed from all its burdens merely because it had been released from slavery. Thomas Nelson Page wrote on the Negro for *McClure's* in May, 1904, and Ray Stannard Baker for *McClure's* and the *American* in 1907 and 1908. In the *Cosmopolitan*, March, 1907, Richard Barry surveyed the conditions under which Negroes worked in the South. He wrote:

The Standard Oil clique, H. M. Flagler's Florida East Coast Railway Company, the turpentine trust, the lumber trust, and other trusts have put in force a system of peonage which is actual slavery, and is done under the legal sanction of state laws— not by direct laws, but by subterfuges and circumventions which nevertheless attain the end in view.

On the whole, people failed to become greatly excited about the problem of the Negro in industry, but they did develop considerable interest in the question of the Chinese. Sensational articles bearing such lurid titles as "The Yellow Pariahs" and "The Dragon in America" appeared in several magazines and served to agitate many otherwise sober American citizens. Charles Frederick Holder, the author of "The

Dragon in America," which appeared in the *Arena* in August, 1904, gave an account of the activities of the Chinese Six Companies, so-called. This organization he described as a Chinese trust which secured Chinese labor, brought it to America, controlled it while here, bribed Americans when necessary, and defied the government. Its head, he asserted, was the Chinese Emperor, and its aim was the population of America with Chinese. The company paid for the transportation, obtained work for the coolies, paid doctors' bills, gave legal protection, and in case of death sent the remains back to China. In return, the coolies became practically the slaves of the company, agreeing to pay $2\frac{1}{2}$ per cent of their income to the company and to make no moves without the company's consent. Each of the Six Companies had its name, its organization, and its headquarters, but they were bound together into one trust. They had started their activities as early as 1848, and between 1850 and 1853 they had sent 15,000 coolies to America. These Chinese went into the laundry business and into truck-farming, and in a little while they controlled both businesses. Their truck-farmers, living on six cents a day, could undersell American producers by 75 per cent and still make money. They sent millions of dollars in gold to China, and this, the author suggested, might explain the mysterious depletion of gold in the United States. These coolies stayed in America until they had earned one or two thousand dollars, and then they returned to their own country to spend the rest of their lives in leisure. They evaded the first act of restriction, passed in 1882, and, despite the increasing strictness of later laws, they continued to come; the Six Companies hoped to create by propaganda a sentiment more favorable to the admission of Chinese. Mr. Holder declared in horrified italics that the activities of the Six Companies were "a menace not only to America but to civilization."

Even the more conservative magazines concerned themselves with the appalling number of accidents in the United
States. The *Century*, for example, published in May, 1911,
an article by Will Irwin on employers' liability. In *Public
Opinion*, May 27, 1905, Daniel T. Pierce stated that each
year there were 66,000 fatal accidents, and at least two million injuries. He placed the estimate for the railroads alone
at ten thousand deaths and seventy-five thousand injuries,
and he declared that most of these railroad accidents could
have been prevented by the employment of safety applian-
ces. The number of accidents in the mines was far greater,
Edgar Allen Forbes pointed out in *World's Work*, February,
1908, than the number in European mines. *Everybody's* was
extremely active in treating the question of accidents in industry and of compensation therefor. William Hard, in an
article called "Making Steel and Killing Men," which appeared in the November, 1907, issue, commented scathingly
on the large number of preventable accidents in the steel
mills, and in other articles he went thoroughly into the subject of compensation laws. In the same magazine, in February, 1907, Arthur B. Reeves, later a successful writer of
detective stories, estimated that half a million people were
killed or maimed annually in our industries, largely because
of the indifference of employers, laborers, and the public.
Several women writers did excellent work on the conditions
of women in industry. In *McClure's* Mary Alden Hopkins
showed that the great loss of life in the Newark factory fire
was due mainly to defective doors and fire escapes. These
articles helped to put over workmen's compensation laws.

After 1907 the *American Magazine* occupied itself with many
aspects of the labor movement and of labor problems. In
1905 *Frank Leslie's Popular Magazine* had been taken over by
a new company, re-christened, and put into the hands of
Ellery Sedgwick, now the distinguished editor of the *Atlantic*

Monthly. The *American Monthly Magazine,* as it was called by the new publishers, sought to shun "the 'exposure' business, the ripping the cover off everything that smells rotten." Sedgwick himself attacked the muckrakers in May, 1906, declaring that they heaped together "exaggeration, perversion, distortion, truths, half-truths, lies." It was Sedgwick, indeed, who first referred to Bunyan's man with the muckrake, thus furnishing Roosevelt with the phrase he popularized.

After two years under Sedgwick's management, the *American* was again for sale, and at just this time several members of the staff of *McClure's* happened to disagree with Mr. McClure over a matter of business policy. Having worked together for many years, and having similar views on the need for unsparing criticism of American life, they determined to band together and to purchase a magazine for themselves. Led by John S. Phillips, who had played a most important part in the editing of *McClure's,* Baker, Steffens, Miss Tarbell, William Allen White, and Finley Peter Dunne purchased the *American.*

The members of this group invested their own funds in the enterprise, and their aim was to edit a magazine as they thought it should be edited. They continued the policy of painstaking investigation initiated by *McClure's,* and they prided themselves on the accuracy of their articles. No episode in the whole movement is more indicative of the spirit behind muckraking at its best. Here were talented men and women, capable of commanding the highest prices for their articles, but content with salaries that barely met their needs so long as they were free to carry on the kind of work in which they believed. Most of them had come into muckraking by way of journalism and had become trained investigators as well as skilled reporters. They had seen at first hand the suffering of the poor and knew from personal experience the devious ways of big business. In the end, they were forced to surrender their control of the magazine, partly because the public was losing its interest in the literature of exposure, partly because influential business men saw fit to withdraw their advertising. But they had several years in which to hammer away at the public. Mr. Baker has said that the happiest days of his life were those he spent on the *American*, days of fine friendship with his colleagues, days of arduous toil for causes in which he believed.

The editors of the *American*, it should be noted, were all, with the possible exception of Lincoln Steffens, liberals rather than radicals, and they believed that at bottom American institutions were sound. One of the aims of this magazine was to point out commendable as well as dangerous tendencies in the life of the nation, and they particularly stressed hopeful developments in their treatment of labor problems. Miss Tarbell, for example, wrote a series on "New Ideals in Business," discussing scientific management, industrial representation schemes, and similar devices for the more efficient and more humane conduct of industry.

The attitude of the *American* toward labor problems admirably illustrates the extent to which muckraking was a middle-class movement. Few of the muckrakers were in any way connected with trade unions; few of them wrote in the interest of trade-union development. As good reporters, they were on the watch for live stories wherever they could be found; as philanthropically minded men and women, they attacked injustice wherever they discovered it; but beyond that they did not go. Baker, for example, had only to adopt a pseudonym in order to write *Adventures in Contentment* and *Adventures in Understanding*. By his own account, he had no program of reform, nor was he fundamentally critical of American life. He described both the good and the bad as he saw them, fully confident that in the end the good would prevail. It is his opinion that the muckraking movement was, for the most part, merely a special development of journalism in response to a special need, and he believes that the movement derived its strength from the fact that the muckrakers did not attempt to prescribe remedies for the evils they depicted.

CHAPTER ELEVEN

CHANGING THE CHURCH

AT FIRST the muckrakers steered clear of religious subjects, not because of excess reverence but because of a feeling that politics and industry offered more fruitful fields. No institution, however, was entirely exempt from their attack, and near the end of the period ecclesiastical questions were dragged out from the cloisters and given prominence in the spotlight of magazine publicity. The writers, as a rule, took pains to record their respect for religion, but they showed no such mercy to the church.

Ray Stannard Baker's articles on "The Spiritual Unrest," which were published in the *American* in 1908 and 1909, are typical of the saner discussions of religion and the church. Mr. Baker, after investigating such subjects as psychic healing, church attendance, city missions, and the like, concluded that a large section of the population was estranged from the church, and he tried to show why this was the case and what religious beliefs were held by these non-churchgoers. He commented on the work of the slum missions, which, he said, "demonstrated again and again the power of living religion to reconstruct the individual human life," but he also noted that only about 5 per cent of the converted remained faithful to their vows. After describing the vast amount of religious dissatisfaction, he put it up to the religious leaders to decide whether the fault lay with them or with the dissentient masses.

In the course of his survey Mr. Baker touched gently on the fact that the churches were sometimes allied in concrete ways with the forces which were demoralizing the national life. Trinity Church in New York, for example, owned and drew income from tenements that were a disgrace to the city. Charles Edward Russell, writing in *Everybody's*, July, 1908, had described the situation the year before, and *Hampton's* had repeatedly devoted editorials to the subject. Mr. Russell wrote:

I have tramped the Eighth Ward day after day, with a list of Trinity properties in my hand, and of all the tenement houses that stand on Trinity land, I have not found one that is not a disgrace to civilization.

Marvelling that a Christian church should be willing to take money from such dens of filth, he studied the situation and found that the communicants of the church, having left the matter in the hands of a small and self-perpetuating body were absolutely ignorant of the extent and nature of the investments. As a result of these various attacks the Trinity Church Corporation tore down one hundred and fifty-seven of the worst tenement houses in New York, and reformed a policy which it had followed for one hundred and twenty years.

Two religious sects were frequently attacked, namely Christian Science and Mormonism. Georgine Milmine wrote for *McClure's* in 1907 a series of twelve articles on "Mary Baker G. Eddy: The Story of Her Life and the History of Christian Science." These articles, to the preparation of which three years were devoted, constituted the most detailed treatment the subject was given, but it was not the only unflattering study of the new sect and its founder. Indeed, so much was written attacking Christian Science that Benjamin Flower, editor of the *Arena*, was moved to protest against the "persistent campaign of falsehood, slander and calumny."

The articles on the Mormon church were directed against its political and economic power rather than against its tenets. Judson C. Welliver, as already noted, had denounced the connection between the sugar trust and the Mormon organization. Burton J. Hendrick, writing in *McClure's*, January and February, 1911, insisted that the Mormon church existed chiefly for criminal purposes, namely the practising of polygamy. In *Pearson's*, October, 1910, Richard Barry argued that the relation between the Mormon church and the government of the state was very close, that polygamy was still practised in Utah, and that business interests were bound up with the religious and political organizations. But the most startling articles were those which Alfred Henry Lewis wrote for the *Cosmopolitan* in 1911. Mr. Lewis named his articles "The Viper on the Hearth," "The Trail of the Viper," and "The Viper's Trail of Gold," and they appeared on pages handsomely adorned with pictures of snakes and moneybags. He announced that Mormonism had already influenced the politics of nine western states, and he declared that, by its method of tithing, the Mormon church had become a powerful financial institution that could even defy Wall Street. These allegations were widely believed and created much alarm.

Mr. W. W. Young tells a story indicating the power which Mormons were able to exert. In 1911, just after *Hampton's Magazine* had been merged with the *Columbian* and Mr. Young had been made editor of what was then called *Hampton's Columbian Magazine*, a new series of articles was announced on the Mormon church. Before the issue in which the series was to begin went to press, the receiver, a lawyer with an office in Wall Street, asked the editor for a table of contents of the forthcoming issue. Then he drew a line

Top left: RAY STANNARD BAKER. *Top right:* C. P. CONNOLLY. *Bottom left:* GEORGE KIBBE TURNER. *Bottom right:* SAMUEL HOPKINS ADAMS. Photograph by Bachrach.

through the article on Mormonism, and ordered its omission. When Mr. Young protested and offered his resignation, the lawyer counseled coolness, explaining that it would be very bad business to publish an attack on Mormonism. Some weeks later the editor was asked how he would like to own the magazine and manage it to suit himself; the only condition was that nothing hostile to Mormonism should appear in it. Young did not accept the offer, but ex-Senator Frank J. Cannon is authority for the statement that since that time the church has been immune from criticism in the public press.

Spiritualism was discussed in its many aspects, from the type that sought to appear scientific to the type that was manifestly fraudulent. Hamlin Garland and Will Irwin were two among many writers to deal with this theme. Irwin, in order to get material for his articles, acquired some of the paraphernalia and learned some of the arts of the more dubious practitioners, and for a week posed as a spiritualist. His experiences he utilized not only in four articles for *Collier's* but also in many short stories.

A more general examination of religion was that contained in a series which Harold Bolce wrote for the *Cosmopolitan* in 1909. Mr. Bolce, after stating that he had studied at or visited most of the leading universities of the country, including Harvard, Yale, Columbia, Wisconsin, Northwestern, Nebraska, and Leland Stanford, asserted that he had heard problems of morality, economics, marriage, divorce, the home, religion, and democracy discussed as if they were fossils, equations, chemical elements, or chimeras. "There is," he said, "scholarly repudiation of all solemn authority. The decalogue is no more sacred than a syllabus." He described the teachings of such men as Edwin L. Earp of Syracuse, Simon Patten of Pennsylvania, Franklin Giddings of Columbia, Edward A. Ross of Wisconsin, Frank A. Fetter of Cornell, Shailer Mathews of Chicago, William Graham Sumner of Yale, and Woodrow Wilson of Princeton. These professors, he said, taught their pupils that an immoral act was merely one contrary to prevailing conceptions of society and that the person who defied the code did not offend any Deity, but simply aroused the venom of the majority. He had been surprised, he said, to find academic warrant for "departure from conjugal restraint," to hear that the home was too narrow a channel for the transmission of progress to the race to come, to hear that conscience is not a safe guide for conduct, to learn that standards of morality change, to be told that "society, by its approval, can make any kind conduct right."

Following the first article, appearing in May, 1909, which Mr. Bolce called "Blasting at the Rock of Ages," came a second in June, which he entitled "Polyglots in the Temples of Babel." This dealt with the iconoclastic teachings of professors of politics and economics, and Mr. Bolce recorded several more things he had been surprised to hear. In the third article, "Avatars of the Almighty," which appeared in July, he dealt with the faith of these iconoclastic professors, recording that they were unequivocally optimistic and undoubtedly believed that what they taught was for the best interests of their students and of the nation. The fourth article, "Christianity in the Crucible," in the August issue, began by describing the tremendous sensation caused by its predecessors. Mr. Bolce asserted that the ministers were charging the teachers with destroying all that had been held sacred, while the professors were countering with the astonishing charge that the church was the leading obstacle to man's spiritual growth. He quoted the professors as expressing their recognition of the many services of the church and their hope that it would yet surrender its antiquated beliefs and devote itself to humanity. The last of the series, entitled "Rallying Round the Cross," appearing in September, consisted of replies to the university professors, mostly from orthodox clergymen, some of whom gave evidence of only a foggy idea of what it was they were attacking.

Mr. Bolce's articles illustrate a type of muckraking that became increasingly frequent in the latter part of the era. Instead of presenting a straightforward exposure of an institution, he tried to wring every possible bit of sensationalism from a complex situation. The primary aim was neither reform nor yet the dissemination of information, but rather the arousing of a factitious interest which would help to sell the paper. The contrast between his articles and those of Mr. Baker makes perfectly obvious one reason, at least, for the decline of muckraking.

A rather significant document on the church appeared somewhat later than the bulk of the articles on the subject. Upton Sinclair's *The Profits of Religion* (1918), is so typical a muckraking document in content and form that it deserves consideration here. The point which Sinclair, characteristically, chose to study was the relation between organized religion and the maintenance of the capitalistic system. He charged the church with being a tool in the hands of the capitalistic classes, aiding them to retain control of the government and of the economic order by teaching the poor that God had allotted to them humble positions, and that it was their duty to be satisfied. The Roman Catholics, he said, had engaged in charity time without end, but had never stopped to consider the causes of misery. The Catholic church was one of the main pillars of capitalism, but Protestantism was, he asserted, almost as bad. He said that many preachers fell in with modern commercialism, eulogizing the rich and powerful no matter how they had acquired their wealth. Some ministers were deliberately used to quiet industrial unrest; Billy Sunday, for example, had been engaged by John D. Rockefeller to speak to 50,000 laborers in 187 meetings. This cost Rockefeller $200,000, but, said Mr. Sinclair, the money was well spent.

Sinclair expressed his admiration for Jesus and for his principles. "Beyond all question," he said, "the supreme irony of history is the use which has been made of Jesus of Nazareth as the Head God of this blood-thirsty system; it is a cruelty beyond all language, a blasphemy beyond the power of art to express." He also recorded his belief in morality, but he thought that a new morality was coming—a morality of freedom, joy, reason, and love. The way in which Sinclair stated his case probably would have failed to secure the approval of a number of his fellow muckrakers, and there may have been much in his attack that was only partially true, but it is almost certain that a majority of the muckrakers would have agreed heartily with his fundamental belief that true religion expresses itself in the service of humanity.

CHAPTER TWELVE

THE PRESS MUZZLED AND UNMUZZLED

IT IS AN interesting and not easily explicable fact that the leading articles and books attacking the press appeared after muckraking in other fields had practically come to end. Why the press had not come in for its share of exposure much earlier is something of a mystery, and it is equally strange that muckraking should continue its attacks on one institution when it had ceased attacking almost all others. It is difficult to believe that there was less corruption in the press before 1910 or 1912 than there was afterwards, but possibly the very fact that a number of muckraking magazines were forced out of existence had something to do with awakening interest in the subject. There is the possibility, also, that the attempt to reform the newspapers appealed to citizens who had grown weary of the sensationalism all too common in the latter days of the muckraking era.

In the whole range of journalistic endeavor no organization came in for such violent denunciations as were visited upon the Associated Press. As early as July, 1909, William Kittle, writing in the *Arena* on "The Making of Public Opinion," had pointed out that the supreme court of Illinois had held the Associated Press to be a monopoly in February of 1900, while the supreme court of Missouri, in December of the same year, had reached a decision that it was not a monopoly. He himself was of the opinion that it was a monopoly and he pointed out that it had all the earmarks. In July, 1914, "Observer," a contributor to the *Atlantic*, discussed the same subject, reaching the conclusion that the Associated Press at least tended toward monopoly control. Other writers were not so moderate, and James H. Barry, editor of the San Francisco *Star*, called it, according to Upton Sinclair, "the damndest, meanest monopoly on the face of the earth —the wet-nurse for all other monopolies."

The organization of the Associated Press, according to its critics, was narrow and exclusive. In 1914 it was reported that there were 894 members, each having one vote, but the actual number of votes cast ran into the thousands. The discrepancy, as was pointed out by Gregory Mason in the *Outlook* for May 30, 1914, and by Will Irwin in *Harper's Weekly* for March 28 of the same year, was due to the fact that for every $25 worth of bonds which an original member took he received one extra vote. Most of the newspapers took $1,000 worth of bonds, which meant, combining these votes with their membership votes, that they had forty-one votes apiece. Since the papers which joined later had only their membership votes, the "old crowd" had absolute and perpetual control. The directors and managers, then, were not chosen by a majority of the approximately nine hundred members, but by the small group of bondholders.

Mr. Irwin, in his article on the subject, went on to describe certain other of the undesirable features of the organization. By the "power of protest" any member of the "A. P." could veto the application for a franchise of any competing newspaper within sixty miles. A gesture of reform, however, had been made in 1900, when it was ruled that any newspaper which had been denied a franchise by the "power of protest" could make application to the annual meeting of the association and could receive a franchise if four-fifths of the members voted in favor of the application and against the protest. This, Mr. Irwin asserted, had happened only two or three times, and usually such an application was voted down without hesitation.

The organization also enjoyed peculiar power because of the fact that, when it was reorganized in New York in 1900, the directors secured their charter under the section of the law which permits "Mutual Companies"—literary, social, and fish and game clubs. In such an organization a member may be expelled for an act derogatory to the interests of the association. This meant, obviously, that no member could criticize the "A. P." without endangering his valuable franchise. Mr. Irwin stated that two or three liberal publishers, after having expressed their opinion of the "A. P. cinch," anxiously insisted that he should not quote them. "For heaven's sake," one of them said, "don't quote me in print, and don't tell anyone I've said this. The fine for such an offense runs from $50,000 up."

Both Mr. Kittle, in the article which he published in the *Arena* in 1909, and Mr. Irwin, in his 1914 *Harper's Weekly* article, were interested in discovering the bias of the Associated Press. Kittle made a study of the attitude of the directors as they revealed it in their own newspapers, for they all controlled big dailies, and of the fifteen directors twelve had held office continuously from 1900 to 1914. He found that the Kansas City *Star-Times*, under William R. Nelson, had published more progressive articles and editorials than the other fourteen combined. These fourteen, he wrote, were

. . . huge commercial ventures, connected by advertising and in other ways, with banks, trust companies, railway and city utility companies, department stores, and manufacturing enterprises. They reflect the system which supports them. They cannot afford to mold public opinion against the net-work of special interests which envelop them.

As between the Democratic party and the Republican party, Mr. Kittle thought, the Associated Press was fairly impartial, but he intimated that progressive movements were exceedingly fortunate if they got a square deal. The only affirmative policy that he could discover was a determination to report the unusual and spectacular because that was what sold papers.

Mr. Irwin also found a conservative, capitalistic attitude but he was inclined to attribute it less to deliberate partisanship and unfairness than to the environment and training of the reporters. These agents, he pointed out, selected from the events of the day such news as squared with their conservative picture of the world, and the organization hindered, or prevented, the rise of publishers who might present the other side. This, to his mind, was the real quarrel with the Associated Press—that it tended to keep young men from exercising a directive influence on its policies. The "power of protest" prevented new men from obtaining franchises in their own territories, and as a result the organization was a powerful force for reaction. More vehement protests were voiced by various writers, among them Charles Edward Russell, who, in an article which he wrote for *Pearson's* in April, 1914, charged the Associated Press with deliberately misrepresenting the strike situation at Calumet, Michigan, in an attempt to turn public sentiment against the strikers. This, he said, was the usual policy of the "A. P."

The charges that were brought against newspapers in general were much the same as those directed against the Associated Press in particular. It was frequently charged and widely believed that the newspapers were dominated by the capitalists, that important news was suppressed or distorted to please the advertisers, that editorials were "slanted" so as to attract advertising, and that "Big Business" lavished money on the newspapers for the purpose of creating public opinion favorable to their interests.

A thorough and revealing survey of the newspaper field was made by Will Irwin in *Collier's* as early as 1911, but eight years later, in 1919, a much more violent and much more famous attack appeared—Upton Sinclair's *The Brass Check*. This book Ernest H. Gruening, writing in the *Nation*, July 17, 1920, under the title "What Every Newspaper Man Knows," called a "fascinating and thorough treatise upon the American press, based on a variety of personal experiences and on contacts, direct and indirect, with newspapers, newspaper stories, and newspaper men." It is, Mr. Gruening maintained, an exposé and an indictment, and he continued:

It marshals fact after fact and arrays incident after incident, waving aside hearsay and rumor. Respecting no locality, it covers metropolitan and country newspapers from coast to coast, pays its respects to magazines, and delves into the workings of news associations. It is a complete, masterful study.

The facts, Mr. Gruening wrote, were incontrovertible; but the conclusions which the author reached were a different matter. Being a Socialist, Sinclair had seen everything through the spectacles of class-consciousness, making no allowances for selfishness, timidity, ignorance, partisanship, lack of public spirit, or downright dishonesty.

Gruening's judgment seems to have been sound. Sinclair's belief that every case of distortion was the result of a capitalistic conspiracy must be regarded with scepticism, but his exposure of conditions prevailing in the newspaper world has a vast amount of documented evidence behind it. With his thesis that since the days of Mark Hanna the betrayal of public opinion has been deliberately planned and systematically carried out we need not long concern ourselves, nor need we believe his statement that high-priced experts sit in council with the masters of industry and determine precisely how this shall be presented and that suppressed. There is, perhaps, some truth in these charges, but how much it is not our duty to decide in the present work. What does concern us is the great mass of carefully supported exposure of the activities and methods of the press.

Of the many instances of suppression and distortion which Sinclair gives two may be selected as typical. During the hearings of the Interstate Commerce Commission in 1914, when the railroads were trying to secure a 5 per cent increase in freight rates, a certain Mr. Thorne of the Iowa State Railway Commission cross-questioned the railroad presidents and showed that 1912 had been the most profitable year in their history, and that in twelve years the capitalization of the roads had been increased 92 per cent and dividends had increased enormously. The country was showing much interest in the investigation, but many of the leading newspapers did not report a single word of Thorne's statements, though they gave columns to the speeches in which the presidents told how much they needed the increase. The other case had to do with Roosevelt's investigation of the packing plants. The people were clamoring for news, but the reporters would not accept any information from Sinclair, who had a first-hand knowledge of the situation. He wrote "They never sent out a single line injurious to the packers, save for a few lines dealing with the Congressional hearings, which they could not entirely suppress."

Other writers cited similar examples of the way in which news was controlled in the interests of the industrialists and financiers. Mr. Kittle, in his *Arena* article of 1909 mentioned above, quoted from a story which Gustavus Meyer told in the Milwaukee *Social Democratic Herald*. Mr. Meyer said that he had investigated the record of Senator Dryden, president of the Prudential Insurance Company, for David Graham

Phillips, who was then engaged in writing his famous series on "The Treason of the Senate" for the *Cosmopolitan*. Mr. Phillips had incorporated the material in his article for October, 1906, but a few weeks before publication the business manager of the *Cosmopolitan* announced his intention to "kill" that part of the article which dealt with Dryden. The Prudential Insurance Company, he said, had sent a four-page advertisement to the magazine, and he doubted if it was worth losing four or five thousand dollars for the sake of printing a few paragraphs. The paragraphs were dropped, and instead of attacking Senator Dryden the October number published an article eulogizing him and his company.

Maxwell Anderson, now a successful dramatist, wrote for the *New Republic*, December 14, 1918, an article called "The Blue Pencil," in which he exposed the inside workings of a large newspaper. Reporters and assistants, he said, despised the editor and his policy, but they had to eschew anything new or progressive if they wanted to keep their jobs. Much earlier, in October, 1914, an anonymous article appeared in *Collier's* with the title, "The Confessions of a Managing Editor." The author stated that the managing editor of a paper was under the thumb of the business office, and was forced to keep from the columns anything that might damage the advertisers. Charles Edward Russell, in his "How Business Controls News," in *Pearson's*, May, 1914, told some interesting stories of what had happened to editors who published news distasteful to the financiers. Will Irwin, writing in *Collier's*, from January to July, 1914, maintained that editorial writers were often required to color their editorials in such a way as to attract advertisers. George Creel, as already noted, charged the papers with distorting facts during labor disputes, and other writers echoed this charge. Many serious thinkers were alarmed by these statements and by the truth they obviously contained, and Professor Edward A. Ross, writing in the *Atlantic* in 1910, stated that the popularity of the muckraking magazines was due to their publishing news which the papers suppressed.

Another charge against the press was that it often prostituted itself to create public opinion favorable to big business. As early as 1906, in one of the first articles on the newspapers, Ray Stannard Baker had shown "How Railroads Make Public Opinion." He stated that in 1905 the railroads, alarmed by the public clamor for railroad legislation and by the passage of the Esch-Townsend bill in the House of Representatives, undertook a sweeping campaign to reach and change public sentiment. A firm of publicity agents was established with headquarters in Boston and branches in New York, Chicago, Washington, St. Louis, and Topeka. In each office was a large corps of employees, directed by experienced newspaper men. These journalists and their assistants undertook a careful survey of all the newspapers, and visited hundreds of editors, noting the views of each on economic and political questions. Then literature which would put the railroads in a favorable light was supplied by them to the editors who frequently, perhaps usually, did not know whence this material came. The results were amazing. In the week ending June 5, 1905, the newspapers of Nebraska published 212 columns of matter unfavorable to the railroads and only two columns of favorable matter. Eleven weeks later, after a careful campaign had been made, the Nebraska papers, in the course of a week, published 202 columns that were favorable to the railroads and only four columns that were unfavorable.

Naturally the railroads were not the only corporations that played this little game. Kittle, for example, in his article, "The Interests and the Magazines," *Twentieth Century* (successor to the *Arena*), May, 1910, showed what the Standard Oil Company was doing. He said that John D. Arch-

bold, vice-president of the company, sent $5,000 to George
Gunton of *Gunton's Magazine* "as an additional contribution
to that agreed upon and to aid you in your most excellent
work," and also promised a subscription of $5,000 to the
Southern Farm Magazine. An anonymous writer in *Collier's* described the activities of Standard Oil publicity agents in the
West. Swift and Company, according to Upton Sinclair,
spent a million dollars a month in the effort to defeat a bill
before Congress which provided for government control of
the packing industry, and Armour's paid farm publications
$2,000 a page for "special articles." An editorial in *McClure's*
charged the Mutual Life Insurance Company with paying
as much as a dollar a line for favorable stories published in
the newspapers, and *Collier's*, on March 18, 1911, denounced
the efforts of the American Wool Company.

The technique of using the papers to influence public
opinion was, Kittle stated in his *Arena* article of 1909, carefully worked out. Numerous well organized bureaus furnished adroitly prepared articles, letters, and interviews to
the newspapers, which printed them without indicating their
source. Corporations paid generously for advertising space
with the tacit agreement that they could control the news
and editorial columns as well. Such an organization as the
Municipal Ownership Publicity Bureau published a magazine and sent out articles and news items to the press in order
to discredit municipal ownership and advance the interests
of the gas, light, water, and traction companies.

It was the hypocrisy of the Press which particularly dis-
gusted Upton Sinclair. He cited the case of General Otis,
a wealthy newspaper owner in Los Angeles. Otis, Sinclair
asserted, appeared in the *Times* as a Republican and advocated the "open shop" policy so fiercely that some outraged
labor leaders blew up the *Times* building with a dynamite
bomb. At the same time he secretly owned the *Herald*, which

was "independent," "Democratic," and favored the "closed-shop." Another large paper preached the virtues of being poor in editorials bearing such titles as "My Lady Poverty," the while it was making a million dollars a year from doubtful advertising. Sinclair declared that the hypocrisy of the press was such that there were two propositions which were invariably true: first, any proprietor of a department store anywhere in America might divorce or be divorced with entire impunity so far as the press was concerned; second, "no radical in America can divorce or be divorced without being gutted, skinned alive, and placed on the red-hot griddle of Capitalistic Journalism." To emphasize his accusations he quoted a New York editor as saying:

The business of the New York journalist is to destroy the truth, to lie outright, to pervert, to vilify, to fawn at the feet of Mammon, and to sell his race and his country for his daily bread. . . . We are the tools and vassals of rich men behind the scenes. We are the jumping jacks: they pull the strings and we dance. Our talents, our possibilities and our lives are all the property of other men. We are intellectual prostitutes.

And he stated that a Los Angeles editor had written, "We are hired poisoners, whose lot it is to kill the things we love most."

Among newspaper owners William Randolph Hearst was several times singled out for attack. Frederick Palmer wrote four articles on "Hearst and Hearstism" for *Collier's* in 1906, and Steffens discussed Hearst in the *American*, November, 1906. Steffens, who, after years of investigations, had come to the conclusion that personally vicious men were comparatively rare, treated Hearst as a social phenomenon, and blamed the times rather than the man for the evils of yellow journalism. This did not altogether please the other members of the staff, and there was a rather warm session of the editorial board. At last it was decided that the article should be published, and Mr. Phillips asked what it should be called. "Why," said Miss Tarbell, who had been acting as peacemaker, "call it 'William Randolph Hearst' by Lincoln Steffens." "Yah," grumbled Finley Peter Dunne, "out of Arthur Brisbane."

The magazines were attacked as well as the newspapers, and here there was the additional point—it was widely believed, and probably pretty well proven, that more than one of the muckraking magazines had been put out of business. In 1912 George French wrote for the *Twentieth Century* two articles, "Masters of the Magazines" (April), and "The Damnation of the Magazines" (June), in which he showed how financial interests controlled the majority of periodicals.

To-day [he wrote] it is the paper-maker that is the master of this magazine, the big advertiser of that one, a financial house of the other; and in the last analysis, this control comes down to a control in the interests of money, whether the root of the matter is a big unpaid paper bill, and "accommodation" note at some bank, or a veiled subscription to stock or bond issue.

Charles Edward Russell, writing in *Pearson's* for February, 1914, under the title, "The Magazine Soft Pedal," illustrated how advertising could influence magazine policy, by saying that when his first article on the Beef Trust appeared seven pages of advertising was withdrawn, and that his article on the Tobacco Trust had a similar effect.

The magazines which engaged in exposure were in danger not merely of losing their advertisers but also of being forced out of existence. The most conspicious example of this danger was the story of *Hampton's*, which has been repeatedly told. Benjamin Hampton purchased the *Broadway Magazine* in 1907, when its circulation was 13,000. He changed the name to *Hampton's*, plunged into muckraking, and in four years had brought the circulation up to 440,000. But he was continually offending the most powerful corporations in the country, and they began to bring pressure to bear upon him. Not only did they try to secure control of the magazine and to weaken it by withdrawing advertisements, but they also kept spies in the office to furnish them with information. A young man with good references applied for a place as accountant, worked diligently for a few months, and then suddenly left—without explanation but with a complete list of the several thousand stockholders of the magazine. Immediately, Russell tells us, these stockholders were flooded with "devilishly cunning" literature designed to undermine their confidence in the magazine.

The climax of the struggle came when, in December of 1910, *Hampton's* published an article attacking the New York, New Haven and Hartford Railroad. Before the article appeared, a representative of the road visited Hampton, discussed the article with him, and warned him that if the article was printed *Hampton's* would be on the rocks in ninety days. The article was published, and the threat was carried out. First came a campaign among the advertisers, and then the stockholders were bombarded. In May, 1911, Hampton found that he had to have money to tide him over the dull summer months, but he could not borrow $30,000 from any bank in New York, despite the fact that his business had been valued at two million dollars and that back of the paper he offered was collateral worth at least two hundred thousand. In the issue of August, 1911, Mr. Hampton stated that he and his magazine had been in a hand-to-hand fight with Wall Street, and all the banks were closed against him. Finally he was forced to sell, for ten thousand dollars, this enterprise into which more than a million had gone, and in less than a year *Hampton's* had ceased to exist.

It is only fair to state that there are other accounts of the decline of *Hampton's*, some of them sponsored by men who are by no means hostile to muckraking in general. It is said that there was bad management, and it has been hinted that Mr. Hampton was not entirely sincere. However this may be, there seems to be strong evidence that financial interests, profiting perhaps by weaknesses in the conduct of the magazine, were quick to seize the first opportunity to put it out of business.

Other magazines suffered from the same pressure. George French, in the articles previously mentioned, stated that when *Success*, of which Orison Swett Marden was editor and Edward E. Higgins business manager, went into muckraking, "Uncle Joe" Cannon, who had been forcefully assailed in an article which Higgins wrote, threw the magazine on the table, crying, "Damn *Success*! Who in hell is E. E. Higgins?" And *Success* was damned! The big interests quietly withdrew their advertisements, the paper-makers demanded cash for paper, the banks were loath to lend money, the sales fell off —and *Success*, for which nearly $400,000 had been offered not long before, was sold for $2,250.

Pearson's, which had started brilliantly in 1899 with a first number circulation of 100,000, and which, under new management, had reached a circulation of nearly 300,000 in 1906, participated in muckraking, especially in the later years of the era. As a result of its unflinching attacks on various corporations, it lost a great deal of advertising; the Armour interests, for example, canceled an order for eighteen pages after the appearance of an article entitled "How Food Prices Are Made." Then the New York *Sun* published an article on *Pearson's* financial status. This article, which came into the office from some outside source, was a distorted version of a circular which Arthur W. Little, the publisher of *Pearson's*, had issued to stockholders, and was intended to weaken his financial standing. Mr. Little, despite his recognized position and the excellent security he offered, was unable to borrow money, and it was only by using the cheapest paper that *Pearson's* was able to struggle on for a little longer.

Other magazines fell by the wayside from time to time. *McClure's*, for example, came to be controlled by the West Virginia Pulp and Paper Company. According to Upton Sinclair, *Human Life*, *National Post*, the *Twentieth Century*, and *Times Magazine* all succumbed to the interests. George French, in a third article for the *Twentieth Century* called "Shall the Tail Wag the Dog?" (May, 1912), stated that many magazines had been taken over by the interests which they had previously fought, and that many of the saner and more dependable muckrakers had been forced by 1912 to give up writing on sociological subjects because there was no market for their articles.

In general, the tendency from 1910 on was against the progressive magazines. In 1909 William Kittle, writing in the *Arena*, recorded that there were four actively liberal magazines: the *Arena*, the *American*, *Everybody's*, and *McClure's*. These four had a combined circulation of a million and a third, and they constantly voiced "the indignant protest against all forms of special privilege," The *North American Review* he listed as the most conservative of the popular journals. The next year he added *Hampton's* and the *Outlook* to his roster of the progressives. In 1912 he studied a large number of magazines, including several national weeklies, and noted their attitude toward the Progressive Party. *Collier's* and *LaFollette's* were leaders in the campaign, but *McClure's* had given up muckraking, and *Hampton's* was practically extinct. In 1919, when Upton Sinclair published *The Brass Check*, he could not find a single popular magazine that was actively opposing Big Business.

The attack on the press has gone on. After the war much was said about the way in which the newspapers had distorted war news and had misrepresented conditions in Sov-

iet Russia. The *Nation* and the *New Republic* were the leaders
in the post-war campaign for honest news, and the latter
published a special supplement entitled "The Crimes of the
Times," in which it exposed the bias shown by the New
York *Times* in reporting events in Russia. Walter Lippmann,
both during and after his connection with the *New Republic*,
has been a careful student of the press, and in two volumes,
Public Opinion (1922), and *Liberty and the News* (1927), he
has dealt with this question. Mr. Lippmann, unlike Upton
Sinclair, attributes the distortion of news not to a great conspiracy but to a variety of causes.

The critics of the press have frequently offered constructive suggestions for the improving of journalism. Professor
Ross has recommended an endowed daily paper, which
would publish the news impartially. Hitchcock and Lippmann have advocated the raising of journalism to a profession with high standards. Upton Sinclair suggests legislation which would prevent the publication of false interviews and fake telegraph and cable dispatches, the forma-
tion of a union of newspaper workers, and the founding of
an impartial newspaper. These propositions and others have
been repeatedly debated, for interest in the whole question
is still keen.

CHAPTER THIRTEEN

THE WAR AGAINST POISON

INADEQUATE as in some ways it is the Pure Food and Drugs Act of 1906 is one of the most important pieces of legislation ever enacted. And this law may justly be regarded as a product of muckraking, since it was the magazines which aroused the public to support a reform for which medical associations had long been pleading in vain. The pioneer work in this field was done by Dr. Harvey Wiley, Chief of the Bureau of Chemistry in the Department of Agriculture. As early as 1889 he began publishing books on the subject, and his treatises undoubtedly paved the way for more sensational exposures, such as Upton Sinclair's *The Jungle* (1906). Another pioneer was Professor E. F. Ladd, Food Commissioner for the State of North Dakota, who, in the summer of 1904, read before the National Pure Food Congress and the Convention of Dairy and Food Departments, assembled at St. Louis, a detailed account of food conditions. He stated that he had never found in North Dakota a can of potted chicken or potted turkey which contained chicken or turkey in recognizable quantities; that 90 per cent of the local meat markets used chemical preservatives such as Freezem, preservaline, iceline, or Bull Meat Flour; that a pound of sausages frequently contained from twenty to forty-five grains of boracic acid, four or five times as much as a physician would think of giving his patient in a day; that the packers as well as the local dealers used boracic acid, making it a common ingredient of dried beef, smoked meats, canned bacon, and canned chipped beef; that 90 per cent of the so-called French peas contained copper salts, while some brands contained aluminum salts as well, that 80 per cent of the canned mushrooms in North Dakota had been bleached by the use of sulphites; that before the food law went into effect there was only one brand of catsup that was free from chemical preservatives and coal tar coloring matter; that about 70 per cent of cocoas and chocolates were adulterated; that ten times as much Vermont maple sugar was sold as the state could produce; that a large proportion of the ground spices were imitations; that jellies, wines, and other liquors were made from cheap substances and then doctored; that butter was made from a mixture of butter and deodorized lard; that ice cream usually contained no cream but was made of neutral lard and condensed milk and that cider vinegars usually contained no apple juice. The adulteration of food was so common, Walter Lippmann said in *Drift and Mastery* (1914), that if conditions were vividly described, "Milk would curdle the blood, bread and butter would raise a scandal, candy—the volume would have to be suppressed." It was as a result of these agitations that the Pure Food and Drug Act of 1906 was passed.

A similar campaign was inaugurated against the patent medicine fraud. The *Ladies' Home Journal* and *Collier's* were the leading magazines in this struggle, and Mark Sullivan, Edward Bok, and Samuel Hopkins Adams were the outstanding writers, with Adams easily at the top. In the first series of articles which he wrote, "The Great American Fraud," beginning in October, 1905, Adams described the contents of certain of the more popular medicines. Peruna, he said, contained 28 per cent of alcohol, and six other drugs went into its composition. The actual cost per bottle (including the bottle) was, he estimated, eight and one-half cents; the consumer paid a dollar. It was supposed to cure catarrh, and according to Dr. Hartman's Peruna Book nearly every ailment was a kind of catarrh. Actually, Adams maintained, the use of Peruna often led to tuberculosis and drunkenness. And in the other eleven articles of this series, appearing in *Collier's* in 1905 and 1906, he described the manufacture and sale of similar panaceas.

After the series had been concluded, the editors of *Collier's* discussed the libel suits and protests which had resulted, and stated that scores of state and national medical societies had praised Adams's work, and that many states had passed laws as a result of his articles. But in 1912 Mr. Adams discovered that there was still plenty of opportunity for muckraking, and he published a second series of articles. Before the passage of the Pure Food and Drug Act in 1906 conditions had been unbelievable—

Floods of potions, avalanches of pills and powders, had been pouring out from the various nostrum shops, without let or hindrance, to overflow the land. Seventy-five million dollars a year is a moderate estimate of the volume of business done by pseudo-medical preparations which "eradicated" asthma with sugar and water, "soothed" babies with concealed and deadly opiates, "relieved" headaches through the agency of dangerous, heart-imparing, coal-tar drugs, "dispelled" catarrh by cocaine mixtures, enticing to a habit worse than death's very self, and "cured" tuberculosis, cancer, and Bright's disease with disguised and flavored whiskies and gins.

For five years, Adams explained, the law was in full operation, but in 1911 the Supreme Court had ruled that the prohibition of falsification referred only to the ingredients of the medicine. That meant that the quacks could go on with their false promises, and this situation demanded further exposure.

Top left: ALFRED HENRY LEWIS. *Top right:* BENJAMIN B. HAMPTON. Courtesy of International News Service, Inc. *Bottom left:* MARK SULLIVAN. Copyright Underwood and Underwood Studios. *Bottom right:* JOHN O'HARA COSGRAVE.

Moreover, as an editorial, "Profitable Food Poisoning," in *Hampton's* for September, 1911, pointed out, the law was not being enforced in such a way as to check the patent medicine evil. The editor stated that the Department of Agriculture had sent out 860 cases of judgment against the violators of the Pure Food and Drug Law. Fines were imposed in 490 cases, the heaviest $500 and the average $43.44. Obviously such light fines did nothing to restrain the poisoners and dopers, who were reaping huge profits from their victimization of the public. H. Parker Willis, writing in *Collier's*, made similar charges, accusing Secretary Wilson of the Department of Justice and Solicitor George P. McCabe of holding up thousands of cases of misbranding and adulteration which had been prepared in the Bureau of Chemistry.

This series of Adams's had first been offered to McClure, who rejected it—one of his few mistakes. Adams then turned to *Collier's*, which was just beginning its career in muckraking. Samuel Hopkins Adams had been studying public health, partly as a result of a suggestion offered by Ray Stannard Baker, and he became interested in patent medicines at just about the time that Collier and Hapgood were considering the possibilities of a series on the topic. Adams's method was to select a medicine and have it analyzed. Then he carefully studied the advertising and if possible collected reliable case histories of people who had used it. He insisted upon complete accuracy, and as a result neither he nor the magazine lost a cent in libel suits, though many suits were threatened and several were actually prosecuted.

One of the most interesting cases which developed as a result of the patent medicine series was the suit which *Collier's* brought against Post, the cereal manufacturer. Post had been advertising grape-nuts as a cure for appendicitis, and *Collier's* published an editorial ridiculing the idea. Post then published throughout the country an advertisement stating that the magazine was attacking him because he had refused to place his advertising on its pages. It happened that the advertising department had in its files letters from Post's company offering advertising matter, which had been rejected. *Collier's* promptly brought suit for $250,000 in damages, and was awarded $50,000, the largest sum ever awarded in a libel suit in New York up to that time. Later the decision was reversed on a technicality, and *Collier's*, having received complete vindication, dropped the suit.

In the course of this case, Adams happened to notice an advertisement of Post's products which told of three cases of people who were dying from drinking coffee and were saved by Postum. He looked up the magazine from which these cases were quoted, and found that it was a dubious medical journal that had failed. From the receivers, however, he learned the address of the doctor, one Underwood, who had reported the cases. He looked him up and discovered that he was a printer, a sort of unconscious quack, who sold pills and assumed the title of doctor. With complete naïveté he told how he believed that coffee was a menace to health, how he had studied three acquaintances, how he had written to Mr. Post about his studies, how Mr. Post had promised to pay him if he could get the account published, and how he actually had found a magazine to publish it and had been paid.

Underwood was immediately secured as a witness in the libel suit, and when Mr. Post was placed on the stand he was asked if he knew Dr. Underwood. He replied that he did not know him personally but knew him by reputation. He was asked if he considered Dr. Underwood a reputable and eminent physician. He replied that he did. Mr. Post was dismissed, and Dr. Underwood was called. This strange old man, shabbily dressed, with long side-whiskers, and none too steady on his feet, took the witness stand. The case was over.

Another phase of *Collier's* effort to protect the public developed in Will Irwin's articles on the liquor industry and the beginnings of the prohibition movement. Irwin had come east from California, had entered journalism, had served for a year on *McClure's*, and had built up a reputation as a writer of articles and stories. Though not himself a prohibitionist, he advanced the thesis that national prohibition was bound to come unless the brewers changed their methods. In the course of getting material for this series, he traveled over much of the country, and on several occasions his life was threatened. His investigations in the South led to the discovery that gin was being advertised among the Negroes in such a way as to suggest that it had aphrodisiac powers, and he realized that there was undoubtedly a connection between this type of advertising and the increase of lynching. His exposure of this situation led to the prosecution of certain manufacturers, and the practice was discontinued, with the result, according to Mr. Irwin, that cases of rape and consequently cases of lynching also decreased.

It was with such articles as these that *Collier's* built up its reputation not only as a live news weekly but also as an agency of reform. The time came when a single editorial in *Collier's* carried tremendous weight, and its political articles and editorials were discussed throughout the country. After 1912, however, its influence declined, partly because of national conditions, partly because of the breakdown of Robert Collier. Valuable members of the staff left it, and at last a different group was in control. It had been active long enough, however, to effect important changes in the life of every American.

CHAPTER FOURTEEN

A VARIETY OF EXPOSURES

WHILE muckraking was at its height, there was no institution which was immune from attack. Not content with exposing corruption at home, the muckrakers frequently attacked conditions in other lands. Russia, Belgium, and Mexico bore the brunt of the attack, but other nations received their share of attention. The confidence with which these reformers assailed evil the world over is an index of the exuberance which characterized the movement in its earlier stages.

The Czarist rule in Russia was constantly under attack. David Soskice, Leroy Scott, Robert Crozier Long, George Kennan, and Albert Edwards denounced the system of exile, the secret police, the methods of terrorism, the bigotry and tyranny of the state church, the extreme reactionism of the government, the poverty of the people, and the suppression of the Baltic provinces. The *Arena, McClure's*, the *Cosmopolitan*, and *Collier's* participated in the assault. *McClure's*, in 1908, published a sensational document, General Kuropatkin's "History of the Russo-Japanese War." Kuropatkin, who had been the commander-in-chief of the Russian forces, and who had therefore borne most of the abuse consequent upon Russia's defeat, prepared a detailed statement of the condition, aim, and development of the Russian Empire. This document the government had immediately suppressed, but in some way, not revealed, *McClure's* had secured a copy, and published extracts translated by George Kennan. The revelations which Kuropatkin made confirmed the widespread impression that sordid causes lay behind the conflict, and *McClure's* received hundreds of letters from foreign countries.

The misgovernment which King Leopold II of Belgium was responsible for in the Congo Free State aroused the horror of the civilized world. W. M. Morrison, a returned Presbyterian missionary, exposed in two articles which he wrote for the *Independent* in July, 1903, the practices of Belgian officials. In the six years that he spent in the Congo he had seen much slave hunting and had witnessed the most horrible treatment of natives, and he described some of the more gruesome scenes. Three years later Robert E. Park wrote for *Everybody's* a more comprehensive account of the Congo situation. In three articles, entitled "A King in Business" (November, 1906), "The Terrible Story of the Congo" (December, 1906), and "The Blood-Money of the Congo" (January, 1907), he explained how Leopold had secured control in 1877, how he had secretly extended his authority until by 1906 he had crowded out or absorbed all private trade in 800,000 out of the 900,000 square miles of territory, how trade was supplemented by taxation, and how the territory was parcelled out among stock companies who paid 50 per cent of their profits to the state for the privilege of assessing and collecting taxes. Park asserted that by 1906 Leopold was deriving from the Congo an annual income of about five million dollars. He had capitalized the industry and sold the stocks on the Antwerp market. In less than twenty years the population of the Congo decreased by fifteen millions. Natives were shot, hanged, or starved when their only crime was their inability to gratify promptly enough the lust and rapacity of their masters. The enormous profits which the king amassed did not benefit Belgium but

were spent on extravagant public buildings and on courte-
sans and favorites.

In the *Cosmopolitan*, in 1906 and 1907, Charles Edward
Russell wrote a rather striking series on the caste system the
world over. In India he found that the ancient and hideous
social system still retarded progress, destroyed ambition,
and discouraged education. In England he observed the
prevalence of a system of snobbery based on special privilege,
and he found that a similar system was developing in American life. He declared that the caste system, wherever found
and in whatever form, was democracy's bitterest foe and the
greatest obstacle to the happiness of mankind.

"Barbarous Mexico," a series of articles published in the
American in 1909, directed a scathing attack against the Diaz
administration. John Kenneth Turner, a business man who
had spent a year and a half in Mexico, visiting nearly every
part of the country and collecting a vast amount of material,
wrote the first three of these articles. He declared that Mexico was only a republic in name and that Diaz ruled like a
Czar. The few at the top grew richer, while the millions were
near the starvation line. Only large standing armies, strong
police, an all-pervasive spy system, and a brutal terrorism
prevented revolution. Outsiders were ignorant of conditions
because Diaz controlled the sources of news and the means
of transmitting it.

After three of Turner's articles had appeared, the editors
of the *American* refused to accept any more from him, though
they continued to publish articles under the title "Barbarous Mexico." Upton Sinclair has asserted that the discon-
tinuing of Turner's articles indicates a change of policy, but
Ida M. Tarbell and John S. Phillips, two of the editors of
the *American* at that time, deny this allegation, insisting
that the staff had reason to believe Turner's statements
unreliable. The remainder of Turner's articles were pub-

lished in the Socialist weekly, *The Appeal to Reason.*

Germany's preparations for war were regarded as cause for alarm, and in November, 1909, *McClure's* published an article, "Germany's War Preparedness," by G. E. Maberly-Oppier, describing the efficiency of the German war machine, the military and financial resources of the country, the development of new and deadly instruments of war, the careful and realistic training for combat, the building of airships, and the activities of the secret service department. In a more general article, "The Ominous Hush in Europe between England and Germany," H. R. Chamberlain, writing for the same magazine in October of the same year, discussed the growth of armaments, the fostering of international suspicion, and the absence of any real cause for war. He expressed the opinion that the armament race was bringing nations dangerously close to bankruptcy and that the time might come when war would prove cheaper than peace.

Talk of war and of the need for preparation was also current in the United States. In three jingoistic articles published in the *Cosmopolitan* in 1907 Captain Richmond Pearson Hobson tried to arouse America to a sense of insecurity. He was especially perturbed by the victory of Japan over Russia, and he wrote: "The supreme duty of America at this moment is to gauge accurately the possibilities of Japan's military power, and to make that power ineffectual by the provision of an unquestionably superior force." The next year he painted another terrifying picture of our helplessness, declaring that our program should be "to send our whole fleet to the Far East and keep it there, and to build quickly two more fleets for the Atlantic and while we are building the fleets we must be prepared 'to eat dirt'. " Others shared the gallant captain's alarm, as is evident from the article by Goldwin Smith, "The World-Menace of Japan" (*Cosmopolitan*, October, 1907).

Our navy was frequently under attack. Henry Reuterdahl, in *McClure's*, January, 1908, and George Kibbe Turner, in the same magazine, February, 1908, attacked the administration of the navy department, and declared that we were unprepared to fight. An editorial in the same magazine, "Naval Incredibilities," marvelled at the numerous inefficiencies of the navy. Ambrose Bierce, writing in *Everybody's*, October, 1909, deplored the lack of coaling stations and of a merchant marine. The absence of a merchant marine also disturbed Lewis Nixon, who contributed to the *Cosmopolitan* in February, March, and April, 1910, a series of articles in which he declared that the United States had become a "serf-nation," paying millions of "tribute" to other nations and unable to assert her rights—simply because her merchant marine was inadequate.

Not all the criticisms of the country's military forces, however, expressed the militaristic point of view. As early as 1904 Edward Crosby, writing in the January *Arena*, deplored the development of a powerful military center in Washington, and in 1910 Bailey Millard asserted in the September *Cosmopolitan* that conditions in the army were so bad that there had been 50,000 desertions in the preceding twelve years. Crosby made the significant point that the development of a strong military force was intended not only for defense against foreign nations but also for the purpose of controlling labor disturbances.

What was perhaps a more important service than could be accomplished by attacks on foreign nations and alarmist diatribes on preparedness was rendered by the exposures of the loan sharks, the crooked promoters, and the bucket shops. In this campaign even the *Saturday Evening Post* took part, though as a rule Lorimer preferred to have his muckraking done in fiction form. Will Irwin, for example, wrote a story for the *Saturday Evening Post* called "Golden Water," and other authors employed the same method to reveal corruption and chicanery. The direct attack was also common, however. Merrill A. Teague, writing a series for *Everybody's* in 1906, described the activities of many companies which were engaged in gambling on the probable rise and fall of stocks. *Collier's* published a number of articles on the ways in which unwary investors were mulcted of their money. In 1907 Elliott Flower wrote for the August issues of that magazine, "The Diary of a Small Investor," and "Promotors and their References"; in 1909 and 1910, J. M. Oskison wrote several articles for *Collier's* on the loan sharks; and on March 2, 1912, Arthur H. Gleason described "Promoters and Their Spending Money." One of the most astounding hoaxes of the period was "The Franklin Syndicate," which Arthur Train exposed in the *American*, December, 1905. This enterprise, which was a forerunner of the notorious Ponzi affair, was started by a certain William F. Miller, who, finding himself hard-up, announced that he had inside information about Wall Street, and would pay 10 per cent interest on loans. His business increased, and he was soon advertising boldly and was receiving money from all over the United States and Canada. What he was doing, of course, was simply paying the interest out of the principal, and at last he became alarmed, and took into partnership a man named Schlessinger. He also consulted a lawyer, Colonel Robert A. Ammon, who thereafter was the moving force of the concern. In due season the public became suspicious. Schlessinger fled to Europe with $175,000. Miller went to Canada, but later returned, and was sentenced to ten years in prison. Ammon received a sentence of five years.

A more dignified kind of thievery was exposed in Martin Foss's "Bucket-Shops of the Book World," which appeared in *Public Opinion* for April 29, 1905. Mr. Foss stated that a large proportion of the books on the market had been published by so-called "coöperative publishers" or "authors' publishers." These concerns issued the books at the authors' expense, and reaped all the profits. They would tell a discouraged author that they would publish his book if he would pay half the expenses. Then they would inform the poor poet or novelist that his share would amount to five or six hundred dollars, an amount which covered the entire cost of publishing the manuscript and left a neat profit for the company besides. It is interesting to note that an article making exactly the same charges appeared in the *Nation* for August 3, 1927.

The problem of prisoners and prisons was as urgent then as it seems to be now. In 1904 Dr. G. W. Galvin of the Emergency Hospital of Boston denounced in the December *Arena* the inhuman treatment accorded prisoners in Massachusetts. Charles Edward Russell, writing in *Everybody's* in June, 1908, portrayed the evils arising out of the Georgia system of hiring out convicts for money. An investigation followed, conditions were found to be fully as bad as he had charged, and the system was changed. Some time after, a more inclusive treatment of the problem of convict labor appeared in *Pearson's*. The author, Julian Leavitt, charged that convict labor created unfair competition for the workers, robbed the state and enriched the capitalists, resulted in injustice for the convicts, and subjected the courts to undue pressure. Russell also discussed prison conditions in a series of articles, "Beating Men to Make Them Good," which appeared in *Hampton's* in 1909.

The situation in the Panama Canal Zone aroused Poultney Bigelow, who, writing a series for *Cosmopolitan* in 1906, attacked the filthy and unsanitary living arrangements, and charged that there was much graft. The same magazine published in October, 1910, an article, "The Theft of the Panama Canal," in which Willis J. Abbott asserted that the canal would be of little value to the public because the company which owned the Panama Railroad also owned the ships, and rates would therefore be maintained at the same level.

From time to time muckrakers denounced the activities of American interests in Mexico, portrayed the filth and disease of the slums, pointed to the menace of the Black Hand, pleaded for the prohibition of liquor, scoffed at the importance attached to college athletics, revealed the inconsistences and injustices of divorce laws, expressed horror at the immorality of the theatre, attacked or defended Socialism, and bewailed the extravagance of the American people. However firmly corruption might be entrenched, there was always some writer fearless enough to attack it; however petty an evil might be, there was always a writer who could make it seem vastly important and well worth the article which he devoted to it.

CHAPTER FIFTEEN

THE BALANCE SHEET

IT IS clear that muckraking is not something that was discovered by a group of men in the first decade of the twentieth century. What does distinguish that decade is the fact that there then existed a muckraking movement, a concerted effort on the part of a large number of writers, using as their medium books and pamphlets but more especially the popular magazines which had sprung up in the late eighties and early nineties and had, by the turn of the century, achieved large circulations. Muckraking, as a movement, began late in 1902, became militant in 1903, in 1904 and 1905, and by 1906 was a force that was felt throughout the nation. By 1908 it was dying down, but the Taft administration revived the interest in the literature of exposure and gave a new incentive to the cause of liberalism in politics. The activities of the insurgents in Congress in 1909 and 1910 provided a center for agitation, and the tariff legislation enacted at that time proved a source of dissatisfaction and a subject for criticism. In 1911 muckraking was again at a high point, and many of the muckrakers participated in the campaign of 1912. But even before that three-cornered struggle, muckraking was again on the decrease, and soon nothing was left that could be described as a movement. Some writers and some magazines continued to expose corruption and vice, but whatever fragments of the movement remained were crushed by the entrance of this country into the war. Since the World War, attempts to revive muckraking have largely proved abortive, and "debunking" was for a time the only popular form of the literature of exposure.

Looking back on the muckraking movement, we can readily see that it was part of a larger social, intellectual, and political development. In the nineties, as was pointed out, the average man acquiesced in the methods of industry and commerce. Industrial expansion seemed as much a matter of "manifest destiny" as geographical expansion had seemed in the days before the Civil War, and no more thought was given to those who were ruined by the ruthless methods of the business men than had been wasted on the Indians and Mexicans whose land was taken from them. For the poor there was sympathy and even charity, but few people stopped to consider the conditions which made poverty inevitable. The majority threw themselves into the struggle for wealth with as little consideration for abstract theories of right and wrong as the pioneers had shown in the struggle for land. Even those who were beaten in the struggle were inclined to look upon their defeat as produced by the very laws of nature, and not through the operation of controllable social forces.

Of course there were movements of protest in the nineties, but it was not until the next decade that there came a definite revolt against Big Business. Gradually, but on the whole with surprising rapidity, people, partly because of the facts which the muckrakers revealed, partly because of the visions of better things which the reformers held before them, partly because of chastening personal experiences, began to regard the corporations as enemies rather than as friends. In particular, the comfortable middle classes, who had viewed the earlier stages of the growth of monopoly with considerable complacency, now began to fear the power of the trusts. And they turned to the government as their bulwark in the struggle against the great interests. Formerly, they had accepted the view that the function of government was to protect and encourage the growth of business enterprise; now they demanded that the state and federal legislatures enact laws which would defend the rights of the common people by restraining the activities of the large corporations.

It is significant that there came to be much talk about the "social conscience." Forward-looking men in the churches and in public life began to say that too much attention had been paid to the sins of the individual. They pointed out that men who were kindly, thoughtful, and high-principled in their private lives condoned and even practised business methods which brought poverty, misery, and disease to millions. Washington Gladden noted our discovery that no society could march hellward faster than a democracy under the banner of unbridled individualism. A "Golden Rule" movement was started in 1901, and it was the intention of the founders that the Golden Rule should be practised in business and political relations. Dr. Max Farrand holds that every twenty or thirty years a wave of "moral hysteria" passes over the country, and practices that were once regarded as proper and honorable come to be condemned and scorned. "Hysteria" may or may not be the right word, but it is true that, with almost the suddenness of conversion, the attitude of the American people toward industry and toward government underwent a complete reversal.

The expression of the attitude was twofold: exposure and reform. It is important to note that, taking the most conservative figures available, those given in Ayer's *American Newspaper Annual and Directory*, we find the total circulation of the ten magazines which engaged in muckraking to run over three million. These periodicals devoted a considerable proportion of their space, sometimes as much as 20 per cent, to articles of exposure. And in addition to the magazines we have books and the newspapers. Several of Russell's books sold more than thirty thousand copies, and both *The Brass Check* and *The Jungle* went over the hundred thousand mark. A few newspapers, particularly the New York *World* and the Kansas City *Star*, aided materially in the campaign. We have every reason, then, to suppose that the muckrakers touched in one way or another the great majority of American citizens.

Parallel with the muckraking movement went a political movement which took shape in a variety of ways. Some of the muckrakers were Socialists, but others, probably the majority, believed that the capitalistic system could be so altered as to meet the needs of the nation. During the Roosevelt administration the hopes of the liberals were pinned on the President, and much of the legislation for which he was responsible met with their approval. With the Taft administration reaction set in, and the liberals linked themselves with the insurgents in Congress. In 1912 the liberal movement was divided. Many of the men who had worked for reform supported Roosevelt and the Progressive party, but others gave their allegiance to Wilson and "The New Freedom" of which he eloquently spoke and wrote. But at no time from 1902 to 1912 were the muckrakers and the reformers without some political figure who seemed to embody more or less adequately the ideals which they held.

Since Roosevelt was the outstanding statesman of the muckraking era, and since he was intimately associated with many of the measures which were intended to remedy the evil situations which the muckrakers exposed, it is interesting to note the judgments expressed in 1922 by some of the leaders. Mr. S. S. McClure, in a letter to the present writer, stated:

President Roosevelt was the most influential force in getting good things done that the country ever possessed. He assisted all good causes and hindered all bad causes.

William Allen White expressed a similar opinion:

Roosevelt was the leader of the liberal movement. At the famous Gridiron Dinner in which Roosevelt spoke about the muckrakers, Uncle Joe Cannon spoke up, and said, "Yes, you're the chief muckraker," which was literally true.

More critical was the verdict of Ray Stannard Baker:

In the beginning I thought, and still think, he did great good in giving support and encouragement to this movement. But I did not believe then, and have never believed since, that these ills can be settled by partisan political methods. They are moral and economic questions. Latterly I believe Roosevelt did a disservice to the country in seizing upon a movement that ought to have been built up slowly and solidly from the bottom with much solid thought and experimentation, and hitching it to the cart of his own political ambitions. He thus short-circuited a fine and vigorous current of aroused public opinion into a futile partisan movement.

John S. Phillips and Charles Edward Russell went even further. The former wrote:

The greatest single definite force against muckraking was President Roosevelt, who called these writers muckrakers. A tag like that running through the papers was an easy phrase of repeated attack upon what was in general a good journalistic movement.

And Russell, when asked what place Roosevelt had in the muckraking movement, replied:

None of any honor. He did much to hamper and discourage it, but never a thing to help it. His speech in which he first misapplied . . . a passage of Bunyan to this work of righteousness, frightened some timid editors and greatly emboldened those malefactors of great wealth to whom he was afterward supposed to be hostile.

But the fact remains, whatever individual muckrakers may think of Roosevelt, that muckraking was closely bound up with the progressive movement for reform, and that both movements were expressions of the attitude of the decade. It was a period not merely of bitter criticism but also of high hopes. The liberals of the period felt that they were getting results, and that they would go on getting results. It seemed as if a new Golden Age were at hand, not only for American business and government, but also for American letters and art. Much of the writing of the nineties, as already observed, was infinitely removed from the realities of life, but the authors of the early nineteen-hundreds were eager to grapple with American problems and to find their subjects on American soil. Robert Herrick, in a series of novels on the American scene, criticized the shallowness and crassness of his contemporaries, especially the women. Theodore Dreiser was beginning his distinguished career. William Allen White's immensely popular *A Certain Rich Man* (1909), portrayed the growth of the Middle West since the Civil War, ending on a note of high optimism and ardent faith. Brand Whitlock was writing about politics; Winston Churchill shifted from historical romances to critical studies of politics, business, and the church; Edith Wharton was achieving realistic works of distinction. In American literature, especially in the novel, a new spirit was evident: a determination to utilize typically American material; a willingness to criticize unflinchingly what was unseemly in American life; a note of confidence in America's future.

Frederic C. Howe, in his *Confessions of a Reformer* (1925), describes the attitude of the liberals in the years just before the outbreak of the war in Europe, and much of what he says is equally applicable to the decade before 1912. He writes:

The years from 1911 to 1914 were a happy interim for me. Working with college men and women who were convinced that the old order was breaking up, living in a world that had confidence in literature and in the power of ideas, it seemed to me that a new dispensation was about to be ushered in. A half-dozen magazines had built up their circulation on disclosures of corruption and economic wrong; Lincoln Steffens, Ida M. Tarbell, Ray Stannard Baker, Charles Edward Russell had the attention of America; forums were being opened in the churches, city reformers were springing up all over the country. A dozen insurgents had been elected to Congress; direct primaries, the direct election of United States senators, the initiative and referendum were being adopted, while municipal ownership, labor legislation, woman suffrage, and the single tax seemed but a short way off. It was good form to be a liberal. Conservative lawyers, bankers, and men of affairs stepped out from their offices and lent their names to radical movements. They presided at meetings and contributed to causes. Branches of the Intercollegiate Socialist League were being organized in the colleges, woman suffrage was enlisting the most prominent women of the country, President Roosevelt was providing catchwords for radicals to conjure with, while Woodrow Wilson was taken from the cloisters of Princeton to be made governor of New Jersey, to be later elected to the presidency.

"The new freedom" was to replace the old serfdom of bosses, the younger generation was to achieve the things that had been denied my own—a generation ignorant of the old Egypt of small capitalism, aware of the crude feudalism of the new. The political renaissance was now surely coming. It would not stop with economic reform; it would bring in a rebirth of literature, art, music, and spirit, not that which came to Italy in the thirteenth century after the *popolo grasso* had made their pile and then turned to finer things. The colleges were to lead it; it was to have the support of the more enlightened business men; it would call forth the impoverished talents of the immigrants and the poor. The spirit of this young America was generous, hospitable, brilliant; it was care-free and full of variety. The young people in whom it leaped to expression hated injustice. They had no questions about the soundness of American democracy. They had supreme confidence in the mind. They believed, not less than I had always believed, that the truth would make us free.

Such was the spirit of the age, and such was the optimism of the muckrakers, the reformers, the leaders of liberal opinion. And now we naturally ask ourselves what was accomplished by these workers, more especially, of course, by the muckrakers. We wish to know not merely what laws were passed as a result of their agitation but also what effect their exposures had on business. For it was business, as we have said many times, that bore the brunt of the muckraking attack. The muckrakers discovered that the great corporations were behind the corruption in municipal, state, and national politics, behind the suppression of liberal magazines, and the perversion of news, behind the pollution of foods and the misrepresentation of medicines. It was the opinion of most of the muckrakers that almost all the evils of American life were directly traceable to the aims and methods of industrialists and financiers, and it was in the hope of arousing public opinion and thus changing these aims and methods that they did their work.

It is impossible to prove that business methods were bettered in such and such a way by such and such an attack, but it is quite possible to argue that the whole tone of business in the United States was raised because of the persistent exposures of corruption and injustice. As early as 1909 John Forbes stated that in his early business career "things were done without a thought of their being wrong that the public would not for an instant stand for to-day." The Rev. Hugh Black declared in 1922, "during the sixteen years that I have been in America the whole basis of commercial morality has changed." In 1921, Dr. Frank C. Doan, comparing the public attitude a quarter-century ago with that of his own

time, said that whereas old men had once advised him to
rid himself of his dreams of social justice, he found intelligent men everywhere willing to listen to talk of the Sermon
on the Mount and the Golden Rule. Even Charles Edward
Russell, who has remained militant in his attitude, believes
that business methods have been remade, that the old tac-
tics of monopoly have been abandoned, that business has
been humanized and made decent so far as that is possible
under our competitive system, that there is a general interest in the conditions of labor, and that competitors are no
longer put out of business without regard to law. President
Wilson, in his message to Congress in January, 1914, sum-
marized an opinion that was widely held when he said, "At
last the masters of business on the great scale have begun to
yield their preference and their purpose, and perhaps their
judgment also, in honorable surrender." One of the most
impressive statements on the subject is to be found in an
article entitled "Higher Standards Developing in American
Business," written by Judge Elbert H. Gary, and published
in *Current History* for March, 1926. Judge Gary, after con-
trasting the business ethics of to-day with the practices current twenty-five years ago, writes:

To my personal knowledge many men of big affairs have completely changed their opinions and methods concerning ethical
questions in business. The majority of business men conduct operations on the basis that right is superior to might; that morality
is on a par with legality and the observance of both is essential
to worthy achievement. They regard employees as associates and
partners instead of servants. Executives have come to understand
that stockholders are entitled to any reasonable information, so
that under no circumstances can there be preferential rights and
opportunities. At last it has been perceived—and this belief is
spreading everywhere—that destructive competition must give
way to humane competition; that the Golden Rule is not an
empty phrase, but a golden principle. Finally, business as a

whole sees that full and prompt publicity of all facts involving the public weal, not only must be made possible, but must be insisted upon as a primary tenet of good faith.

It is something to have great industrialists and financiers rendering even lip-service to ethical principles and humane considerations.

The achievements of muckraking and the liberal movement in the field of legislative accomplishments can be more easily tabulated. The list of reforms accomplished between 1900 and 1915 is an impressive one. The convict and peonage systems were destroyed in some states; prison reforms were undertaken; a federal pure food act was passed in 1906; child labor laws were adopted by many states; a federal employers' liability act was passed in 1906, and a second one in 1908, which was amended in 1910; forest reserves were set aside; the Newlands Act of 1902 made reclamation of millions of acres of land possible; a policy of the conservation of natural resources was followed; eight-hour laws for women were passed in some states; race-track gambling was prohibited; twenty states passed mothers' pension acts between 1908 and 1913; twenty-five states had workmen's compensation laws in 1915; a tariff commission was established in 1909, abolished in 1912, and revived in 1914; an income tax amendment was added to the Constitution; the Standard Oil and the Tobacco companies were dissolved; Niagara Falls was saved from the greed of corporations; Alaska was saved from the Guggenheims and other capitalists; and better insurance laws and packing-house laws were placed on the statute books. Some changes can be traced directly to specific muckraking articles. *Hampton's* maintained that Charles Edward Russell's articles on the Southern Pacific Railroad were instrumental in breaking the power of that corporation in California politics. Mr. Russell himself states that the articles of John L. Mathews were responsible for defeating the plans of the Water Power Trust. And it is fairly clear that it was because of Russell's articles that Trinity Church destroyed the vile and unsanitary tenements from which it had long been drawing income.

The period also witnessed a number of important changes in the machinery of government: the popular election of United States senators, direct legislation through the initiative, referendum, and recall, direct primaries, corrupt practices acts, campaign expense laws, commission form of government for cities, and women suffrage—reforms all of which were intended to remedy the abuses pointed out by the muckrakers. William Allen White, in 1909, stated that the shackles of democracy—direct bribery, party bribery, machine rule, and unresponsive legislative control of the states —had been thrown off. The muckrakers probably deserve credit also for the introduction of congressional investigations, for the development of sociological surveys, for the devising of methods of popular exposition which the later essayists and the conservative magazines adopted, and for the destruction of the awe and reverence in which wealth had been held. *Everybody's*, in 1909, offered a somewhat exuberant summary of what had been accomplished:

Wall Street cannot gull the public as it once did. Insurance is on a sounder basis. Banking is adding new safeguards. Advertising is nearly honest. Rebating is unsafe. Food and drug adulteration are dangerous. Human life is more respected by common carriers. The hour of the old-time political boss is struck. States and municipalities are insisting upon clean administrators. The people are naming their own candidates. Independent voters, and that means thinking men, are legion. The children are having their day in court. Protection is offered to the weak against the gambling shark and saloon. Our public resources are being conserved. The public health is being considered. New standards of life have been raised up. The money god totters. Patriotism, manhood, brotherhood are exhalted. It is a new era.

A new world. Good signs, don't you think? And what has brought it about? Muckraking. Bless your heart, just plain muckraking. By magazine writers and newspapers and preachers and public men and Roosevelt.

We may discount as much as we like the enthusiasm of the editor of *Everybody's* and of other commentators on the achievements of the era, but it still remains obvious, even from so cursory a survey as we have offered, that a great many important and valuable reforms were adopted, as the result, in part at. least, of muckraking. What the muckrakers tried to do was necessary; the evils were there, and there was no hope of removing them until the public was aroused to a recognition of their existence. What they accomplished was significant; the public was aroused and conditions were improved. Why, then, did muckraking cease?

The first, and most obvious answer, in view of what has just been said, is that muckraking was no longer needed because the conditions against which it was directed had been abolished. This seems plausible enough, and there is indeed some truth in it. The more flagrant evils, both in politics and in industry, had been eliminated. Moreover, the public had been aroused, and Congress, together with the state legislatures, was carrying on investigations of its own and was apparently committed to a policy of reform. On the other hand, in 1911, when muckraking ceased, many important reforms, some of which were adopted during the first Wilson administration, were still unrealized, and, furthermore, it was already apparent that many of the old evils were appearing in new guises. Monopoly had been abolished in theory, but it still existed in fact. Despite the amendment providing for direct election, senators were frequently chosen by the same old bosses. The direct primary, for which so much had been hoped, was proving a disappointment in many states. Business might be less open in its defiance of law, but there were many subtle ways of evading legislation that clamored for exposure. Finally, it is to be noted that many of the muckrakers were themselves dissatisfied with what had been achieved, while the liberals in politics put forth their greatest efforts in 1912, a year in which there was almost no muckraking. Quite probably belief that muckraking was no longer needed had something to do with the decline of public interest in exposure, a point which will be discussed shortly, but it is wrong to suggest that the muckrakers ceased their efforts of their own accord because they believed that their work was finished.

We must go on, then, to discuss other factors in the cessation of muckraking, and immediately there comes to mind another possibility: perhaps muckraking did not stop; perhaps it was stopped. We have repeatedly commented on the extent to which muckraking was made possible by the rise of the popular magazines, and we have already seen, in the chapter on the press, that a number of muckraking magazines were forced out of existence or compelled to change their policies. It is difficult to analyze the facts, but as already seen, there is considerable evidence to show that financial interests did manage to suppress more than one magazine that had been antagonistic to Big Business.

William Allen White, however, believes it was a "natural phenomenon" that the liberal magazines should fall into the hands of their creditors, mostly financiers, when liberalism declined and with it the popularity of these periodicals. He writes, "There is absolutely no truth in the story that there was a deliberate plot on the part of the great financial interests to grab the magazines." And we have, in support of his position, the fact that the costs of publishing had greatly increased, making advertising necessary if magazines were to survive.

To the present writer it seems possible to find much truth in both these statements. To him the evidence seems overwhelming that some muckraking magazines, which might otherwise have survived for some time longer, were deliberately and ruthlessly put out of business by the interests which they had antagonized. On the other hand, it is reasonable to suppose that these magazines could have continued, in defiance of the financiers, if the public interest in muckraking had been maintained and circulation had remained large. And it is quite clear that other magazines gave up muckraking, not because their existence was threatened by the financiers and industrialists, but because articles devoted to exposure did not serve to sell copies. Financial pressure may have hastened the demise of muckraking, but there is no conclusive evidence that it was a case of murder in the first degree.

We come inevitably, then, to the conclusion that muckraking ceased, primarily, because the American people were tired of it. John S. Phillips, in a letter to the author, states:

This phase of journalism died down because of the unwarranted and exaggerated imitations done without study and containing much that was untrue. The result of these things was a revulsion and a loss of public interest. Journalistically, the scheme was given up because readers didn't want to read that sort of thing any more. The same thing happened in the political field. Victor Murdock and Senator Beveridge both told me they couldn't get any response to the former kind of speech. The people at large, as readers and auditors, are changeable and when they get tired of a certain kind of thing they stop reading and stop attending lectures and speeches.

John O'Hara Cosgrave, editor of *Everybody's* during the muckraking period, says much the same thing: "The subject was not exhausted but the public interest therein seemed to be at an end, and inevitably the editors turned to other sources for copy to fill their pages."

But why the change in public interest? Why, indeed? Why does public interest permit one play to run on Broadway for five years, while another, and a much better, according to the critics, dies in its first week? Why does public interest send this book, rather that that, to the head of the list of best-sellers? Why did the public interest in muckraking ever develop? These questions cannot be conclusively answered, for public taste is largely incalculable. "The wind bloweth where it listeth." But, even as we tried to show some of the reasons for the beginning of public interest, so we can now seek a partial explanation for its decline.

In the first place, as already suggested, it is possible that many people believed so many important reforms had taken place that there was no need for muckraking. In the second place, it may be that the excitement wore off in time, with the result that the magazine readers found more of a thrill in stories about cowboys and bandits than they did in articles about senators and industrialists. In the third place, as Mr. Phillips says, the increased sensationalism of the latter years of the era may have sickened people with the whole business. In the fourth place, intelligent citizens may have become impatient with exposure and may have begun to demand what they should do to remedy conditions. And, in the fifth place, the mere fact that muckraking had gone on for ten years may be enough to explain why the reading public was weary of it.

We come, in short, to the conclusion that to a considerable extent muckraking was little more than a fad. Many writers took up muckraking because, for the time being, it was more profitable than other forms of writing. They gave up writing pretty romances, western thrillers, or ingenious yarns about detectives, in order to "expose" real or imagined abuses.

Naturally they turned to other fields the moment it seemed likely that greater profit lay therein. Some of the editors were much the same. They had little of the social vision which brought the *Arena, McClure's, Collier's,* and *Hampton's,* to mention without invidious intent only a few names, into the muckraking campaign. They sought only to capitalize a tendency of the times. Such writers and such editors, of course, did not hesitate over sensationalism, and accuracy was of only minor concern. By their attitude and their conduct they did much to bring muckraking into discredit, and when the public would have no more of it, they blithely turned to other things.

We have said enough, perhaps, to explain why muckraking ended, but it is important to devote a little more attention to those writers who were both purposeful and competent, to those periodicals whose editors were sincerely devoted to the general good, to that section of the public which examined with seriousness and intelligence the literature of exposure. Probably the decline of muckraking was hastened by the insincerity of certain writers and editors, the cheapness of what they wrote and published, and the superficiality of the interest they aroused. But we should study the movement at its best, noting the criticisms which have been directed against it, and endeavoring to discover if there were inherent weaknesses that may have contributed to its cessation.

It has been frequently charged that the muckrakers were not fundamental enough in their diagnoses and in their prescriptions. Walter Lippmann, for example, in *Drift and Mastery* (1914), charges the muckrakers with failing to understand the great changes in American life. They did not realize how the nature of industry had been altered, and they were content to denounce this abuse and remedy that evil without ever touching the bases of the whole problem. William Archer reached a similar conclusion, declaring in his article on "The American Cheap Magazine" that the muckrakers were never willing to admit that collectivism was the only permanent check upon the enslavement of the people by the most amazing plutocracy the world had ever seen. Frederic C. Howe, in his *Confessions of a Reformer* (1925), argues that the whole liberal movement was on the wrong basis. The liberals thought that it was enough to make people see what was wrong; they did not realize that the mind "refused to work against economic interest."

In all these criticisms there is more than a grain of truth. Of course it cannot be said that all the muckrakers were afraid of collectivism, for Sinclair and Russell, and at one time Lincoln Steffens, were Socialists. But most of the muckrakers described themselves as "liberals," meaning by that term much or little, as the case might be, and even the Socialists did not seem fully to understand how their dogmas were to be applied to American life. As Lippmann has said, the muckrakers were not leaders, showing men and women how to rise above the chaos of individualistic industrialism; they were, rather, symptoms and expressions of that chaos. Their exposures were unquestionably fruitful, but more than muckraking was necessary for healing the sores of American civilization. Of far-reaching and fundamental philosophy the muckrakers had little; as a result their movement could be only a passing phase in the long struggle for justice and liberty.

Other criticisms have been leveled against these men. It has been charged that the muckrakers were not sufficiently accurate and painstaking in their studies, and that their articles consisted of rhetoric instead of facts. This was true of the more sensational muckrakers, but it was not true of the revolutionary exposures made by such investigators as Steffens, Tarbell, Baker, Connolly, and their confreres. John

S. Phillips, who served on both *McClure's* and the *American*, says: "So thorough was the work then, that, although we dealt with libelous materials all the time, there was only one suit for libel sustained against the magazine [*McClure's*]." And this suit was successful simply because a document on which an article was based turned out to be inaccurate.

It is amazing, when one considers the kind of material these men were using, how few successful libel suits were brought against them. A single article might blast a political reputation or ruin a business. Naturally, the people who were attacked sued for damages if they dared. Samuel Hopkins Adams says that he was threatened with suit after suit but usually all he needed to do was to point out that he had far more information than he had thus far used, and the threat was forgotten. Of all the threats produced by his patent medicine articles, comparatively few materialized into cases, and of these cases he lost but one. Will Irwin had six suits filed against him, but only one was brought to trial. Connolly, as already mentioned, filed a suit for libel himself and won it. Steffens, despite the fact that he was constantly destroying the prestige of eminent politicians, never had to pay a cent in damages. The victims of muckraking were on the lookout for the slightest inaccuracy and yet the muckrakers lost very few cases.

This is some indication of the reliability of the better type of muckraking, but there are other proofs. We have already mentioned the time and money expended in preparing some of the series, and have called attention to the fact that many articles were based entirely on official documents. It should also be noted that articles were subjected to the most rigorous editorial scrutiny, and that the advice of experts was occasionally obtained. In the better type of muckraking, matters of hearsay were entirely eliminated, and merely personal charges were never included. Of course there were muckrakers who were reckless, and there were muckrakers who could not distinguish between evidence and rumor, but the general level of accuracy in the leading magazines was astoundingly high.

If we wish to find other criticisms of the movement, criticisms many of which were voiced by men who took part in it, we need only turn to the *Survey Graphic* for February, 1926, in which are printed twenty-three answers to the question, "Where are the pre-war radicals?", raised by Mr. Howe in his *Confessions of a Reformer*. The criticisms contained in these statements are directed against the liberal movement, but some of them apply to muckraking. Stuart Chase pleads for a more careful study of facts, declaring that "the Uplift . . . is comatose if not completely ossified—strangled both by the war and its own ineptitude. It was inept because its moral judgments took the place of sound analysis." Ray Stannard Baker says that he and his fellows were on the wrong track because they believed that what they wanted could be had by "adopting certain easy devices or social inventions," and he insists that more understanding is necessary. "Think of us," he writes, "as having gone back to get acquainted with life; of liking better for a while to ask questions than to answer them; of *trying to understand.*" And William Hard says that the liberals have depended too much on legislation and political reform, not realizing that to create a bureaucracy is to put a weapon into the hands of the classes they are trying to fight.

These criticisms all point to the conclusion stated a moment ago: muckraking, however necessary and however valuable it might have been for the time being, was essentially a superficial attack upon a problem which demanded—and demands—fundamental analysis and treatment. If we paraphrase Mr. Howe's provocative question and ask ourselves "Where are the pre-war muckrakers?" we are likely to find some indication of what happened to the movement.

We see, in the first place, that the spirit of many of these men remains unchanged. Upton Sinclair is still a muckraker, but, until very recently, he has found it necessary to publish his own books in order to get them before the public. Charles Edward Russell also remains critical, but, unable or unwilling to follow Sinclair's example, he has failed to secure a medium through which his political and social ideas could reach the reading public. Thus these two writers illustrate the influence which economic pressure has had in checking the movement.

Others of the old muckrakers are engaged in what is a modern approximation of muckraking. Will Irwin has done important service in his exposures of the horrors and the futility of war and in his articles on the scandal in the Veterans' Bureau. Samuel Hopkins Adams, devoting himself chiefly to fiction and writing under a pseudonym as well as under his own name, has used one of his novels, *Revelry*, in order to make a startling exposure of the Harding regime. And George Creel, writing for *Collier's* under the name of "Uncle Henry," frequently offers friendly but acidulous criticisms of things-as-they-are.

In one way or another, the muckrakers have adapted themselves to the changes that have taken place in the life of the nation. The transformation which brought us David Grayson in place of Ray Stannard Baker is significant because it reveals Baker's belief that we must have understanding, and Baker's present devotion to the history of the Wilson administration still further illuminates his decision that quiet study rather than noisy assertion is the present need. Mark Sullivan, though writing on politics, seems to have tempered his views, and he, too, is devoting himself to history. Ida M. Tarbell, apparently, has made an even more drastic change; at least her life of Judge Gary shocked those readers who remembered with approval her history of the Standard Oil Company. Steffens, after a long stay in Europe, is back in this country and, as mentioned above, has just published his *Autobiography*. He has come to the conclusion that the movement toward union of big business with politics is inevitable. Like an old contented lover he accepts conditions as they are. "I have been contending," he writes, "with all my kind, always against God. . . . The world which I tried so hard, so honestly, so dumbly, to change has changed me. . . . And as for the world in general, all that was or is or ever will be wrong with that is my—our thinking about it." Then there are some of the muckrakers who, like the late Thomas Lawson, went scurrying back to the swine and their husks.

Because muckraking was to some extent merely a fad— of which the public grew tired, because of the pressure of financial interests, because some of the evils exposed had been remedied, and because of inherent weakness in the movement itself, muckraking came to an end. Even liberalism, of which muckraking was but a part, received a stunning blow when the United States entered the World War.

After this colossal "atrocity" the public mind was in no mood to become excited over mere political and business exposures at home. The absolute apathy in the face of the Teapot Dome scandals is sufficient indication of the way "times have changed." The genteel sort of exposure which such periodicals as the *Nation*, the *New Republic*, and the *World Tomorrow* carried on could hardly be dignified with the term muckraking. The editorials and books of Mr. Mencken, the novels of Mr. Lewis, the many critical biographies of Washington and the "eminent Victorians"—these represent a social philosophy quite unlike that of the muckrakers.

Is muckraking likely to return? A few years ago the historian would probably have answered that the era of the muckrakers was a unique phenomenon in American history, and that the chapter was definitely closed. Today he is not so sure. Liberalism seems to be coming back. The fanaticism and provincialism and conservatism of the post-war period are passing away; and Progressives can carry elections, as was demonstrated in 1930.

Is there need for further muckraking? What brought about muckraking in 1902? S. S. McClure's desire to satisfy the people—for journalistic reasons—on such vexing subjects as the trusts, labor unions, municipal corruption. Are there any public problems that puzzle the American people to-day? Certainly. There is the problem of the gangsters. Everybody is interested in it and very few understand it. There is the whole problem of the relation of the underworld to the so-called respectable classes. There is the problem of the relation of the police to communists and other "undesirables," there is the problem of prohibition, and there is the old alliance of business and politics, in state and nation. These are a few of the things that need to be exposed.

At present (1932) we find ourselves in a world-wide depression. Millions of working men and women are out of employment because, so they are told, they have "produced" too much. The Kansas farmer sells his wheat for twenty-five cents a bushel—the lowest figure in forty years. The Texas farmer dumps many tons of fruit and vegetables to rot in the sun while the West Virginia or Pennsylvania coal miner starves for want of food. People are beginning to ask fundamental questions. Has capitalism failed? Or has it not been allowed to go far enough? Perhaps political power should be delegated to the managers of capital as well as economic power. In that case we should approach the contemporary Russian ideal of unified control, only we should reach it from the opposite direction. Or should our government definitely and finally give up the old theory of laissez faire and actually plan and enforce a unified and harmonious scheme of economic, cultural, and political life for all of its citizens? We want to know; and before we can know much we must have the facts; and how can we get the facts except by further honest and scientific exposures? It would almost seem that before we can have another intelligent progressive movement we will have to have some more muckraking. How this can be brought about it is not easy to see. What magazine would undertake such a task? What magazine has a staff of trained social scientists who can write interestingly and significantly, and is willing to pay them for their investigations? Or is there any other plan of bringing such information before all the citizens who would care to read it?

In conclusion we shall quote two prominent muckrakers on the value of muckraking magazines and on the need for further exposures. Charles Edward Russell wrote thus to the present writer: "Looking back, it seems to me clear that the muckraking magazine was the greatest single power that ever appeared in this country. The mere mention in one of these magazines of something that was wrong was usually sufficient to bring about at least an ostensible reformation." And Ray Stannard Baker wrote a few years ago that "there is a greater opportunity now than ever before for clear-headed criticism by writers, and a greater need than ever for an illuminating presentation of conditions."

BIBLIOGRAPHY

The following is a selective bibliography. It would be well-nigh impossible to compile a complete one on this subject, and if it were possible, it would be far too bulky. Much of the information contained in this study was obtained directly from leading muckrakers by means of correspondence and personal conferences. Some of the books listed below appeared in serial form in one or another of the popular magazines. In such cases, they have usually been listed both as books and as magazine articles.

BOOKS

Allen, Philip Loring, *America's Wakening: The Triumph of Righteousness in High Places*. New York, Chicago, Fleming H. Revell Company, 1906.

Baker, Ray Stannard, *Following the Color Line: An Account of Negro Citizenship in the American Democracy*. New York, Doubleday, Page and Company, 1908.

————, *The Spiritual Unrest*. New York, Frederick A. Stokes Company [c1910].

Bok, Edward, *The Americanization of Edward Bok: The Autobiography of a Dutch Boy Fifty Years After*. New York, Charles Scribner's Sons, 1923.

Brooks, John Graham, *As Others See Us: A Study of Progress in the United States*. New York, The Macmillan Company, 1908.

Day, James Roscoe, *The Raid on Prosperity*. New York, D. Appleton and Company, 1907.

De Witt, Benjamin Parke, *The Progressive Movement: A Non-Partisan Comprehensive Discussion of Current Tendencies in American Politics*. New York, The Macmillan Company, 1915.

Howe, Frederic C., *The Confessions of a Reformer*. New York, Charles Scribner's Sons, 1925.

King, Willford Isbell, *The Wealth and Income of the People of the United States.* New York, The Macmillan Company, 1915.

Lawson, Thomas, *Frenzied Finance: The Crime of Amalgamated.* New York, The Ridgway-Thayer Company, 1905.

Lindsey, Benjamin B., and O'Higgins, Harvey J., *The Beast.* New York, Doubleday, Page and Company, 1910.

Lippmann, Walter, *Drift and Mastery.* New York, Henry Holt and Company, 1914.

————, *Liberty and the News.* New York, The Macmillan Company, 1927.

————, *Public Opinion.* New York, The Macmillan Company, 1922.

McClure, S. S., *My Autobiography.* New York, Frederick A. Stokes Company [c1914].

Older, Fremont, *My Own Story.* New York, The Macmillan Company, 1926.

Ross, Edward Alsworth, *Changing America: Studies in Contemporary Society.* New York, The Century Company, 1912.

————, *Sin and Society: An Analysis of Latter-day Iniquity.* Boston and New York, Houghton Mifflin Company, 1907.

Russell, Charles Edward, *Business, The Heart of the Nation.* New York, John Lane Company, 1911.

————, *Greatest Trust in the World, The.* New York, The Ridgway-Thayer Company, 1905.

————, *Lawless Wealth: The Origin of Some Great American Fortunes.* New York, B. W. Dodge and Company, 1908.

————, *Stories of the Great Railroads.* Chicago, Charles H. Kerr and Company, 1912.

————, *Uprising of the Many, The.* New York, Doubleday, Page and Company, 1907.

————, *Why I Am a Socialist.* New York, Hodder and Stoughton, George H. Doran and Company (new and rev. ed.) [c1910].

Sinclair, Upton, *Brass Check, The.* Pasadena, Cal., published by the author, 1919.

————, *Jungle, The.* New York, Doubleday, Page and Company, 1906. New ed., New York, The Vanguard Press, 1926.

————, *Metropolis, The.* New York, Moffat, Yard and Company, 1908.

————, *Profits of Religion, The.* Published by the author in 1918. New ed., New York, The Vanguard Press, 1927.

Spargo, John, *Underfed School Children.* Chicago, Charles H. Kerr and Company, 1906.

Steffens, Lincoln, *Autobiography.* New York, Harcourt, Brace and Company, 1931.

————, *Shame of the Cities, The.* New York, McClure, Phillips and Company, 1904.

————, *Struggle for Self-Government, The; Being an Attempt to Trace American Political Corruption to Its Sources in Six States of the United States, with a Dedication to the Czar.* New York, McClure, Phillips and Company, 1906.

————, *Upbuilders, The.* New York, Doubleday, Page and Company, 1909.

Tarbell, Ida M., *History of the Standard Oil Company, The.* New York, McClure, Phillips and Company, 1904. Reissue, New York, The Macmillan Company, 1925.

————, *Tariff in Our Times, The.* New York, The Macmillan Company, 1911.

Tassin, Algernon, *The Magazine in America.* New York, Dodd, Mead and Company, 1916.

Thayer, John Adams, *Astir: A Publisher's Life-Story.* Boston, Small, Maynard and Company, 1910.

White, William Allen, *A Certain Rich Man.* New York, The Macmillan Company, 1909. Ed. by Mildred B. Flagg (Modern Readers' Series), The Macmillan Company, 1926.

————, *The Old Order Changeth: A View of American Democracy.* New York, The Macmillan Company, 1910.

Wiley, Harvey W., *Chemical Examination of Canned Meats.* Washington, Government Printing Office, 1899.

————, *Drugs and Their Adulteration and the Laws Relating Thereto.* [Washington, 1902.] Reprinted from *Washington Medical Annual*, Vol. II, No. 3, 1903.

————, *Lard and Lard Adulteration.* Washington, Government Printing Office, 1889.

ARTICLES IN PERIODICALS

Abbott, Lyman, "Flaws in Ingersollism," *No. Am. Rev.*, CL (Apr., 1890), 446-57.

————, "Theology of an Evolutionist," *Outlook*, LV (Jan. 2-April 10, 1897). Thirteen articles.

Abbott, Willis J., "Necessity of an Independent School of Economics," *Arena*, XXII (Oct., 1899), 472-81.

————, "The Theft of the Panama Canal," *Cosmopol.*, XLIX (Oct., 1910), 539-52.

Adams, Samuel Hopkins, "Fraud Above the Law," *Collier's*, XLIX (May 11, 1912), 13-15.

————, "Fraud Medicines Own Up," *Collier's*, XLVIII (Jan. 20, 1912), 11-12.

————, "Great American Fraud, The," *Collier's*, XXXVI and XXXVII (Oct. 7, 28, Nov. 18, Dec. 2, 1905; Jan. 15, Feb. 17, Apr. 28, July 14, 21, Aug. 4, Sept. 1, 22, 1906).

————, "Law, the Label, and the Liars, The," *Collier's*, XLIX (Apr. 13, 1912), 10-11.

————, "Tricks of the Trade," *Collier's*, XLVIII (Feb. 17, 1912), 17-18.

Addams, Jane, "A New Impulse to an Old Gospel," *Forum*, XIV (Nov., 1892), 345-58.

Alden, Henry Mills, "Magazine Writing and Literature," *No. Am. Rev.*, CLXXIX (Sept., 1904), 331-40.

Alger, George W., "The Literature of Exposure," *Atlan.*, XCVI (Aug., 1905), 48-52.

Anderson, Maxwell, "The Blue Pencil," *New Repub.*, XVII (Dec. 14, 1918), 192-94.

Anonymous, (By "An American Journalist"). "Bondage of the Press, The," *Twentieth Cent.*, I (Oct., 1909), 48-52.

————, "Can the Wool Trust Gag the Press?", *Collier's*, XLVI (March 18, 1911), 11-12.

————, "Confessions of a Managing Editor," *Collier's*, XLVIII (Oct. 28, 1911), 18-20.

————, "Confessions of a New York Detective," *Cosmopol.*,

xxxix (Sept., Oct., 1905); 473-82, 607-15; xl (Nov.-Jan., 1906), 105-12.

————, "Other Side, The," *Atlan.*, cxiii (March, 1914), 357-62.

————, "Patent Medicine Conspiracy against the Freedom of the Press," *Collier's*, xxxvi (Nov. 4, 1905).

————, (By "An Observer"). "Problem of the Associated Press, The," *Atlan.*, cxiv (July, 1914), 132-37.

————, "Professor's Freedom of Speech, A," *R. of Rs.*, xx (Dec., 1899), 713-16.

————, "Scottish View of American Literature, A," *Pub. Op.*, Feb. 14, 1891.

————, "Southern Delegates, The," *Collier's*, xlix (Apr. 6, 13, 27, May 4, 18, 25, June 1, 8, 1912).

Archer, William, "The American Cheap Magazine," *Fortn. Rev.*, lxxxvii (May, 1910), 921-32.

Baker, Ray Stannard, "Black Man's Silent Power, The," *Am. Mag.*, lxvi (July, 1908), 288-300.

————, "Capital and Labor Hunt Together," *McClure's*, xxi (Sept., 1903), 451-63.

————, "Case Against Trinity, The," *Am. Mag.*, lxviii (May, 1909), 2-6.

————, "Color Line in the North, The," *Am. Mag.*, lxv (Feb., 1908), 345-57.

————, "Corner in Labor, A," *McClure's*, xxii (Feb., 1904), 368-78.

————, "Following the Color Line," *Am. Mag.*, lxiii (April, 1907), 563-79; lxiv (May-Aug., 1907), 3-18, 135-48, 297-311, 381-95.

————, "Godlessness of New York, The," *Am. Mag.*, lxviii (June, 1909), 117-27.

————, "How Railroads Make Public Opinion," *McClure's*, xxvi (March, 1906), 534-49.

————, "Lift Men from the Gutter? Or Remove the Gutter? Which?" *Am. Mag.*, lxviii (July, 1909), 227-39.

————, "Negro in a Democracy, The," *Ind.*, lxvii (Sept. 9, 1909), 584--88.

———, "Negro in Politics, The," *Am. Mag.*, LXVI (June, 1908), 169-80.

———, "Negro's Struggle for Survival, in the North, The," *Am. Mag.*, LXV (March, 1908), 473-85.

———, "Organized Capital Challenges Organized Labor," *McClure's*, XXIII (July, 1904), 279-92.

———, "Ostracized Race in Ferment," *Am. Mag.*, LXVI (May, 1908), 60-70.

———, "Railroad Rate, The," *McClure's*, XXVI (Nov., 1905), 47-59.

———, "Railroad Rebates," *McClure's*, XXVI (Dec., 1905), 179-94.

———, "Railroads and Popular Unrest," *Collier's*, XXXVII (Aug. 11, 1906).

———, "Railroads on Trial," *McClure's*, XXVI (Jan.-Mar., 1906), 318-31, 398-411, 535-49.

———, "Reign of Lawlessness, The," *McClure's*, XXIII (May, 1904), 45-57.

———, "Riddle of the Negro, The," *Am. Mag.*, LXIII (March, 1907), 517-21.

———, "Right to Work, The," *McClure's*, XXI (Jan., 1903), 323-36.

———, "Spiritual Unrest, The," *Am. Mag.*, LXVII (Dec., 1908, Jan., 1909), 192-205, 231-44; LXVIII (July, Sept., Oct., 1909), 227-39, 439-49, 590-603; LXIX (Dec., 1909), 176-83.

———, "Subway Deal, The," *McClure's*, XXIV (Feb., 1905), 451-69.

———, "Tragedy of the Mulatto, The," *Am. Mag.*, LXV (April, 1908), 582-98.

———, "Trust's New Tool—The Labor Boss," *McClure's*, (November, 1903), 30-43.

———, "Way of a Railroad with a Town, The," *McClure's*, XXVII (June, 1906), 131-45.

———, "What is Lynching," *McClure's*, XXIV (Jan., Feb., 1905), 299-314, 422-30.

———, "What the United States Steel Corporation Really Is and How It Works," *McClure's*, XVIII (Nov., 1901), 3-13.

Barry, David S., "The American House of Lords," *Pearson's*, XXI (March, 1906), 331-35.

Barry, Richard, "Mormon Evasion of Anti-Polygamy Laws," *Pearson's*, XXIV (Oct., 1910), 443-51.

———, "Mormon Method in Business, The," *Pearson's*, XXIV (Nov., 1910), 571-78.

———, "Political Menace of the Mormon Church, The," *Pearson's*, XXIV (Sept., 1910), 319-30.

———, "Slavery in the South To-day," *Cosmopol.*, XLII (March, 1907), 481-91.

Bierce, Ambrose, "Have We a Navy?", *Everybody's*, XXI (Oct., 1909), 517-20.

Bigelow, Poultney, "Panama—the Human Side," *Cosmopol.*, XLI (Sept., Oct., 1906), 455-62, 606-12; XLII (Nov., 1906), 53-60.

Bingham, Theodore A., "The Organized Criminals of New York," *McClure's*, XXXIV (Nov., 1909), 62-67.

Blankenburg, Rudolph, "Forty Years in the Wilderness, or, Masters and Rulers of 'The Freemen' of Pennsylvania," *Arena* XXXIII and XXXIV (Jan.-Aug., 1905). A Serial.

Bolce, Harold, "Avatars of the Almighty," *Cosmopol.*, XLVII (July, 1909), 209-18.

———, "Blasting at the Rock of Ages," *Cosmopol.*, XLVI (May, 1909), 665-76.

———, "Christianity in the Crucible," *Cosmopol.*, XLVII (Aug., 1909), 310-19.

———, "Polyglots in the Temple of Babel," *Cosmopol.*, XLVII (June, 1909), 52-65.

———, "Rallying Round the Cross," *Cosmopol.*, XLVII (Sept., 1909), 491-502.

Bradford, Gamaliel, "The American Pessimist," *Atlan.*, LXIX (March, 1892), 363-67.

Brandeis, Louis D., "The Greatest Insurance Wrong," *Ind.*, LXI (Dec. 20, 1906), 1475-80.

Bray, F. C., "Recent Phases of Journalism," *Chaut.*, XLVI (March, 1912), 100-3.

Browne, Junius Henri, "The Philosophy of Meliorism," *Forum*, XXII (Jan., 1897), 624-32.

Burton, Richard, "The Healthful Tone for American Literature," *Forum*, xix (April, 1895), 249-56.

Chamberlain, H. R., "The Ominous Hush in Europe between England and Germany," *McClure's*, xxiii (Oct., 1909), 598-612.

Chandler, William E., "Free Competition versus Trust Combinations," *Munsey*, xxii (Jan., 1900), 569-70.

Clark, Sue Ainslie, and Wyatt, Edith, "Working-Girls' Budgets," *McClure's*, xxxv (Oct., 1910), 595-614; xxxvi (Nov., Dec., Feb., 1911), 70-86, 201-11, 401-14, 708-14.

Coler, Bird S., "The Political Wrecking of Business Enterprises," *Munsey*, xxiii (May, 1900), 277-80.

Collier, Robert J., "1879-1909," *Collier's*, xlii (Jan. 2, 1909), 13.

Connolly, C. P., "Ballinger—Shyster," *Collier's*, xlv (April 2, 1910), 16-17.

————, "Barnes of Albany," *Collier's*, xlix (Sept. 14, 1912), 10-11.

————, "Big Business and the Bench," *Everybody's*, xxvi (Feb.-June, 1912), 146-60, 291-306, 439-53, 659-72, 827-41; xxvii (July, 1912), 116-28.

————, "Fight for the Minnie Healy," *McClure's*, xxix (July, 1907), 317-32.

————, "Fight of the Copper Kings," *McClure's*, xxix (May-June, 1907), 1-16, 214-28.

————, "Freight Tariffs," *Collier's*, xliii (April 3, 1909), 13-14.

————, "Gallinger of New Hampshire," *Collier's*, xlii (Jan. 9, 1909), 7.

————, "Governor Glynn of New York," *Collier's*, lii (March 7, 1914), 7-8.

————, "Labor Fuss in Butte," *Everybody's*, xxxi (Aug., 1914), 205-8.

————, "More Loopholes," *Collier's*, xlii (Feb. 20, 1909), 9.

————, "Moyer-Haywood Case, The," *Collier's*, xxxix (May 11, 18, 25, June 22, 29, July 6, 20, 27, 1907).

————, "Protest by Dynamite," *Collier's*, xlviii (Jan. 13, 1912), 9-10.

————, "Raiding the People's Land," *Collier's*, XLIV (Jan, 8, 1910), 18-19.

————, "Story of Montana, The," *McClure's*, XXVII (Aug., Sept., Oct., 1906), 346-61, 451-65, 629-39; XXVIII (Nov., Dec., 1906), 27-43, 198-210.

————, "Trial at Los Angeles, The," *Collier's*, XLVIII (Oct. 14, Dec. 23, 1911, Jan. 13, 1912).

————, "Who is Behind Ballinger?", *Collier's*, XLV (April 9, 1910), 16-17.

Crane, Frank, "The Man with a Muck-rake and the Man with a Job," *Collier's*, XXXVIII (Dec. 22, 1906).

Creel, George, "Poisoners of Public Opinion," *Harp. W.*, LIX (Nov. 7, 14, 1914), 436-38, 465-66.

Crosby, Ernest Howard, "Dangers of an Aristocracy, The," *Ind.*, LIV (May 1, 1902), 1055-58.

————, "Man with the Hose, The," *Cosmopol.*, XLI (July, 1906), 341.

————, "Militarism at Home," *Arena*, XXXI (Jan., 1904) 70-74.

————, "Our American Oligarchy," *Cosmopol.*, XLII (March, 1907), 549-50.

————, "Our Senatorial Grand Dukes," *Cosmopol.*, XLI (June, 1906), 121.

————, "Wall Street and Graft," *Cosmopol.*, XLII (Feb., 1907), 439-40.

————, "Why I Am Opposed to Imperialism," *Arena*, XXVIII (July, 1902), 10-11.

Donohoe, Denis, "The Truth about Frenzied Finance," *Pub. Op.*, XXXVIII (Jan., 1905), 69-74; (Jan. 26), 109-13; (Feb. 2), 149-52; (Feb. 11), 189-95; (Feb. 18), 229-32.

Dorr, Rheta Childe, "The Prodigal Daughter," *Hampton's* XXIV (April, 1910), 526-38.

Dutton, J. Frederic, "Forms of Agnosticism," *Pub. Op.*, IX (Aug. 16, 1890), 439. (Quoted from *The Unitarian Rev.*, 1890.)

Eaton, Charles Henry, "A Decade of Magazine Literature," *Forum*, XXXVI (Oct., 1898), 211-16.

Edmunds, George F., "Should Senators Be Elected by the People?", *Forum*, XVIII (Nov., 1894), 270-78.

Ely, Richard T., "An Analysis of the Steel Trust," *Cosmopol.*,
    XXXI (Aug., 1901), 428-31.
Farrar, Frederick William, "A Few Words on Colonel Ingersoll,"
    No. Am. Rev., CL (May, 1890), 594-608.
Field, Henry M., "The Influence of Ingersoll," *No. Am. Rev.*,
    CLXIX (Sept., 1899), 322-28.
Flower, B. O., "Crucial Movements in National Life," *Arena*,
    X (July, 1904), 260-62.
————, "Dead Sea of Nineteenth Century Civilization, The,"
    Arena, V (March, 1892), 523-27.
————, "Earnest Word to Young Men and Women of America,
    An," *Arena*, XXIV (Nov., 1900), 538-41.
————, "Eternal Vanguard of Progress, The," *Arena*, XXVI
    (July, 1901), 91-99.
————, "Fountain-Head of Municipal Corruption, The,"
    Arena, XXVI (July, 1901), 95-98.
————, "Fundamental Conflict of the Present, The," *Arena*,
    XXIX (Jan., 1903), 89-90.
————, "Keynote of the Present Revolutionary Movement in
    the Political and Economic World," *Arena*, XXVIII (July,
    1902), 84-90.
————, "Program of Progress, A," *Arena*, XXV (Jan., 1901),
    79-84.
————, "Pure Democracy Versus Governmental Favoritism,"
    Arena, VIII (July, 1893), 260-72.
————, "Report of the Steel Trust as an Object Lesson for
    American Voters, The," *Arena*, XXVIII (July, 1902), 90-94.
Flower, Elliott, "The Diary of a Small Investor," *Collier's*, XXXIX
    (Aug. 10, 17, 24, 1907). A Serial.
————, "Promoters and Their References," *Collier's*, XXXIX
    (Aug. 31, 1907).
Flynt, Josiah, "In the World of Graft," *McClure's*, XVI (Feb.,
    April, 1901), 327-34, 570-6; XVII (June, 1901), 115-21.
————, "Men Behind the Pool Rooms, The," *Cosmopol.*, XLII
    (April, 1907), 636-45.
————, "Pool Room Spider and the Gambling Fly," *Cosmopol.*,
    XLII (March, 1907), 513-21.

————, "Pool Room Vampire and Its Money-Mad Victims," *Cosmopol.*, XLII (Feb., 1907), 543-49.

————, "Tammany Commandment, The," *McClure's*, XVII (Aug., 1901), 543-49.

————, "Telegraph and Telephone Companies as Allies of the Criminal Pool Rooms," *Cosmopol.*, XLIII (May, 1907), 50-57.

Folk, J. W., "Municipal Corruption," *Ind.*, LV (Nov. 26, 1903), 2804-6.

Forbes, Edgar Allen, "The Human Toll of the Coal-Pit," *World's Work*, XV (Feb., 1908), 9928-32.

French, George, "Damnation of the Magazines, The," *Twentieth Cent.*, VI (June, 1912), 99-111.

————, "Everybody's Business," *Twentieth Cent.*, VI (July, 1912), 241-49.

————, "Masters of the Magazines," *Twentieth Cent.*, V (April, 1912), 501-8.

————, "Shall the Tail Wag the Dog?", *Twentieth Cent.*, VI (May, 1912), 19-26.

Galvin, G. W., "Inhuman Treatment of Prisoners in Massachusetts," *Arena*, XXXII (Dec., 1904), 577-86.

————, "Our Legal Machinery and Its Victims," *Arena*, XXXII (Nov., 1904), 471-80.

Gary, Elbert H., "Higher Standards Developing in American Business," *Cur. Hist. Mag., N. Y. Times*, XXIII (March, 1926), 775-79.

Glavis, L. R., "Whitewashing of Ballinger, The," *Collier's*, XLIV (Nov. 13, 1909), 15-17.

Gleason, Arthur H., "Promoters and Their Spending Money," *Collier's*, XLVIII (March 2, 1912), 13-14.

Grant, Percy Stickney, "Are the Rich Responsible for New York's Vice and Crime?", *Everybody's*, V (Nov., 1901), 555-60.

Gruening, Ernest H., "What Every Newspaper Man Knows," *Nation*, III (July 17, 1920), 72-73.

Hampton, Benjamin B., "Statement by Mr. Hampton, A," *Hampton's*, XXVII (Aug., 1911), 258-59.

————, "Vast Riches of Alaska, The," *Hampton's*, XXIV (April, 1910), 451-68.

Hard, William, "De Kid Wot Works at Night," *Everybody's*, xviii
    Jan., 1908), 25-37.

———, "Labor in the Chicago Stockyards," *Outlook*, lxxxiii
    (June 16, 1906), 366-73.

———, "Law of the Killed and Wounded," *Everybody's*, xix
    (Sept., 1908), 361-71.

———, "Making Steel and Killing Men," *Everybody's*, xvii
    (Nov., 1907), 579-91.

———, "Uncle Joe Cannon," *Collier's*, xli (May 23, 30,
    1908).

Hendrick, Burton J., "Astor Fortune, The," *McClure's*, xxiv
    (March, 1905), 564-78.

———, "Governor Hughes and the Albany Gang," *McClure's*,
    xxxv (Sept., 1910), 495-512.

———, "Gould Fortune, The," *Am. Mag.*, lxi (Jan., 1906),
    300-13.

———, "Great American Fortunes and Their Making," *Mc-
    Clure's*, xxx (Nov.-Jan., 1907-8), 33-48, 236-50, 323-38.

———, "Mormon Revival of Polygamy," *McClure's*, xxxvi
    (Jan., Feb., 1911), 245-61, 449-64.

———, "Most Powerful Man in America, The," *McClure's*,
    xxxvi (Oct., 1909), 641-59.

———, "Race for Bigness, The," *McClure's*, xxviii (Nov.,
    1906), 61-73.

———, "Story of Life Insurance, The," *McClure's*, xxvii (May-
    Oct., 1906), 36-49, 157-70, 237-51, 401-12, 539-50, 659-71;
    xxviii (Nov., 1906), 73.

———, "Street Railway Financiers," *McClure's*, xxx (Nov.-
    Jan., 1907-8), 33-48, 236-50, 323-38.

———, "Surplus: The Basis of Corruption," *McClure's*, xxvii
    (May, 1906), 36-49.

Heydrick, Benjamin A., "As We See Ourselves," *Chaut.*, lxiv,
    lxv. A Series.

Hobson, Richmond Pearson, "Defense of Our Outlying Posses-
    sions, The," *World To-Day*, xv (July, 1908), 741-44.

———, "If War Should Come," *Cosmopol.*, xliv (May, 1908),
    584-93; xlv (June, Sept., 1908), 38-47, 382-87.

Holder, Charles Frederick, "The Dragon in America," *Arena* (Aug., 1904), 113-22.

Holly, Flora Mai, "Notes on Some American Magazine Editors," *Bookm.*, XII (Dec., 1900), 357-68.

Hopkins, Mary Alden, "The Newark Factory Fire," *McClure's*, XXXVI (April, 1911), 663-72.

Howe, Frederic C., "Men of Honor and Stamina Who Make the Real Success in Life—I. Joseph W. Folk," *Cosmopol.*, XXXV (Sept., 1903), 554-58.

Ingersoll, Robert G., "Agnostic Side, The," *No. Am. Rev.*, CLXIX (Sept., 1899), 289-321.

————, "Why Am I an Agnostic?", *No. Am. Rev.*, CXLIX (Dec., 1889), 741-49; CL (March, 1890), 330-38.

Irwin, Will, "American Newspaper, The," *Collier's*, XLVI, XLVII (Jan. 21-July 29, 1911).

————, "Awakening of the American Business Man," *Cent.*, LXXXI (March, April, 1911), 689-92, 946-51; LXXXII (May, 1911), 118-22.

————, "Industrial Indemnity," *Cent.*, LXXXII (May, 1911), 118-22.

————, "Tainted News Methods of the Liquor Interests," *Collier's*, XLII (March 13, 1909), 27-28.

————, "Unhealthy Alliance, The," *Collier's*, XLVII (June 3, 1911).

————, "What's Wrong with the Associated Press?", *Harp. W.*, LVIII (March 28, 1914), 10-12.

Kelly, Elisha Warfield, "Gambling and Horse Racing," *Pub. Op.*, XXXIX (July 22, 1905), 109-12.

Kennan, George, "Count Tolstoy and the Russian Government," *Outlook*, XCVI (Dec. 2, 1910), 769-71.

————, "Fight for Reform in San Francisco, The," *McClure's*, XXIX (Sept., 1907), 547-60; XXX (Nov., 1907), 60-71.

————, "General Kuropatkin's History of the Russo-Japanese War," *Outlook*, XCIV (Jan. 1, 1910), 36-40.

————, "Holding Up a State, The True Story of Addicks and Delaware," *Outlook*, LXXIII (Feb. 7, 14, 21, 1903), 277-83, 386-92, 429-36.

————, "Military and Political Memoirs of General Kuropatkin," *McClure's*, xxxi (Sept., 1908), 483-99.

————, "Problems of Suicide, The," *McClure's*, xxxi (June, 1908), 218-29.

Keys, C. M., "Large Corporations, The," *World's Work*, xvi Aug.-Sept., 1908), 10571-90, 10683-792.

————, "Money Kings, The," *World's Work*, xiv (Oct., 1907), 9475-81; xv (Nov., Dec., 1907, Feb., 1908), 5919-34, 9705-11, 9907-12.

Kittle, William, "Interests and the Magazines, The," *Twentieth Cent.*, ii (May, 1910), 124-28.

————, "Making of Public Opinion, The," *Arena*, xli (July, 1909), 433-50.

————, "What Makes a Magazine Progressive?", *Twentieth Cent.*, vi (Aug., 1912), 345-50.

Lathrop, John E., and Turner, George Kibbe, "Billions of Treasure," *McClure's*, xxxiv (Jan., 1910), 339-54.

Lawson, Thomas W., "Fools and Their Money," *Everybody's*, xiv (May, 1906), 545-49.

————, "Frenzied Finance; The Story of Amalgamated," *Everybody's*, xii xiii, xiv (Jan., 1905-Feb., 1906).

————, "Friday, the Thirteenth," *Everybody's*, xv (Dec., 1906), 821-33c; xvi (Jan.-March, 1907), 41-53, 193-208, 262-77.

————, "Muck-Raker, The," *Everybody's*, xv (Aug., 1906), 204-8.

————, "To My Readers," *Everybody's*, xv (Nov., 1906), 714-18.

————, "Why I Gave Up the Fight," *Everybody's*, xviii (Feb., 1908), 287.

Leavitt, Julian, "Convict Labor Versus Free Labor," *Pearson's*, xxix, 1-11, 179-88, 360-69, 490-98, 539-46, 754-62.

————, "Man in the Cage, The," *Am. Mag.*, lxxiii (Feb.-April, 1912), 397-409, 533-44, 719-29.

Lewis, Alfred Henry, "Apaches of New York, The," *Pearson's*, xxv, xxvi, xxvii (1911-1912), A series.

————, "Betrayal of a Nation, The," *Pearson's*, 1909.

————, "Lesson of Platt, The," *Cosmopol.*, xl (April, 1906), 639-45.

————, "Owners of America," *Cosmopol.*, XLV, XLVI (1908-1909). A series.

————, "Trail of the Viper, The," *Cosmopol.*, (April, 1911), 693-703.

————, "Trust in Agricultural Implements, A," *Cosmopol.*, XXXVIII (April, 1905), 666-72.

————, "Viper's Trail of Gold, The," *Cosmopol.*, L (May, 1911), 823-33.

————, "Viper on the Hearth, The," *Cosmopol.*, L (March, 1911), 439-50.

————, "What Is Joe Cannon?", *Cosmopol.*, XLVIII (April, 1910), 569-75.

Lindsey, Benjamin B., "The Beast and the Jungle," *Everybody's*, XXI, XXII (Oct., 1909-May, 1910). A serial.

London, Jack, "My Life in the Underworld," *Cosmopol.*, XLIII (May-Oct., 1907). A serial.

Mabie, Hamilton Wright, "American Literature and American Nationality," *Forum*, XXVI (Jan., 1899), 633-40.

Maberly-Oppler, G. E., "Germany's War Preparedness," *McClure's*, XXXIV (Nov., 1909), 108-11.

Maclaren, Ian, "The Shadow on American Life," *Outlook*, LXV (Sept. 9, 1899), 116-18.

McClure, S. S., "Chicago as Seen by Herself; Epidemic of Crime," *McClure's*, XXIX (May, 1907), 67-73.

————, "Increase of Lawlessness in the United States, The," *McClure's*, XXIV (Dec., 1904), 163-71.

————, "Tammanyizing of a Civilization, The," *McClure's*, XXIV (Nov., 1909), 117-28.

McCumber, Porter J., "Alarming Adulteration of Food and Drugs, The," *Ind.*, LVIII (Jan. 5, 1905), 28-33.

McEwen, Arthur, "The Trust As a Step in the March of Civilization," *Munsey*, XXII (Jan., 1900), 570-74.

Manners, Mary, "The Unemployed Rich," *Everybody's*, VII (Sept., Oct., 1902), 282-87, 486-93; VIII (Nov., Dec., 1902), 83-89, 412-18.

Markham, Edwin, "The Hoe-Man in the Making," *Cosmopol.*,

XLI (Sept., Oct., 1906), 480-87, 567-74; XLII (Nov., Dec., 1906), 20-28, 143-50.

Marsten, Joseph Freeman, "The Maelstrom of the Betting-Ring," *Munsey*, XXIX (1904), 705-11.

Mason, Gregory, "The Associated Press—A Criticism," *Outlook*, CVII (May 30, 1914), 237-40.

Mathews, John L., "Trust That Will Control All Other Trusts The," *Hampton's*, XXIII (Aug., 1909).

————, "Water Power and the Pork Barrel," *Hampton's*, XXIII (Oct., 1908).

————, "Water Power and the Price of Bread," *Hampton's*, XXIII (July, 1909), 1-14.

Millard, Bailey, "The Shame of Our Army," *Cosmopol.*, XLIX (Sept., 1910), 411-20.

Miller, George M., "Academic Center for the New Education, An," *Arena*, XXIV (June, 1903), 601-10.

Mills, J. Warner, "Economic Struggle in Colorado, The," *Arena*, XXXIV, XXXV, XXXVI. A Series.

Milmine, Georgine, "Mary Baker G. Eddy," *McClure's*, XXVIII, XXIX, XXX, XXXI (Jan., 1907-June, 1908). A Serial.

Moody, John, "Conservation of Monopoly, The," *Arena*, XXXIV (Oct., 1905), 337-43.

————, and Turner, George Kibbe, "Masters of Capital in America, The," *McClure's*, XXXVI (Nov., Dec., 1910-Jan., March, 1911), 3-24, 123-40, 334-52, 564-77.

Morrison, W. W., Misgovernment of the Congo Free State," *Ind.*, LV (July 9, 1903), 1604-8.

Moss, Frank, "Municipal Misgovernment and Corruption," *Cosmopol.*, XXXII (Nov., 1901), 102-7.

Nixon, Lewis, "Conquering the Seven Seas," *Cosmopol.*, XLVIII (Feb., 1910), 263-72.

————, "Crime of Our Vanished Ships, The," *Cosmopol.*, XLVIII (April, 1910), 606-13.

————, "Selling a Nation's Birthright," *Cosmopol.*, XLVIII (March, 1910), 445-54.

Norcross, Charles P., "Beet-Sugar Round-Up, The," *Cosmopol.*, XLVII (Nov., 1909), 713-21.

————, "Rebate Conspiracy, The," *Cosmopol.*, XLVIII (Dec., 1909), 65-73.

————, "Tragedies of the Sugar Trust," *Cosmopol.*, XLVIII (Jan., 1910), 192-98.

————, "Trail of the Hunger Tax, The," *Cosmopol.*, XLVII (Oct., 1909), 588-97.

Norris, Frank, "A Deal in Wheat," *Everybody's*, VII (Aug., 1902), 173-80.

————, "Life in the Mining Region," *Everybody's*, VII (Sept., 1902), 241-48.

Older, Mrs. Fremont, "The Story of a Reformer's Wife," *McClure's*, XXXIII (July, 1909), 277-93.

Oskison, J. M., "Competing with the Sharks," *Collier's*, XLIV (Feb. 5, 1910), 19-20.

————, "Round-up of the Financial Swindlers," *Collier's*, XLVI (Dec. 31, 1910), 19-20.

Page, Thomas Nelson, "The Negro: The Southerner's Problem," *McClure's*, XXIII (May, 1904), 96-102.

Palmer, Frederick, "Abe Ruef of the Law Offices—San Francisco's, Fight to Free Herself of His Rule," *Collier's*, XXXVIII (Jan. 12, 1907).

Park, Robert E., "Bloody-Money of the Congo, The," *Everybody's*, XVI (Jan., 1907), 60-70.

————, "King in Business, A," *Everybody's*, XV (Nov., 1906), 624-33.

————, "Terrible Story of the Congo, The," *Everybody's*, XV (Dec., 1906), 763-72.

Parsons, Frank, "Great Conflict, The," *Arena*, XXVI (Aug., 1901) 141-53.

————, "Preservation of the Republic," *Arena*, XXIII (June, 1900), 561-65.

————, "President and the Trusts, The," *Arena*, XXVIII (Nov., 1902), 449-56.

Perkins, George C., "The United States Senate and the People," *Ind.*, LX (April 12, 1906), 839-43.

Phillips, David Graham, "David B. Hill," *Everybody's*, VII (Nov., 1902), 446-51.

————, "Delusion of the Race Track, The," *Cosmopol.*, xxxviii (Jan., 1905), 251-62.

————, "Treason of the Senate, The," *Cosmopol.*, xl, xli, xlii (1906). A Series.

Pierce, Daniel T., "Waste of Human Life in America, The," *Pub. Op.*, xxxviii (May 27, 1905), 808-10.

"Q. P.," "Changes in the 'Big Three' Companies," *World's Work*, xi (Nov., 1905), 7379-91.

————, "Irresponsible Insurance Millions," *World's Work*, xi (Jan., 1906), 7100-6.

————, "Life Insurance Corruption," *World's Work*, xi (March, 1906), 7317-23.

————, "Life Insurance Machine, The," *World's Work*, xi (Nov., 1905), 6841-48.

————, "Life Insurance Remedy, The," *World's Work*, xi (Feb., 1906), 7212-18.

Reeves, Arthur B., "Our Industrial Juggernaut," *Everybody's*, xvi (Feb., 1907), 147-57.

Reuterdahl, Henry, "Needs of Our Navy," *McClure's*, xxx (Jan., 1908), 251-63.

Ridpath, John Clark, "Invisible Empire, The," *Arena*, xix (June, 1898), 828-40.

————, "Open Letter to President Andrews," *Arena*, xviii (Sept., 1897), 399-402.

————, "Prosperity: The Sham and the Reality," *Arena*, xviii (Oct., 1897), 486-504.

Rockefeller, John D., "Business Experiences and Principles," *World's Work*, xvii (April, 1909), 11470-78.

————, "Difficult Art of Getting, The," *World's Work*, xvii (Feb., 1909), 11218-28.

————, "Experiences in the Oil Business," *World's Work*, xvii (March, 1909), 11341-55.

Ross, Edward A., "The Suppression of Important News," *Atlan.*, cv (March, 1910), 303-11.

Rubinow, I. M., and Durant, Daniel, "The Depth and Breadth of the Servant Problem," *McClure's*, xxxiv (March, 1910), 576-85.

Russell, Charles Edward, "American Diplomat Abroad, The," *Cosmopol.*, XLVII (Nov., 1909), 739-46.

————, "Associated Press and Calumet, The," *Pearson's*, XXXI (April, 1914), 437-48.

————, "At the Throat of the Republic," *Cosmopol.*, XLIV (Dec., 1907, Jan., March, 1908), 146-57, 259-71, 361-68.

————, "Beating Men to Make Them Good," *Hampton's*, XXIII (Sept., Oct., Nov., 1909).

————, "Burglar in the Making, A," *Everybody's*, XVIII (June, 1908), 753-60.

————, "Caste—The Curse of India," *Cosmopol.*, XLII (Dec., 1906), 124-35).

————, "Colorado—New Tricks in an Old Game," *Cosmopol.*, L (Dec., 1910), 45-58.

————, "England's System of Snobbery," *Cosmopol.*, XLII (Jan., 1907), 276-85.

————, "Greatest Trust in the World, The," *Everybody's*, XII (Feb.-Sept., 1905). A Series.

————, "Growth of Caste in America, The," *Cosmopol.*, XLII (March, 1907), 524-34.

————, "Keeping of the Kept Press, The," *Pearson's*, XXXI (Jan., 1914), 33-43.

————, "Magazine Soft Pedal, The," *Pearson's*, XXXI (Feb., 1914), 179-89.

————, "Railroad Revolution, The," *Pearson's*, XXIX, XXX.

————, "Scientific Corruption of Politics," *Hampton's*, XXIV (June, 1910), 843-58.

————, "What Are You Going to Do About It?", *Cosmopol.*, XLIX, L (July, 1910-Jan., 1911). A Series.

————, "Where Did You Get It, Gentlemen?" *Everybody's*, XVII, XVIII (Aug., 1907-March, 1908). A Series.

Savage, Minot J., "Agencies That Are Working a Revolution in Theology," *Arena*, I (Dec., 1889), 1-14.

Seaber, Louis, "Pennsylvania's Palace of Graft," *Ind.*, LXII (May 30, 1907), 1235-41.

Sedgwick, Ellery, "The Man With the Muck-Rake," *Am. Mag.*, LXII (May, 1906), 111-12.

Seward, Theodore F., "Spiritual Birth of the American Nation," *Arena*, XXVII (Jan., 1902), 22-27.

Shearman, Thomas G., "The Coming Billionaire," *Forum*, X Jan., 1891), 546-557.

Sinclair, Upton, "Condemned Meat Industry, The," *Everybody's*, XIV (May, 1906), 608-16.

———, "Is Chicago Meat Clean?", *Collier's*, XXXV (April 22, 1905), 13-14.

———, "Metropolis, The," *Am. Mag.*, LXV (Jan.-March, 1908), 227-36, 370-80, 506-17. A Serial.

———, "My Cause," *Ind.*, LV (May 14, 1903), 1121-26.

———, "Stockyard Secrets," *Collier's*, XXXVI (March 24, 1906).

———, "What Life Means to Me," *Cosmopol.*, XLV (Oct., 1906), 591-95.

Small, Albion W., "Limits Imposed by Responsibility," *Arena*, XXII (Oct., 1899), 463-72.

Smith, Goldwin, "Christianity's Millstone," *No. Am. Rev.*, CLXI (Dec., 1895), 703-19.

———, "Is There Another Life?", *Forum*, XXI (July, 1896), 607-19.

———, "Prophets of Unrest," *Forum*, IX (Aug., 1890), 599-614.

———, "World-Menace of Japan," *Cosmopol.*, XLIII (Oct., 1907), 604-7.

Smyth, Newman, "The Old Testament," *Cent.*, L (June, 1895), 295-306.

Snyder, Carl, "Our Judicial System," *Collier's*, XLVIII (1911-1912).

1. "Ripping Up Mr. Morgan's Model Trust," Nov. 11, 1911.
2. "The Encouragement to Kill," Nov. 25, 1911.
3. "The Monstrous Breakdown of Criminal Law," Dec. 2, 1911.
4. "The Scandal of Lawless Law," Dec. 23, 1911.
5. "The Extravagant Cost of Law, "Dec. 30, 1911.
6. "The Defeat of Justice by Law's Delay," Jan. 6, 1912.
7. "Judicial Tyranny," Feb. 10, 1912.
8. "Justice vs. Technicality, Courts in Reform," Feb. 24, 1912.

————, "Charles S. Mellon to the Bar," *Collier's*, L (Jan. 4, 1913).

————, "Mr. Mellon's Wonderful Top," *Collier's*, L (Jan. 11, 1913).

Somerville, Charles, "The Yellow Pariahs," *Cosmopol.*, XLVII (Sept., 1909), 467-75.

Spargo, John, "The Underfed Children in Our Public Schools," *Ind.*, LVIII (May 11, 1905), 1060-65.

Stead, F. Herbert, "The Story of the World's Parliament of Religions," *R. of R's.*, IX (March, 1894), 299-310.

Steffens, Lincoln, "Breaking into San Francisco," *Am. Mag.*, LXV (Dec., 1907), 140-51.

————, "Enemies of the Republic," *McClure's*, XXII (March, 1904), 587-99; "Illinois," *McClure's*, XXIII (Aug., 1904), 395-408; "Wisconsin," *McClure's*, XXIII (Oct., 1904), 564-579; "Rhode Island: A State for Sale," *McClure's*, XXIV (Feb., 1905), 337-53; "New Jersey: A Traitor State," *McClure's*, XXIV (April, 1905), 649-64; and XXV (May, 1905), 41-58; "Ohio: A Tale of Two Cities," *McClure's*, XXV (July, 1905), 293-311.

————, "Hearst, the Man of Mystery," *Am. Mag.*, LXIII (Nov., 1906), 3-22.

————, "It: An Exposition of the Sovereign Political Power of Organized Business," *Everybody's*, XXIII, XXIV (Sept., 1910-March, 1911). A Series.

————, "Mote and the Beam, The," *Am. Mag.*, LXV (Nov.-Dec., 1907), 26-40, 140-51.

————, "Philadelphia: Corrupt and Contented," *McClure's*, XXI (July, 1903), 249-63.

————, "Pittsburgh, A City Ashamed," *McClure's*, XXI (May, 1903), 24-39.

————, "Roosevelt—Taft—LaFollette," *Everybody's*, XVIII (June, 1908), 723-36.

————, "Shamelessness of St. Louis, The," *McClure's*, XX (March, 1903), 545-60.

————, "Shame of Minneapolis, The," *McClure's*, XX (Jan., 1903), 228-39.

Stewart, William M., "Great Slave Power, The," *Arena*, XIX
    (May, 1898), 577-82.

Strangeland, Charles Emil, "The Preliminaries to the Labor War
    in Colorado," *Pol. Sc. Q.*, XXIII (March, 1908), 1-17.

Sullivan, Mark, "The Way of a Railroad," *Collier's*, XXXVII (June
    9-Aug. 11, 1906).

Sutcliffe, Stephen, "In a New York Gambling House," *Munsey*,
    XXIX (Sept., 1903), 923-25.

Tarbell, Ida M., "Commercial Machiavellianism," *McClure's*,
    XXVI (March, 1906), 453-63.

————, "History of the Standard Oil Company," *McClure's*,
    XX-XXIII (Nov., 1902-Oct., 1904). A Serial.

————, "How Chicago Is Finding Herself," *Am. Mag.*, LXVII
    (Nov., Dec., 1908), 29-41, 124-38.

————, "Hunt for a Money Trust, The," *Am. Mag.*, LXXV
    (May, 1913), 11-17; LXXVI (June, July, 1913), 42-47.

————, "John D. Rockefeller; a Character Sketch," *McClure's*,
    XXV (July, Aug., 1905), 227-249, 386-98.

————, "Mysteries and Cruelties of the Tariff, The," *Am. Mag.*,
    LXXI-LXXII (Nov., 1910-Oct., 1911). A Series.

————, "Roosevelt vs. Rockefeller," *Am. Mag.*, LXV (Dec.,
    1907-Feb., 1908), 115-31, 267-81, 425-34.

————, "What Kansas Did to the Standard Oil Company,"
    McClure's, XXV (Oct., 1905), 608-22.

————, "What the Standard Oil Company Did in Kansas,"
    McClure's, XXV (Sept., 1905), 469-81.

Teague, Merrill A., "Bucket-Shop Sharks," *Everybody's*, XIV
    (June, 1906), 723-35; XV (July, Aug., Sept., 1906), 33-43,
    245-54, 398-408.

Thompson, Vance, "War Against Christ," *Everybody's*, XVI
    (March, 1907), 310-17.

Tolman, William H., "The League of Social Service," *Arena*,
    XXI (April, 1899), 473-76.

Train, Arthur, "Colonel Ammon and the Franklin Syndicate,"
    Am. Mag., LXI (Dec., 1905), 204-13.

————, "Up for Trial," *Collier's*, XXXVII (March 31, April 21,
    July 28, 1906).

Turner, George Kibbe, "Actors and Victims in the Tragedies, The," *McClure's*, XXIX (April, 1907), 524-29.

————, "City of Chicago, The," *McClure's*, XXVIII (April, 1907), 575-92.

————, "Daughters of the Poor," *McClure's*, XXXIV (Nov., 1909), 45-61.

————, "Our Navy on Land," *McClure's*, XXXII (Feb., 1909), 397-411.

————, "Tammany's Control of New York City by Professional Criminals," *McClure's*, XXXIII (June, 1909), 117-34.

————. See Lathrop, John E.

Turner, John Kenneth, "The Slaves of Yucatan," *Am. Mag.*, LXVIII (Oct., 1909), 525-36.

Turner, William Jewett, "The Progress of the Social Conscience," *Atlan.*, CXVI (Sept., 1915), 289-303.

Van Horst, Bessie and Marie, "The Woman That Toils," *Everybody's*, VII (Sept.-Dec., 1902), 211-25, 361-77, 413-25, 540-52; VIII (Jan., 1903), 3-17.

Vrooman, Carl S., "Railway Corruption," *Twentieth Cent.*, I (Dec., 1909), 221-28.

Vrooman, Hiram, "The Organization of Moral Forces," *Arena*, IX (Feb., 1894), 348-58.

Walker, John Brisben, "The World's Greatest Revolution," *Cosmopol.*, XXX (April, 1901), 677-80.

Ward, Herbert D., "Peonage in America," *Cosmopol.*, XXXIX (Aug., 1905), 423-30.

Ward, Lester F., "Causes of Belief in Immortality," *Forum*, VIII (Sept., 1889), 98-107.

Webster, Henry Kitchell, "Cotton Growing and Cotton Gambling," *Am. Mag.*, LXI (March, 1906), 550-61.

————, "Lords of Our Streets," *Am. Mag.*, LX (Sept., 1905), 503-11.

Welliver, Judson C., "Mormon Church and the Sugar Trust, The," *Hampton's*, XXIV (Jan., 1910), 82-93.

————, "National Water Power Trust, The," *McClure's*, XXXIII (May, 1909), 35-39.

————, "Secret of the Sugar Trust's Power, The," *Hampton's*, XXIV (May, 1910), 717-22.

White, William Allen, "Folk," *McClure's*, XXVI (Dec., 1905), 115-32.

————, "Roosevelt and the Postal Frauds," *McClure's*, XXIII (Sept., 1904), 506-20.

————, "Roosevelt: A Force for Righteousness," *McClure's*, XXVIII (Feb., 1907), 386-94.

Will, Thomas E., "College for the People, A," *Arena*, XXVI (July, 1901), 15-20.

————, "City Union For Practical Progress, The," *Arena*, X (July, 1894), 263-73.

Wister, Owen, "The Keystone Crime," *Everybody's*, XVII (Oct., 1906), 435-48.

Woodruff, Clinton Rogers, "Philadelphia's Election Frauds," *Arena*, XXIV (Oct., 1900), 397-404.

Younger, Maud, "The Diary of an Amateur Waitress," *McClure's*, XXVIII (May, 1907), 543-52, 665-77.

EDITORIALS

"Alaska and the Press Agents," *Hampton's*, XXVI (May, 1911), 659-70.

"Aldrich Senators, The," *Collier's*, XLIII (Aug. 28, 1909).

"*Arena's* Policy, The," *Arena*, XXI (Jan., 1899), 124-25.

"Big Politics Versus the Magazines," *Hampton's*, XXVI (April, 1911), 521-23.

"Bribers and the Bribed," *Ind.*, LV (June 11, 1903), 1409-11.

"Editorial Announcement," *Arena*, XXII (Oct., 1899), 538-39.

"Editorial Announcement of Kuropatkin's History of the Russo-Japanese War," *McClure's*, XXXI (Aug., 1908), 363-66.

"Hail to the Chief," *Collier's*, XLII (March 6, 1909).

"Idea Back of *Collier's*, The," *Collier's*, XLII (Jan. 2, 1909).

"Introduction," *Arena*, XXII (Oct., 1899), 539-40.

"Is the Declaration of Independence a Treasonable Document that Menaces Modern Imperialistic Republicanism?", *Arena*, XXVII (May, 1902), 538-39.

"Keynote of a Modern Magazine, The," *Hampton's*, XXVI (Jan., 1911), 131-36.

"Little Talk About an Important Group of Magazines, A," *Hampton's*, XXVII (Aug., 1911), 264-68.

McClure, S. S., Editorial, *McClure's*, XXII (Jan., 1903), 336.

"Magazines in the Grip of Privileged Wealth, The," *Arena*, XLI (Jan., 1909), 106.

"Miss Tarbell's History of the Standard Oil Company," *McClure's*, XIX (Oct., 1902), 589-92.

"Nation That Cleans Out Its Muck, The," *Hampton's*, XXIV (June, 1910), 875-76.

"Naval Incredibilities," *McClure's*, XXXII (Feb., 1909), 454.

"Our First One Hundred Thousand," *McClure's*, IV (May, 1895), 487-92.

"Our Stimulating Enemies," *Collier's*, XLII (Jan. 2, 1909).

"Paying of the Bill, The," *Hampton's*, XXV (Oct., 1910), 507.

"Profitable Food Poisoning," *Hampton's*, XXVII (Sept., 1911).

"Public Peril in City Franchises," *Cent.*, LX (June, 1900), 311-12.

"Statement by Mr. Hampton, A," *Hampton's*, XXVII (Aug., 1911), 258-59.

"Strangling the Magazines," *Nation*, XCIV (May 2, 1912).

"Stroke to the People, A," *Arena*, XVIII (July, 1897), 134-36.

"Tendencies in Literature," *Dial*, XXX (May 16, 1901), 325-27.

"Titanic Conflict of the Present, The," *Arena*, XXVII (Feb., 1902).

"To Our Patrons and Friends," *Arena*, XVIII (Dec., 1897), 720.

"Trinity Church," *Hampton's*, XXIV (April, 1910), 594.

"*Twentieth Century Magazine* and What It Stands For, The," *Twentieth Cent.*, I (Oct., 1909), 77-78.

"What Has Been Gained by Recent Religious Controversy?", *Chaut.*, XIII (Aug., 1891).

"Why *Hampton's* Has Succeeded?", *Hampton's*, XXIV (April, 1910), 596-97.

"With Everybody's Publishers," *Everybody's*, XII (April, 1905), 857; XX (Jan., 1908), 143-44.

"Word to the Muck-Rakers, A," *Ind.*, LXX (Feb. 9, 1911), 319-20.

Zueblin, Charles, Editorial, *Twentieth Cent.*, V (Nov., 1911), 4.

INDEX

on prostitutes, 81; on the states, 83-98, 106; on the federal government, 108-109, 148, 155, 156; on Hearst, 174-75, 200, 210, 211; later philosophy of, 214
Steunenberg, Frank, 103, 149
Stewart, William M., 27, 29
Stillman, James, 102
Stimson, John Ward, 53
Stockton, Frank, 15
"Stockyard Secrets," 135
Stone, William J., 5, 112
"Story of Montana, The," 102
Strong, Josiah, 30
Struggle for Self-Government, The, 97
Suburban Traction Deal, 61
Success Magazine, 118, 177
Sullivan, Mark, 103, 119, 138, 181
Sumner, William Graham, 162
Sunday, Billy, 163
Supreme Court of the U. S., 7
Survey-Graphic, 212
Susan Lenox, 110
Sussex (Del.), 106
Sutcliffe, Stephen, 82
Swift and Company, 173
Swifts, The, 144
"System, The," 84, 108, 127, 129

Taft, William H., 66, 115, 118
Tammany, 78, 79, 80
"Tammanyizing of a Civilization, The," 79
Tanner, John R., 87
Tarbell, Ida M., on McClure's staff, 56; begins work on Standard Oil, 57; 18 articles by, 58; in Chicago, 74, 84; biographical sketch of, 121-22; History of Standard Oil Co., by, 123-26; on tariff, 144-45; starts American, 155, 148, 156, 175, 188, 200, 210; has changed, 213
Tarkington, Booth, 80
Tax School (of Cleveland), 96
Teague, Merrill A., 190
Teapot Dome, 214
Ten-Cent Magazine, The, 12-17
Ten Great Religions, 37
"Terrible Story of the Congo, The," 187
Texas, 112-15
"Theft of the Panama Canal, The," 192

"Theology of an Evolutionist," 36
Third Avenue Railroad Company of New York, 51
Thorne, of the Iowa State Railway Commission, 170
Tikas, the "Peacemaker," 150
Times Magazine, 178
Titusville, Pa., 122
Tobacco Trust, 175, 203
Tobias, J. J., 35
Tolstoy, Count Leo, 38
Tontine, the, 140
Topeka, 172
Toronto Week, 36
Towle and Patch, lawyers, 128
"Trail of the Vipers, The," 160
Train, Arthur, 191
Traveller from Altruria, A, 45
"Treason of the Senate, The," 111-113, 171
Trinity Church (New York), and its tenements, 159, 204
"Trust That Will Control All Trusts, The," 118
"Truth About Frenzied Finance, The," 129
Turner, George Kibbe, 76, 77, 78, 80, 81, 116, 149-50, 190
Turner, John Kenneth, 188
Twain, Mark, 15
"Tweed Days in St. Louis," 55, 59
Twentieth Century Magazine, 18, 138, 172, 175, 178
Twist, "Kid," 78
Tyner, Paul, 19

"Uncle Henry" (George Creel), 213
Uncle Tom's Cabin, 50
"Under the Lion's Paw," 46
Under the Wheel, 46
Underwood, Dr., 184
"Unemployed Rich, The," 55
Union for Practical Progress, 30
Union Theological Seminary, 41
Unitarian Review, 39
United Railroads of San Francisco, 73, 74
United States Commissioner of Corporations, 4
United States Steel Corporation, 4
"Up the Coulee," 46
Utah, 160

F